EAT *the* YEAR

366 FUN AND FABULOUS FOOD HOLIDAYS TO CELEBRATE EVERY DAY

STEFF DESCHENES

RUNNING PRESS
PHILADELPHIA · LONDON

CARI, DELL, JEFFREY . . . THANK YOU.

© 2014 by Steff Deschenes
Illustrations © 2014 by Mike Lowery
Published by Running Press,
A Member of the Perseus Books Group

All rights reserved under the Pan-American and International Copyright Conventions

Printed in China

Books published by Running Press are available at special discounts for bulk purchases in the United States by corporations, institutions, and other organizations. For more information, please contact the Special Markets Department at the Perseus Books Group, 2300 Chestnut Street, Suite 200, Philadelphia, PA 19103, or call (800) 810-4145, ext. 5000, or e-mail special.markets@perseusbooks.com.

ISBN 978-0-7624-5094-7
Library of Congress Control Number: 2013958112

E-book ISBN 978-0-7624-5187-6

9 8 7 6 5 4 3 2 1
Digit on the right indicates the number of this printing

Designed by Ashley Haag
Edited by Jordana Tusman
Typography: Blockhead, Verlag, and Vonnes

Running Press Book Publishers
2300 Chestnut Street
Philadelphia, PA 19103-4371

Visit us on the web!
www.offthemenublog.com

CONTENTS

INTRODUCTION

At the end of 2011, I had gained a following of sorts. People had watched me—a silly twenty-something with perpetually bad hair—take a photo of myself at dinner every night for two years and started to connect because I was a real person going through real events. They saw friends come and go from my life, traveled where I traveled, and I never tried to hide the days when I was sad, sick, or lonely. At the end of that year—around December 29—I began wondering if I should evolve my daily photoblogging project into something different.

I had been watching more and more folks post on social media about national food holidays, and thought it might be interesting to see if I could *eat* a food holiday every day. I pitched the idea to a couple friends, and, literally, forty-eight hours later (just an hour or so before the clock struck midnight on 2012), with their help, my food blog, *Almanac of Eats*, was born.

So my journey to "eat the year" began.

Now since you're reading this, I'm sure you've realized that I successfully *did* eat a food holiday of some kind every day for one year. I fully acknowledge that I wasn't the first person to eat the national food holidays, and I know I won't be the last. (Actually, I'm hoping this book inspires you to try it!) But I'm particularly proud of the unique way in which I accomplished my own adventure to do so; not once did I compromise my vegetarian values. Also, the first year I celebrated the national food holidays over one-third of the year ended up being sponsored by companies who believed in what I had to say—the bottom line of which was, is, and always will be *inclusivity*.

Nobody *tells* you how to celebrate Christmas (if that's your holiday of choice in December), do they? For the most part—if you remove the commercialism from it—it's one part tradition and one part instinct. Holidays are both very personal and a reflection of the person celebrating them. So it shouldn't be expected that everyone believes in, does, or practices the same thing. Though less serious, the same is true for food holidays. Know that I never have and never will push my personal or dietary beliefs on you or *tell* you how to celebrate any of the days. Some foodies believe their opinion is far too important than what it really is, and unfortunately they will try to tell you there is a right and wrong way to celebrate. Do not listen.

Food holidays are about capturing the essence of the day—*whatever* that means to *you*. They're about having fun, exploration, education, trying new things, and camaraderie. Embrace the days, make them uniquely your own, and do what feels right. And if you're feeling uninspired one day, but still want to partake, don't feel guilty getting something premade or celebrating a couple days late!

There are some things you should be armed with, though, before beginning your own feat to Eat the Year. You should know I did *not* make up any of these holidays. Through researching food holidays I simply culminated what *I* thought was the ultimate list based entirely on what the *majority* of people seem to be celebrating.

Also, I guarantee that between the time of my writing this introduction and you reading it, a new food holiday will have no doubt popped up, so forgive my inability to include it here! Also, the food calendar can be very frustrating. Trust me, I know! There are loads of repeated days, but that's because somewhere along the line people lobbied for those days to be recognized (perhaps without realizing it already existed). Which brings me to my last point.

People often ask how food holidays become food holidays, which are really just daily observances held in honor of a certain food (or drink). Usually they're created (and then promoted) by food or health organizations, public relation firms, food bloggers, or through petition to a governmental body (sometimes local, sometimes national) for consideration. So the majority of these aren't actually "national" holidays, but that's what they've been coined as. You will see that there *are* actually a couple days that the president himself has proclaimed as legitimate national holidays, though I don't know why we don't get the day off for them!

Cheers—and happy food holidays to come!

Steff

JANUARY IS...

JANUARY IS ALSO...

International Gourmet Coffee Month
National Bread Machine Baking Month
National Diet Month
National Fat-Free Living Month
National Hot Tea Month
National Meat Month
National Oatmeal Month
National Prune Breakfast Month
National Slow Cooking Month
National Soup Month
National Wheat Bread Month

. . .

3rd Saturday—National Soup Swap Day

NATIONAL BLOODY MARY DAY

"When people ask me if Dean Martin drank, let me put it this way. If Dracula bit Dean in the neck, he'd get a Bloody Mary."—Red Buttons

When I was younger, my mom taught me a really valuable lesson about New Year's resolutions: You *never* start them on January 1st, especially if your resolution is to lose weight.

After cruising through a couple months of holidays, indulging and binging on all manner of sinful things, do you really think on *the very first day* of the new year you're gonna have the willpower to say no to all those holiday leftovers that are giving you the come-hither look?

C'mon, it's too much pressure! If you give in to even one piece of pie making sexytime eyes at you, you're gonna feel defeated.

And that's no fun.

So let's postpone this whole New Year's resolution to eat healthy and get fit until tomorrow. Besides, who really wants to start some new regimented diet when they're hungover? I know I don't.

The only thing I want to do on January 1st is eat my weight in greasy foods and sneer at people who are existing too loudly.

Oh, and crawl into a hot bath while nursing a tall Bloody Mary, which I'm pretty sure is the *only* thing that cures the "what the hell did I just do last night?" feeling.

Besides, it sorta has vegetables in it . . . right? So it's totally okay to drink if your resolution is to up your daily veggie intake. Maybe even have two! I've got only your best interests at heart—I'm making sure you get your vitamins now because if you're eating the year with me, trust me, there's going to be plenty of days ahead where we do nothing but damage to your body.

So bottoms up!

Today is also Apple Gifting Day.

BEST BLOODIES

Makes 2 to 4 drinks

1 cup vodka

3 cups organic tomato juice

1 tablespoon Worcestershire sauce

2 teaspoons black pepper

2 teaspoons celery salt

1 celery stalk for each drink (2 to 4 needed)

In a pitcher, stir together the vodka, tomato juice, Worcestershire, pepper, and celery salt. Pour the drink into ice-filled glasses, add a celery stalk to each drink, and serve.

Tip! Some Worcestershire sauces are made with anchovies. If you've got a plant-based diet, you might want to double-check the ingredients. Personally, I always go with Annie's Organic Worcestershire Sauce.

JANUARY 02 — NATIONAL BUFFET DAY

"I went to this restaurant last night that was set up like a big buffet in the shape of an Ouija board. You'd think about what kind of food you want, and the table would move across the floor to it." —Stephen Wright

According to Templeton the rat in *Charlotte's Web*, "a fair [not "life" . . . though that's applicable, too] is a veritable smörgåsbord, orgåsbord, orgåsbord," and I tend to agree . . . especially today.

The *smörgåsbord*—which translates to a "table of (open-faced) sandwiches"—originated in Sweden. Personally, I'm no stranger to this "buffet" concept. My family gatherings were always

epic affairs because there were so many people. It only made sense to serve food stuffs in giant containers from which people could serve themselves whenever, whatever, and however much they wanted. It also taught me survival skills: If you wanted stuffed mushrooms (a coveted food on my dad's side), you stalked the oven until the moment they came out. Then you filled your plate and fled the scene. You could always let them cool once they were in your possession, but if you waited too long after they hit the "buffet table," you risked the chance of not getting any at all.

Family Buffet Tactics 101, right there.

Even if you're not serving a clan tonight, you can still celebrate like you are—which is how I did—with tubs and tubs of food that I could stuff myself silly on and that I didn't have to compete for.

(In case you haven't figured it out yet, yesterday I lied to you. You're not starting your New Year's resolution today. Actually, why don't we just go ahead and scratch that idea altogether now.)

Today is also National Cream Puff Day.

- -

JANUARY 03

NATIONAL CHOCOLATE COVERED CHERRY DAY

"Break open a cherry tree and there are no flowers, but the spring breeze brings forth myriad blossoms." —Ikkyu Sojun

No one seems to quite know why January 3rd was declared National Chocolate Covered Cherry Day. It just is. My thoughts are that it was created because A) there are a lot of these confectionaries left over from Yankee Swap/Mean Santa, and B) to excite and remind us about the next holiday coming up . . . Valentine's Day!

I'm not usually a huge fan of commercially promoted love or naked babies shooting arrows at people (that just kind of freaks me out), but I *am* a fan of anything chocolate. And juicy, sweet cherries are always a nice surprise to find bursting out of the center of a rich, creamy coating of white, milk, or dark chocolate.

Although, truth be told, I originally ended up celebrating today a little nontraditionally. I purchased chocolate ice cream and a pound of fresh cherries. After one bite, I realized it wasn't going to be the dainty "single scoop topped with perfectly sliced fruit while curled up on the couch with a good book" moment I had originally envisioned. It ended up being more like a "plop down on the kitchen floor, gorge myself on the entire pint of ice cream and bag of cherries while attempting to fend off the pet bunny with my elbows and knees as he tried to lunge for a bite" kind of moment!

LISA'S CHOCOBUTTER CHERRIES

Makes 20 cherries
(or however many are in the jar)

1 (16-ounce) jar maraschino cherries, drained
½ (8-ounce) bag chocolate chips (about 1 cup)
½ (8-ounce) bag peanut butter chips (about 1 cup)

Line a baking sheet with waxed paper and set it aside.

Drain the cherries, place them on paper towels, and dry them thoroughly, as any moisture on the cherries will prevent the other ingredients from sticking to them.

Melt the chocolate chips and peanut butter chips together in a double boiler (or a microwave), stirring occasionally until blended and smooth.

Holding a cherry by its stem, dip it into the mixture, covering completely, and place it on the baking sheet. Repeat until you've run out of cherries. Place the baking sheet in the refrigerator to let the cherries harden, about 20 to 30 minutes. (During this time, keep your burner on low so that the remaining chocolate and peanut butter mixture stays melty; stir frequently.)

Take the sheet out of the refrigerator, dip the cherries a second time, place them back on the baking sheet and back into the refrigerator. Once the cherries have set, another 45 minutes or so, enjoy these little nuggets of love!

JANUARY 04 — NATIONAL SPAGHETTI DAY

"Everything you see I owe to spaghetti." —Sophia Loren

The word *spaghetti* comes from the Italian plural of *spaghetto* meaning "thin rope." And there's little sexier in the food world than sharing a big bowl of it.

If the Disney movie *Lady and the Tramp* taught me anything, it's that true love overlooks the differences between socioeconomic classes, and when life gives you a long strand of pasta with tomato sauce and a hot fella, you dive right in. Why? Because a sexy pasta scene like that is guaranteed to end in four things:

1. A full belly.
2. A feeling of camaraderie when both parties inevitably splash sauce all over the place.
3. Smooching.
4. A family-friendly morality lesson that despite how much or little money we have, we're essentially all the same. Every one of us—in spite of our lot in life—absolutely needs to eat to stay alive.

Oh, and *we all* deserve a little lovin', too.

So find a hungry friend—or a ravenous lover—and get your spaghetti on.

NATIONAL WHIPPED CREAM DAY

"Whipped cream isn't whipped cream at all if it hasn't been whipped with whips, just like poached eggs isn't poached eggs unless it's been stolen in the dead of the night." —Roald Dahl, Charlie and the Chocolate Factory

Unlike many of its counterparts, today's food holiday actually has an origin!

On January 5, 1914, a man named Aaron "Bunny" Lapin (not such a creative nickname, by the way: *lapin* means "bunny" in French) was born in St. Louis, Missouri. He would grow up to become the founder of Reddi-wip. Yes, whipped cream totally existed before 1948, but it wasn't until then that Lapin put Reddi-wip inside the super-convenient, disposable aerosol spray canisters, thus revolutionizing the whipped cream world.

And here I bet you thought I was gonna talk about that time in college when me and all my super cute girlfriends had a wild, crazy whipped cream fight in our skimpy pajamas, right? Have you ever actually *had* a whipped cream fight? Your skin feels like it has a layer of film on it, and you smell like rotting dairy for days. I don't wanna ruin anyone's fantasy, but no matter what the movies may say, it's really best to just eat your whipped cream (straight outta the can like I did today) and avoid getting it all over your private bits.

Trust me on this one.

DID YOU KNOW?

Whipped cream cans use nitrous oxide, aka "laughing gas," to dispense the sweet white stuff.

NATIONAL BEAN DAY

"Beans are neither fruit nor musical." —Bart, The Simpsons

One of the best skills to have is the ability to cook a delicious meal. Not only does it feel good to be able to provide for yourself in such a simple way, but also people feel indebted to you when you satiate their hunger with something tasty (and, while I can't guarantee it, this may result in you getting lucky).

The very first two things I learned to make as a self-sufficient young lass were tacos and chili, which are a lot more alike than you might realize. And over the years, both dishes have evolved with me—especially my chili. I originally made it by tossing some kidney beans, a mega can of crushed tomatoes, a bag of soy meat crumbles, and a package of chili seasoning into a big pot. Once it seemed cooked "enough," I'd eat it smothered in a ton of raw onions, cheese, and sour cream. It was uncomplicated, cheap to make, and tremendously filling (eating raw onions, however, will most likely *not* result in you getting lucky).

But I've since stepped up my game and have started exploring the fascinating world of beans. And I mean that sincerely. They all have such unique textures and flavors that finding the perfect balance for my big-girl chili has been a fun experiment. The waxy kidney beans, creamy pinto beans, and meaty garbanzo beans that I use in today's recipe is by far my best combo to date.

Tossing it all on a bed of crispy french fries and melting cheese on top doesn't hurt either, I suppose!

Today is also National Shortbread Day.

VEG CHILI THAT'LL MAKE GROWN MEN WEEP

Makes 6 to 8 servings

1 large onion, diced
2 garlic cloves, minced
2 tablespoons olive oil
6 large tomatoes, roughly chopped
1 (15-ounce) can crushed tomatoes
1 (15-ounce) can dark red kidney beans,
    drained and rinsed
1 (15-ounce) can great northern beans,
    drained and rinsed
1 (15-ounce) can garbanzo beans,
    drained and rinsed
1 (15-ounce) can cannellini beans,
    drained and rinsed
1 (4.5-ounce) can diced green chilies
1 (1.25-ounce) packet chili seasoning
2 tablespoons lime juice (about 1 lime)
1 (6-ounce) can tomato paste
Cheese, sour cream, and raw onions, toppings
    (optional)

Place the onions, garlic, and olive oil into a large pot and sauté them on medium-high heat until the onions are translucent, about 3 to 5 minutes.

Add the tomatoes and stir, cooking for 5 minutes. Add the crushed tomatoes and stir, cooking for another 5 minutes.

Add the red kidney beans, great northern beans, garbanzo beans, cannellini beans, green chilies, chili seasoning, lime juice, and tomato paste. Stir thoroughly and turn the heat down to medium-low and—this is the ultimate practice in patience—let the whole thing simmer for at least 2 hours. (Be sure to stir every so often to prevent anything from sticking to the bottom.) Serve in a big bowl topped with cheese and/or sour cream and/or raw onions, grab a beer, and eat until your piggy heart can't eat no more.

NATIONAL TEMPURA DAY

"Food is our common ground, a universal experience." —*James Beard,* Beard on Food

Tempura, introduced to Japan in the late sixteenth century by Portuguese Jesuits who abstained from eating meat on occasion for religious reasons, is battered, deep-fried vegetables. And it's absolutely delicious. If ever there was a way to get kids to eat veggies—this is definitely it!

Tempura batter is generally made from cold water (which prevents the batter from absorbing too much oil, keeping the coating light and crispy), wheat flour, and eggs. And while it sounds easy enough, after cooking the first few food holidays of the year, I really needed a break from my kitchen (which I was never intimate with before this project; now she's like a needy lover!). So I decided to treat myself today and go out for tempura. It was the first time I took my project of eating the year "to the streets" as the kids say. At the Thai restaurant, I excitedly told my server that it was National Tempura Day as I ordered some.

And I'm pretty sure he thought I was making it up. (What I didn't know then was that this would be a reoccurring theme throughout the year, as would blatant stares from folks nearby wondering why I was taking pictures of myself.)

NATIONAL ENGLISH TOFFEE DAY

"It is impossible to read English novels without realizing how important a part food plays in the mental as in the physical life of the Englishman." —Elisabeth Luther Cary and Annie M. Jones, Books and My Food

One of the best parts about traveling is the chance to immerse yourself in the local culture—do what they do, speak how they speak, eat what they eat. It's that whole "When in Rome . . . " idea, which I totally think is valid. (If you play tourist all the time, you're never really going to get to know the rest of the world, and that would be a mighty shame.)

When I lived in England, I tried my best to fully adapt to the British lifestyle. One of my favorite parts was the food—which was much different than what I was expecting. Some of it was awful. Case in point: I was invited to my friend's very, *very* elderly grandparents' house, where they made us steak-and-kidney pie. It was traumatic. But I suffered through the meal (mostly in thanks to overusing the potent Coleman's mustard on every single bite I took), and then went out for pizza afterward.

But some of the food I loved so much that I eventually became notorious for eating it. Like my obsession with sticky toffee pudding. I had never had anything so harmoniously rich and warm before. The combination of sweet toffee syrup and moist, date cake was one of the finest mouthgasms I've ever had.

And while I tried to recreate that moment today, nothing is ever as memorable as your first time!

DID YOU KNOW?

The Oxford English Dictionary first featured the word *toffee* in 1825.

JANUARY 09 NATIONAL APRICOT DAY

"I love apricots. They're so fuzzy they're furry. They're like little pets you can eat legally." —Jarod Kintz

Poor apricots. Stateside, I think they're one of the more unloved fruits in the produce kingdom. Personally, I think it has something to do with their fuzzy little skins (fruit should *never* be hairy). But did you know that in Latin *apricot* means "precious?" And that they've been around since prehistoric times? According to English folklore, dreaming about apricots is said to bring good luck; and in Turkey there's a saying that goes, *"Bundan iyisi Şam'da kayısı."* Translated, it means, "The only thing better than this is an apricot in Damascus," or "It doesn't get better than this."

Many cultures respect apricots, and even if they're not your favorite fruit (they definitely aren't mine, especially dried, which is how I ate them today, because finding a fresh apricot in January in New England is an impossible task)—today's our day to do the same!

After all, *bundan iyisi Şam'da kayısı!*

For today? No, it certainly doesn't!

DID YOU KNOW?

There are seventeen calories in an apricot.

NATIONAL BITTERSWEET CHOCOLATE DAY

"That's why I hate bittersweet chocolate. I don't even—what's the point of that? Why not just sweet? I mean who—who are you helping?" —Michael Scott, The Office

Generally, "bittersweet" describes something that is both enjoyable and regretful.

When it comes to chocolate, I'm not sure there's much to regret except maybe that there wasn't enough, that you "accidentally" forgot to share, or that you left some in your pants' pocket and didn't remember until you took them out of the dryer only to find chocolate goo everywhere.

When it comes to bittersweet chocolate, there's even less to regret. Containing 35 percent or more of chocolate liquor, it's filled with antioxidants. So the next time your doctor tells you that you need to lower your blood pressure or reduce the risk of a stroke or heart attack, use it as an excuse to feed your inner chocoholic!

In all honesty, I wasn't totally sure how to celebrate today besides buying a bar of bittersweet chocolate and eating it. But that just seemed so pedestrian and *so* literal to me. I knew there would be plenty of other days throughout the year where I wouldn't have as much wiggle room in the interpretation of whatever the food was. (Baklava is baklava, yeah?) In the end, I made an enormous batch of bittersweet chocolate cookies dusted in powdered sugar. It yielded about a thousand cookies, which is far too much for one girl to handle.

But, hey, if you're gonna feed your inner chocoholic, you might as well appeal to your inner kid, too. And what better way to do that than with a never-ending pile of cookies—am I right?

DID YOU KNOW?

Chocolate is less sweet when there's a higher percentage of cacao in it.

NATIONAL HOT TODDY DAY

"Alcohol gives you infinite patience for stupidity." —Sammy Davis Jr.

I always assumed a hot toddy was a rich, creamy, frothy, butterscotchy tasting alcohol . . . or a term someone might call a sassy or promiscuous gal in the 1920s. ("She's a real hawt toddeh, that one is!") Well, it's neither. A hot toddy is a mixture of either whiskey or spiced rum or brandy, with tea or water, and honey, sugar, lemon, cinnamon, cloves, or nutmeg. It's served hot with the intention of relaxing you before bedtime (and thus assisting you into dreamland) or curing your cold or flu. (Please note: Alcohol causes dehydration, so most health professionals now advise against using it as a remedy.) Personally, I also think it's incredibly soothing to the soul after a heartbreak.

I was perhaps *the most* relaxed and immune-to-every-illness-possible girl there ever was when I celebrated this holiday. I definitely messed up my tea-to-whiskey ratio. Actually, I think I screwed up my whiskey-to-every-other-ingredient-in-a-hot-toddy ratio. I was just so nervous that the combination of tea, agave, cinnamon, lemon juice, and whiskey was gonna be weird tasting that I overcompensated with more whiskey. At least if it *was* a little weird tasting, I'd be buzzed enough not to notice. Or care.

But in the end, it was actually quite pleasant. It had a full-bodied black tea flavor with rich, charcoal undertones of whiskey. And to counteract either one of those flavors being too pungent, the lemon added the perfect amount of acidity while the agave and cinnamon left a sweet note to finish.

And now you can understand why I was feeling so chill and healthy. (Read: Just-plain-old-drunkydrunk.)

Today is also National Milk Day.

HEARTBREAK TODDY

Makes 1 cup

- 1 (8-ounce) cup hot black tea
- 1 ounce Irish whiskey
- ½ teaspoon lemon juice
- 2 teaspoons honey or agave syrup
- 1 cinnamon stick

Prepare a mug of the hot black tea. Stir in the whiskey, lemon juice, and honey (you are layering the flavors). Lastly, stir the whole thing with a cinnamon stick. Let cool a bit before drinking.

Tip! Need an extra kick in the pants? Up the whiskey to 1½ or even 2 ounces!

JANUARY
12

NATIONAL CURRIED CHICKEN DAY

"Where life is colorful and varied, religion can be austere or unimportant. Where life is appallingly monotonous, religion must be emotional, dramatic, and intense. Without the curry, boiled rice can be very dull." —C. Northcote Parkinson

The best chicken curry—which is the anglicized version of *kari*, which comes from the Tamil language and refers to a spiced sauce—I've ever had was at a place called Redfort Tandoori in Overton, England.

The first time my friends took me there the staff rushed out to greet our crew with big smiles and overly emphasized handshakes. They then gave us the best seats in the house and flooded our table with mounds of colorful, delicious-smelling food. Either they were super impressed that some freckled kid from the States was gracing their humble restaurant with her presence, or my mates frequented their fine establishment more than they had let on (it was the latter, in case you had any doubt). The folks I was living with heard about how much I loved it and made me a homemade chicken curry and mango chutney a few weeks later. My appreciation for Indian food was really developed during that period.

There are lots of ways to celebrate today—you can make your own curry from scratch, which isn't that difficult, buy a premade jar of the sauce (this book is a no-judgment zone, friends—you wanna use premade, then use premade), or find your own version of a Redfort and eat like a queen!

Today is also National Glazed Doughnut Day and National Marzipan Day.

JANUARY 13 — NATIONAL PEACH MELBA DAY

"Life is better than death, I believe, if only because it is less boring and because it has fresh peaches in it." —Thomas Walker

Peach Melba was invented for the Australian opera singer Dame Nellie Melba by the famous French chef Georges Auguste Escoffier at The Savoy. He made it for her when she came to London's Covent Garden at the end of the nineteenth century to perform *Lohengrin* by Wagner. I don't know about you, but I've never had a fella try so hard to impress me with a dessert. (Dear eligible bachelors, I'm easy to impress when it comes to food, so don't feel like you need to be too creative.)

So what is Peach Melba anyway? Basically, it's peaches in syrup topped with a raspberry drizzle and ice cream or whipped cream.

My teeth hurt just reading that.

Because I was born a hard-headed Yankee tomboy, I don't think I could ever truly appreciate this holiday like I should. I did try, though!

Here's hoping in my next life I'll be born a soprano-singing dame, a traditional Southern belle, or a dentist so I can enjoy this holiday properly!

DID YOU KNOW?

Besides Peach Melba, Auguste Escoffier also created Melba toast for Dame Nellie, as well!

JANUARY 14

NATIONAL HOT PASTRAMI SANDWICH DAY

"I find the pastrami to be the most sensual of all the salted cured meats."
—Vivian, Seinfeld

Pastrami is a cured meat, originally created before refrigeration was available to preserve meat. It was brought to the States in the latter half of the nineteenth century by Jewish immigrants. But who actually gets the credit for creating the sandwich?

Most agree that Sussman Volk in New York made the first sandwich in 1887. He claimed that the recipe was given to him by a Romanian friend. The sandwich became wildly popular, and Volk eventually converted his kosher butcher shop to a restaurant focused entirely around the meaty treat.

Today, though, many people think of Katz's Deli when they think about the sandwich. The deli, located in the Lower East Side of Manhattan, considers itself the oldest in the city (it was established in 1888). Their one-pound pastrami sandwiches are iconic, as is the locale itself; one of the most famous scenes from movie history—Meg Ryan's fake orgasm in *When Harry Met Sally . . .* —was shot here.

Who knows . . . maybe it wasn't all that fake, after all. Perhaps you really oughta have what she's having (especially if it's a hot pastrami sandwich)!

DID YOU KNOW?

A variation of the Reuben (corned beef and sauerkraut on rye) is the Rachel (pastrami and coleslaw on rye).

NATIONAL FRESH SQUEEZED JUICE DAY

JANUARY 15

"Even bees, the little almsmen of spring bowers, know there is richest juice in poison-flowers." —John Keats, "Isabella, or The Pot of Basil"

We're a couple weeks into the new year . . . are you ready to start that diet yet? By now I expect you've eaten all your leftovers, so it's the perfect time to start thinking about dropping a pound or twelve (unless you're perfectly happy with the polar bear insulation you gain annually to help stay warm during the winter months like I am). It's also important to rid the body of built-up toxins stored from two months of eating crap (assuming you started around Halloween, like I did). To regain your natural homeostasis, you need to detoxify. And a juice cleanse—done in a healthy manner—is a great way to do just that.

This doesn't mean you have to dive in headfirst and purchase a juicer to make some carrot, beet root, sprout, and spinach concoction (though you'd be doing your body a real service if you did!). Try blending together some strawberries, bananas, and oranges to start off (a regular old blender will do just fine)! Or buy a bottle of that green-colored superfood smoothie you've been eyeing at the grocery store for weeks. Today's the perfect day to try it.

Your body will thank you.

Today is also National Strawberry Ice Cream Day.

JANUARY 16

INTERNATIONAL HOT AND SPICY FOOD DAY

"Know how to garnish food so that it is more appealing to the eye and even more flavorful than before." —Marilyn vos Savant

Are you a pyro-gourmaniac? It's totally cool if you are, since that's just the name for someone who loves spicy foods. But how hot do you like it?

The Scoville scale is a measurement of heat in chili peppers. It was created in 1912 by Wilbur Scoville. He found that by measuring the amount of capsaicin present (that's the chemical compound that makes a chili hot and triggers your nerve endings—think about when you touch a jalapeño, and then accidentally touch your eyes), one could determine how hot a food is going to be.

Peperoncini, for example, is between 100 and 500 SHUs (that's Scoville Heat Units). Chipotle is between 5,000 and 10,000. Habanero peppers are between 100,000 and 350,000. And the Trinidad Scorpion Butch T pepper? Over 1.4 *million* units.

So how freaky of a pyro-gourmaniac are you?

(Don't bother asking me; I'm a big baby when it comes to this sort of thing. I'll stick with something on the safe side, like a poblano absolutely smothered in cheese, which at 1,000 to 2,000 SHUs is about as hot and spicy as this girl likes it.)

Today is also National Fig Newton Day.

JANUARY 17
INTERNATIONAL DAY OF ITALIAN CUISINES

"Piatto ricco, mi ci ficco." *(The dish is rich, so I dive in.)* —Italian proverb

Don't you hate *fauxtalian* food? It seems it's trendy these days to serve "Italian" even if consumers don't entirely realize that Alfredo sauce, for example, is an American thing. International Day of Italian Cuisines (IDIC) was created *specifically* to promote and protect authentic, quality Italian dishes while educating consumers on what traditional Italian food really is.

Each year, IDIC and the Virtual Group of Italian Chefs (itchefs-GVCI) honor a specific food. At the IDIC's inception in 2008, it was Spaghetti alla Carbonara; in 2009, it was Risotto alla Milanese; Tagliatelle al ragù Bolognese in 2010; Pesto Genovese in 2011; Ossobuco in Gremolata alla Milanese in 2012; tiramisù in 2013; and in 2014 it's all about Spaghetti Pomodoro e Basilico. I don't know about you, but I'll be annually checking now what the IDIC's food of the year is!

I celebrated this holiday with a thick slab of creamy, flavorful tiramisù, of course! Dessert for dinner? Y'know, being a grown-up has its perks!

Today is also National Hot Buttered Rum Day.

NATIONAL PEKING DUCK DAY

"Peking Duck is different from Russian Caviar. But I love them both. —James Bond, You Only Live Twice

Until today, whenever I heard "Peking duck" the only mental image I could conjure up was of the smiling duck served at the end of the movie *A Christmas Story.*

The dish is actually considered one of the most traditional and nationally loved foods of Beijing (which used to be called Peking), China. It's made from the Pekin duck—the big, white, adorable, fluffy kind, in case you were wondering. The crispy skin of the animal is usually served with a garlic sauce, while the meat is eaten with spring onions, cucumbers, and a hoisin or sweet bean sauce on a thin pancake.

I'm always intrigued by representative dishes of other cultures. Just because I don't eat meat doesn't mean I can't enjoy the flavors of this food (actually, when I celebrated this day I made a version with tempeh that I called "Faking Duck"), and the importance it's had in the culinary world over centuries. Don't shy away from challenges like this—whether because of your diet, your kitchen know-how, or your budget.

Everything is doable with a little creativity and a smile(ing duck)!

Today is also National Gourmet Coffee Day.

NATIONAL POPCORN DAY

"The laziest man I ever met put popcorn in his pancakes so they would turn over by themselves." —W.C. Fields

Do you know the difference between butterfly- and mushroom-shaped popcorn? I know it sounds like a question a psychologist might ask while holding up a card with an inky image that resembles a uterus, but it actually has to do with the popcorn flakes (what a popped kernel of corn is known as) themselves.

Butterfly popcorn is shaped irregularly. In my opinion, it kind of looks like an octopus—you know, one big bump with a bunch of little protruding bumps. Mushroom popcorn is ball-shaped, and is preferred when using coatings (like caramel or "buffalo chicken with bleu cheese sauce," which I've seen recently) because it doesn't crumble quite as easily.

Personally, I'm not really a huge fan of popcorn. Anybody who's worked at a movie theater (or dated someone who worked at a movie theater) can tell you that the smell of the stuff can become nauseating pretty quickly. So to avoid that today, I thought I would make Parmesan and olive oil–flavored popcorn, which smells like stuffing.

Anybody else wonder when popcorn stopped smelling and tasting like popcorn?

DID YOU KNOW?

There are six varieties of corn: dent, flint, flour, pod, popcorn, and sweet.

DILLCORN

1 (20-ounce) bag microwave popcorn, unbuttered
and unsalted

4 tablespoons unsalted butter

2 garlic cloves, finely minced

½ teaspoon salt

¼ teaspoon black pepper

1 tablespoon fresh dill, diced

¼ cup grated Parmesan cheese (the shaker kind)

Pop the popcorn according to package directions.

While the popcorn is popping, melt the butter in a pan. Add the minced garlic and cook until fragrant, about 2 to 3 minutes, being careful not to burn it. Add the salt, pepper, and fresh dill.

Empty the popcorn into a large bowl and toss it with the dill mixture. Top with Parmesan cheese, and serve!

JANUARY 20 — NATIONAL CHEESE LOVER'S DAY

"How can you govern a country which has 246 varieties of cheese?" —Charles de Gaulle

Cheese lovers love cheese for a reason.

One of those reasons—whether they realize it or not—is that cheese is addictive. Literally. Did you know there are trace amounts of morphine in cow's milk? It was discovered by Eli Hazum and his team in the early 1980s at the Wellcome Research Lab in Park, North Carolina. It's there because it has a calming effect on calves; it also helps them to bond with their mother while drinking the milk from the udders. Dairy also contains something called casein. Casein, when digested by the body, releases opiates. And since cheese is a highly concentrated dairy product, guess what? You're getting even more than you would in milk.

So does that mean cheese is a legal way to do drugs?

If so, I'm an addict. In England my favorite cheese was the blue-veined, tangy, and über-stinky Stilton. Manchego, with its nutty, subtle sheep's milk flavor was on my dinner plate nearly every night when I lived in Spain. When I was in Ireland, I think I ate my weight in Dubliner—I couldn't get enough of the sweet and sharp cheese with a bite. Stateside, if you ever find yourself in the Pacific Northwest, try Beecher's Flagship cheese, which is a delicious and robust semi-hard cow's milk cheese.

I think I can say that today's food holiday was definitely made for *lovers* like me!

DID YOU KNOW?

To become a professional cheesemonger one must undergo formal education, hands-on experience, and years of taste testing.

Today is also National Buttercrunch Day and National Coffee Break Day.

POUTINE

Makes 2 to 4 servings

1 (28-ounce) bag frozen crinkle-cut french fries
½ cup (1 stick) unsalted butter
½ large Vidalia onion, diced (about 1 cup)
2 garlic cloves, minced
1 cup finely diced Bella and/or Shiitake mushrooms
2 tablespoons all-purpose flour
2 tablespoons soy sauce or Bragg's Liquid Aminos
2 cups veggie stock, divided
½ pound cheese curds (or chunks of Cheddar)

Bake the french fries according to package directions.

While the fries are baking, melt the butter in a medium sauce pan on medium-high heat. Add the onions and garlic, cooking until translucent and fragrant, about 3 to 5 minutes.

Add the mushrooms and cook them down until they begin to shrink. Whisk in the flour to thicken, add the soy sauce, and one cup of the stock. If the gravy still seems too thick, slowly add the second cup of stock until the gravy has reached a desired thickness.

Once the fries have baked, place them on a platter or in a large bowl, top them with the cheese curds, and cover with the hot gravy. Serve immediately.

NATIONAL NEW ENGLAND CLAM CHOWDER DAY

"(Clam Chowder) is rude, rugged, a food of body and substance—like Irish stew, Scottish haggis, English steak and kidney pie—a worthy ration for the men and women of a pioneer race and for their offspring." —Louis P. De Gouy, The Soup Book

When I first got my license, my dad sent me to pick up fish chowder from my aunt's house. Unfortunately, the lid on the container it came in didn't close properly. Driving home, I hit a bump and the watery chowder—filled with pink, fleshy pieces of unidentifiable fish—splashed all over the inside of my Volvo.

And it stank for days.

I think it was at that (severely traumatizing) point that I stopped being a fan of any seafood chowder. That being said, as a New Englander I still feel passionately about defending what *real* clam chowder is—and it doesn't involve the use of any kind of tomato product. That's not genuine clam chowder, my friends—that's something silly New Yorkers do. And to us, total culinary blasphemy.

Today was the day to face my fears. It had been long enough since the fish chowder incident of my teenage years that perhaps my mind had been changed about the regionally beloved food. So I attempted to make a vegan version of traditional New England clam chowder today. I wasn't sure how I was going to bring to life the distinct clam flavor, so I purchased a bag of powdered kelp at the natural foods store. As I was bringing it home, the twist tie on the bag came undone, dumping the contents all over the inside of my purse.

Powdered kelp, by the way, smells like the ocean farted.

Dear Universe: I know when to take a hint.

DID YOU KNOW?

A bill passed by the Maine legislature in 1939 made adding tomatoes to clam chowder illegal.

Today is also National Granola Bar Day.

NATIONAL BLONDE BROWNIE DAY

"I want to be president someday, so I have not smoked marijuana. I ate a brownie once. At a party in college. It was kind of indescribable really. I felt like I was floating. It turns out that there wasn't any marijuana in it, it was just an insanely good brownie." —Leslie Knope, Parks and Recreation

When I was younger, I was terrified of blonde brownies sold at bake sales. Not only did they confuse me, but they also made me nervous. Why would anybody want a brownie without chocolate in it? Didn't that sort of defeat the purpose of what that particular baked good was all about? It just seemed like a deplorable act of hatred toward brownies by parents who were health conscious.

I know better now, but that doesn't mean I'm any more eager to reach for a blonde brownie at a bake sale when something sinfully chocolate is sitting next to it!

Blondies are usually made from brown sugar and vanilla as opposed to cocoa powder. However, they may include butterscotch or toffee chips, a variety of nuts, shredded coconut, candy pieces, or even chocolate chunks. Blonde brownie purists may balk at this, though, as certain quantities and combinations of any of the aforementioned ingredients may turn the dessert into a Congo bar. Even if they do blur the line, does it really matter? It's sugar. It's delicious. And what's in a name, anyway?

Why not just go to town and make blonde Congo brownie bars like I did? Listen, these food holidays are all about indulgence. So if you're gonna celebrate, do it up right.

Chocolate optional.

Today is also National Southern Food Day.

JANUARY 23 — NATIONAL PIE DAY

"A boy doesn't have to go to war to be a hero; he can say he doesn't like pie when he sees there isn't enough to go around." —Edgar Watson Howe

On this day in 1986, the American Pie Council (yes, there really is one!) declared it to be National Pie Day.

And why shouldn't it be? Pie rocks.

Growing up, my parents used to take my sister and me on the most random, spontaneous road trips. Sometimes we'd go to L.L. Bean at three in the morning just to walk around; other times we'd end up in Canada for a hockey game; and every now and then we'd take a drive a few hours up the coast just to get a slice of pie.

No distance is too great when good pie is involved.

What about you? How will you celebrate? With something homemade, or will you, like we used to do, travel for that special piece? Sweet or savory? Fruit or cream? Cheese or ice cream on your slice of apple? Conventional like peach, or nontraditional like cherry chipotle?

Splurge and celebrate with all of the above! After all, National Pie Day only comes around once a year.

Today is also National Rhubarb Pie Day.

JANUARY 24 — NATIONAL LOBSTER THERMIDOR DAY

"A woman should never be seen eating or drinking, unless it be lobster salad and Champagne, the only true feminine and becoming viands." —Lord Byron

It's probably safe to assume that the average person will go through his or her whole life without having ever tried lobster Thermidor. I mean, seriously, I've never heard of this elegant and expensive dish showing up on anyone's comfort *or* favorite foods lists ever. And yet, someone, somewhere, adored this meal *so much* they lobbied to have it celebrated as an annual food holiday.

So what exactly *is* lobster Thermidor? It's a French dish made of lobster meat, Cognac or brandy, and a béchamel sauce that's stuffed back into the lobster shell, topped with cheese (like Gruyère) and baked until golden-brown. I told you: It's extremely extravagant.

Here's my advice to you: No matter how you celebrate today, budget and plan ahead! Both lobsters and lobster mushrooms (for those of you eating the year on a plant-based diet) can be (A) outrageously priced and (B) impossible to find. In other words: Don't get stuck ordering a baggy of lobster mushrooms off the Internet from some sketchball website at the last minute like I did, because my local grocers only carry them for a few weeks a year in August!

DID YOU KNOW?

Lobsters have blue blood.

Today is also National Eskimo Pie Day and National Peanut Butter Day.

NATIONAL IRISH COFFEE DAY

"Only Irish coffee provides in a single glass all four essential food groups: alcohol, caffeine, sugar, and fat." —Alex Levine

The origin of Irish coffee is sweet. In 1942, Joe Sheridan was the chef of a restaurant near the airbase in Foynes, County Limerick, Ireland. One night, in particularly bad weather, a flight that was en route to North America ended up doubling back to Foynes. Sheridan decided to prepare a special drink that would warm up the cold and exhausted passengers upon re-arrival. When one American asked if they were drinking Brazilian coffee, Sheridan responded, "No, it's Irish coffee!"

When I celebrated National Irish Coffee Day the first time, I took a ton of crap from people for using Jack Daniel's as my whiskey of choice. As a result, I was told I didn't do the holiday justice because I was drinking a brand of sour mash Tennessee whiskey. Despite it being the best-selling American whiskey in the whole wide world, it apparently wasn't good enough to go in a proper Irish coffee—because it wasn't Irish.

Yeah, okay, that makes sense to me.

I guess this just means I'll have to celebrate it again and again until I get it right. Twist my arm, why don't ya?

Today is also National Dinner Party Day.

NATIONAL PEANUT BRITTLE DAY

"Come, my little peanut of brittle. I will help you. Wait for me. Wait."
—Pepé Le Pew

Sometimes I cook naked. It's never intentional. I'm usually getting ready to take a shower, and as I'm undressing I think, "Maybe I should start cooking the such-and-such so that when I get out of the shower it'll be partly ready." And it just so happens that every time I do cook naked, it involves molten-lava levels of heat.

Like making peanut brittle.

The first time I made this, I called my friend—a professional pastry chef—and the moment she picked up I frantically yelled, "I'm standing naked in front of a boiling pot of corn syrup and sugar. And I'm trying to make peanut brittle. I don't have a candy thermometer, which I didn't realize I would need. And now I'm afraid I'm gonna burn my nipples off! Should I be scared?!" To which she, unruffled by my antics, calmly replied, "Yes, you should be. I mean, who cooks peanut brittle without a candy thermometer?"

"Who cooks peanut brittle naked?! My nipples are literally trying to crawl back inside my body because they're afraid of being scorched off. Now tell me what I'm supposed to do!"

She then talked me through making peanut brittle—considered to be one of the first candies ever made, by the way—based on my description of what colors the mixture was turning. For example, after it comes to a rolling boil and turns foamy, it should then turn a golden color similar to the top of a hot dog bun. I'd give her credit for the awesome instructions she gave me, but really I think the reason my peanut brittle came out so darn good was because of my obviously innate ability to cook anything masterfully while nekkid.*

* *Please don't try this at home. Or anywhere else for that matter.*

Today is also National Pistachio Day.

JANUARY 27 — NATIONAL CHOCOLATE CAKE DAY

"Let's face it, a nice creamy chocolate cake does a lot for a lot of people; it does for me." —Audrey Hepburn

High five to Duff and Sons for making today a piece of cake!

Sometime in the late 1920s, Duff and Sons—originally a molasses company—created the first quick mix (read: today's boxed mix) cake. However, they—along with other companies jumping on this bandwagon—couldn't quite master the problems there seemed to be with packaging and subsequent spoilage, so it didn't gain popularity right away. Enter General Mills. In 1947, after some serious R&D, they released the "just add water and mix" boxed cakes for Betty Crocker.

Today, chocolate cake is the most popular variety of quick mix cakes in the U.S. Probably because "it does a lot for a lot of people." I mean, just ask Audrey. This graceful, captivating, forward-thinking fashion and film icon knew *exactly* what she wanted from life . . . and apparently it included plenty of good chocolate cake.

So have a slice—or four—today.

DID YOU KNOW?

The word *cake* is of Viking origin. It stems from the Old Norse word *kaka*.

JANUARY 28 — NATIONAL BLUEBERRY PANCAKE DAY

"He who goes to bed hungry dreams of pancakes." —Proverb

When I first started dating, I fell in love with the fantasy of some unreasonably attractive, shirtless boy in a pair of well-fitting jeans effortlessly flipping pancakes for me while undressing me with his steel-gray eyes. That actually sounds like the cover of some steamy erotica for foodies, doesn't it?

While I've waited for this ridiculous fantasy to happen, I've had to learn how to make a stack on my own. Which is a lot less exciting, lemme tell you. But I'm pretty good at it now. So good, in fact, that a friend from California flew across country just to meet me for breakfast and celebrate today's food holiday with me. While I—an unreasonably tired girl in a pair of baggy blue PJ pants—made disproportionately sized pancakes for my friend, he told me that when he makes pancakes for his wife (she's living the dream), he always puts a few in plastic baggies and freezes them. "That way, if I want a snack later, I can just pull one out of the freezer!"

Absolutely brilliant.

Why didn't I think of this great culinary tip?

(Probably because I'm too busy daydreaming of boys making pancakes.)

JANUARY 29 — NATIONAL CORN CHIP DAY

"I believe in a benevolent God not because He created the Grand Canyon or Michelangelo, but because He gave us snacks." —Paul Rudnick, I Shudder

Just eating a bag of corn chips today seemed altogether too boring for me. Surely there had to be something more exciting to do with them than simply chow down by the fistful with a diet soda while playing video games and screaming at n00bz on my headset. How cliché. Actually, I couldn't think of a more perfect way to celebrate today.

Fritos is one of the oldest and most widely recognized brands of corn chips in the States. How did it all start? In 1932, a fella named C.E. Doolin purchased the recipe for some corn chips he particularly liked from a small business eager to sell out. Doolin began to sell his Fritos out of his Model T Ford. (In 1961, the Frito Company would merge with H.W. Lay—a potato chip company—to become Frito-Lay, Inc. Today, they account for 59 percent of the U.S. snack chip industry.)

(Oh, and hey, if you're ever playing Halo online and some girl starts telling you she's wearing a bra made entirely of Cheetos . . . that's me.)

NATIONAL CROISSANT DAY

"Do you know on this one block you can buy croissants in five different places? There's one store called Bonjour Croissant. It makes me want to go to Paris and open up a store called Hello Toast." —Fran Lebowitz

I have a love-love relationship with croissants.

When I was younger, there was this nondescript bakery near our house that made glazed croissants. Yes, you read that right: *glazed* croissants. (Caloric restraint? What's that?) And they were delicious. Think of the way croissants are buttery, flaky . . . the way each bite seems to effortlessly melt in your mouth. Now, on top of that add the same sticky, sweet glaze that's used on doughnuts. Only, unlike doughnuts, the glaze doesn't sit like a film on the surface, as it has the tendency of doing. Instead, it seeps into the first few layers of the croissant, hardening just slightly on the top like an edible lacquer.

Did I mention they were delicious?

One day, however, that bakery ceased to exist: Overnight it had become a kitschy souvenir and trinkets market. And the glazed croissants were never to be had again (breaking my little foodie heart forever; to this day it remains an open wound).

I attempted to make my own croissants today. Just in case you didn't know, the process to do so involves taking puff pastry and layering it with butter by folding it over and over again before baking it. That process is called *laminating* or (as I like to fondly call it) excruciatingly long. My opinion? Skip the labor and just find a bakery near you that makes chocolate-stuffed croissants instead!

DID YOU KNOW?

The croissant is a "descendant" of the Austrian *kipferl*.

NATIONAL HOT CHOCOLATE DAY

"I know all about you. You're the people waiting on the shoreline with the warm towels and the hot chocolate after the woman swims the English Channel."
—Gwen Moore

Don't be fooled: There *is* a difference between hot cocoa and hot chocolate. Cocoa is generally made from a powdered mix of cocoa and sugar that's combined with either hot milk or water. Proper hot chocolate, on the other hand, is made from melted chocolate and hot cream. And it's totally healthy for you to drink. Well, kind of. Back in the day, hot chocolate was used to medically treat things like upset stomachs.

When I first celebrated today's food holiday, it snowed. Which is really the most appropriate thing to have happened, right?

It's true what they say, however: Every time I take that initial big sip of my hot chocolate, the velvety heat from it catches me off guard, warming my entire physical and psychic being in the deepest, darkest, snowiest days of winter.

Like love does, I suppose.

Without the calories.

Or mini marshmallows.

Which kind of makes love sound boring in comparison, doesn't it?

DID YOU KNOW?

Chocolate comes from the Aztec word *Xocolatl*.

Today is also National Brandy Alexander Day and National Popcorn Day.

FEBRUARY IS...

FEBRUARY IS ALSO...

National Bake for Family Fun Month
National Berry Fresh Month
National Canned Food Month
National Cherry Month
National Chocolate Lover's Month
National Fiber Focus Month
National Fondue Month
National Grapefruit Month
National Heart Healthy Month
National Hot Breakfast Month
National Potato Lover's Month
National Return Shopping Carts to the Supermarket Month
National Snack Foods Month
National Sweet Potato Month

. . .

1st Friday—National Bubble Gum Day
1st Saturday—Día Nacional del Pisco Sour (National Pisco Sour Day in Peru) and International Eat Ice Cream for Breakfast Day
2nd Monday—Oatmeal Monday
4th Thursday—National Chili Day
Shrove Tuesday—Pancake Day

NATIONAL BAKED ALASKA DAY

Rose: "I found out that baked Alaska can be baked locally."
Dorothy: "Rose, I know something else. Mars Bars are made right here on Earth."
—The Golden Girls

It doesn't matter if you call it *glace au four, omelette à la norvégienne* (Norwegian omelette), or *baked Alaska*, the sponge-cake-and-ice-cream dessert covered in meringue and then baked in an extremely hot oven is a total mind-boggling masterpiece. Yes, scientifically speaking, I understand that the meringue acts like insulation, thus preventing the ice cream from melting, but still: You're sticking ice cream *in an oven*. And it doesn't turn to soup! That's just crazy, that's what that is.

The folks behind the original concept of this dessert—most likely the Chinese—first used pastry dough instead of meringue. But the evolution of the dessert as we know it today is heavily debated by food historians. So instead of putting in my two cents, let me just say this, in case you missed it the first time: It's ice cream. That's baked. And it doesn't turn to soup.

How has your mind not been blown yet?

I couldn't imagine sticking ice cream into a very hot oven—and apparently neither could any of the restaurants in my neighborhood. (That's because it's not science; It's black magic that's behind this crazy dessert.) As a result, I was forced to celebrate today with baked Alaska–flavored coffee.

Y'know what? It. Still. Counts.

Today is also National Dark Chocolate Day.

JOUR DES CRÊPES

"À la Chandeleur, l'hiver cesse ou reprend vigueur." *(On Candlemas, winter ends or strengthens.)* —A traditional French saying

February 2nd is the Catholic holiday Candelmas (in French: *La Chandeleur*), which honors the day that baby Jesus was presented to the temple and his mother, the Virgin Mary, was purified after giving birth. Candlemas also goes by the name *Jour des Crêpes* (Crêpe Day) since its tradition is to commemorate the day with a whole lotta crêpe eating. It's also customary for a person to flip a crêpe with one hand (in the pan, obviously—could get kinda messy otherwise) while holding a coin in the other. If the person can do it successfully, it ensures happiness and wealth for the year to come.

It may seem silly to you, but remember, February 2nd is also Groundhog Day. A day when many of us in the States watch to see if a rodent is spooked by his shadow, which then determines whether or not winter is over yet. Yup. M'hmm. That happens.

I'm not from-France-French, and I'm not Catholic, but since I like food holidays (and dig Jesus), I thought I would celebrate today. Obviously, if you're attempting to eat the year, there's no pressure to do so since you have other options (it's also National Heavenly Hash Day and National Tater Tot Day, which may or may not be "real"), but who doesn't love crêpes?

Side note: I can't seem to flip my crêpes, because they stick to the edges slightly. Does this mean that in the coming year I will not live long and prosper?!

Today is also National Heavenly Hash Day and National Tater Tot Day.

FEBRUARY 03

NATIONAL CARROT CAKE DAY

"Vegetables are a must on a diet. I suggest carrot cake, zucchini bread, and pumpkin pie." —Jim Davis

Carrot cake will always have a special place in my heart (and on my hips). I once saw a neurologist who encouraged me to eat more carrots. "Juice, soup, in stick form . . . however you want. Just eat more carrots," he said. But what I heard was: "I give you my blessing as a medical professional to eat as much carrot cake as you want."

So that's what I did.

While I was binging on it for my health, folks during the Middle Ages were enjoying the precursor to it—carrot pudding—out of necessity. Carrots naturally contain sugar, and since sweeteners were both expensive and generally unavailable to the common man back then, it only made sense to use what was available to get their dessert on. And in this case that was the humble carrot.

Today we celebrate this dessert borne out of a desire to fix a sugar craving that then turned into a "health" food fad in the 1970s, and has now become a staple dessert on menus everywhere.

NATIONAL HOMEMADE SOUP DAY

"Onion soup sustains. The process of making it is somewhat like the process of learning to love. It requires commitment, extraordinary effort, time, and will make you cry." —Ronni Lundy

Whether it's coming home to the inviting smell after being out in the cold, wet snow all day or having a steaming bowl brought to you when you're feeling sick, homemade soup has a way of restoring our bodies and souls.

Soup is considered to be one of the first foods ever made or served in public restaurants. I know the former to be true; after all, it was one of the first foods my sister and I ever made while playing outside. (Shh! Don't tell our guests, but the pine needles we used in our "soups" were the same pine needles we used as both our beds and wall dividers in our "house.")

During college it also seemed to be the only thing my guy friends knew how to make. They called it man stew, and they would throw anything leftover that couldn't be considered a meal on its own into a big pot to cook down together for a couple of hours. (I'm guessing not that much has changed since that very first soup was ever made 'lo those thousands of years ago.) They made some absolutely genius creations that way. Then again, they made some really repulsive concoctions that way, too. Never were we more grateful for the pizza delivery man than in those moments (a luxury early man would have also loved in underwhelming culinary moments, no doubt).

Give it a go today—chuck some stuff into a pot, invite some friends over to chuck some stuff into a pot, wait a couple of hours, and then try your masterpiece!

(And maybe have the delivery guy's number on speed dial, just in case.)

Today is also National Stuffed Mushroom Day.

SQUASH AND CIDER SOUP

Makes 4 servings

1 medium butternut squash
1½ cups whole milk, divided
1 cup apple cider, divided
⅛ teaspoon black pepper
¼ plus ⅛ teaspoon salt
½ teaspoon crushed red pepper flakes

Preheat the oven to 350°F.

Cut the squash in half. Scoop out the seeds and pulp and discard them. Place the squash, flesh-side down, on a nonstick baking sheet and bake for

45 minutes to 1 hour, or until a knife can be easily inserted through the skin. Remove the squash from the oven and let it cool slightly.

Scoop the squash's soft flesh out of its skin and into a blender. Add ¾ cup of the milk, ½ cup of the cider, pepper, salt, and pepper flakes. Blend until creamy. The soup will be thick, so add a little more of the milk and cider, alternating back and forth, until the soup is of a consistency to your liking. Serve immediately.

Tip! This soup freezes very well.

FEBRUARY 05

WORLD NUTELLA DAY

"Giving chocolate to others is an intimate form of communication, a sharing of deep, dark secrets." —Milton Zelman

There were a few things about me that stuck out when I lived in Europe. Besides my obviously American accent and the way I drank my tea (black), the other was my total and utter disgust of Nutella.

I just didn't "get it." I had tried Bacio gelato from a *gelateria* in Tenerife, Spain, once, and it tasted gritty to me. Maybe because of that, the idea of chocolate and hazelnut *anything* turned me off.

Years later I tried actual Nutella for the first time. I was hungry, and the only things to eat in my home were Nutella, frozen waffles, and fresh blueberries. My gastronomical world changed for the better that day! (Seriously: Stop reading this book right now, go to the store, purchase those three things, come home, toast the waffle, top it with the Nutella and blueberries, and shove in your face. Eat. Repeat. Eat. Repeat.)

Now I'm sad I spent so many years Nutella-less. But today—and every February 5th from here on out—I get to make up for that. Created in 2007 by Sara Rosso and Michelle Fabio, two American writers living in Italy, World Nutella Day is all about spreading the (Nutella) love.

So what will you spread it on? Waffles and berries like me? Maybe you'll use it instead of peanut butter in your PB&J sandwiches? I bet it might be fun to lick off someone's body, too! Or maybe you're a purist and you just eat yours with a spoon.

There is no shame in this, friends. None at all.

Today is also National Chocolate Fondue Day.

HEALTHY(IER) CHOCOFILBERT SPREAD

Makes roughly 1½ cups

- 1 cup raw hazelnuts
- ⅓ cup cocoa powder
- 2 tablespoons (or more if you want it really sweet) honey or agave syrup, divided
- ½ cup plus 2 tablespoons heavy whipping cream (or water for lower fat), divided

Preheat the oven to 350°F.

Roast the raw hazelnuts in the oven for 10 minutes.

Remove the hazelnuts from the oven and put them in a blender. Add the cocoa powder, 1 tablespoon of honey, and ¼ cup of heavy cream. Blend until everything is combined.

Add the other tablespoon of honey and another ¼ cup of heavy cream. Continue to blend until the nuts are completely broken down. If necessary, add the additional 2 tablespoons of heavy cream, a little at a time, until the spread is the smoothest consistency possible.

NATIONAL CHOPSTICKS DAY

"When I'm at a Chinese restaurant having a hard time with chopsticks, I always hope that there's a Chinese kid at an American restaurant somewhere who's struggling mightily with a fork." —Rick Budinich

Chopsticks, or *kuàizi* as they're known in Chinese, have been in use for over 5,000 years. As food was cut into smaller pieces to help it cook faster, chopsticks became the preferred utensil. It's also believed that the widespread use of chopsticks *may* have had something to do with Confucius, who said, "The honorable and upright man keeps well away from both the slaughterhouse and the kitchen. And he allows no knives on his table." A peaceful and wise philosopher, Confucius believed that knives were symbolic of aggression and murder, something that went against the vegetarian's gentle, nonviolent way of life.

Even though I have my doubts about whether or not this is a legit food holiday, I still celebrated.

How could I not—there was a restaurant in the town I was living in actually called Chopsticks! And any time I have an excuse to use chopsticks, I do.

Probably because I'm an honorable and upright vegetarian (wo)man.

DID YOU KNOW?

The English word *chopstick* may have derived from Chinese Pidgin English, in which *chop chop* meant *quickly*.

Today is also National Frozen Yogurt Day.

NATIONAL FETTUCCINE ALFREDO DAY

"Fettucini Alfredo is macaroni and cheese for adults." —Mitch Hedberg

I think that fettuccine Alfredo is one of the first dishes young adults order at a restaurant when they want to feel mature. I know my friends and I did it when we were teens. If we were trying to act older than we actually were, we'd go out to eat at the semi-fancy Italian restaurant in town where they served water in wine glasses.

We'd each order the fettuccine Alfredo (probably because it sounded foreign and impressive rolling off our young tongues), act as posh as possible, and discuss the woes of our incredibly complicated lives. ("Really, how do they expect me to get *all the way* to my locker to pick up my books when they've placed my classes on like opposite ends of the building?!") Much like younger versions of the women from *Sex and the City*.

The funny thing is, Alfredo sauce as we know it, which is made from cream, isn't really a popular Italian thing like we'd like to believe it is (which we learned on January 17, International Day of Italian Cuisine). Their version of the dish is *pasta al burro*, or pasta with butter. And that's where our version originates. Specifically, in 1914 a Roman man named Alfredo di Lelio used far more butter than the dish usually called for as a way to tempt his pregnant wife into eating again. It became very popular, and the rest is history.

Sono un felice giorno fettuccine Alfredo! (Happy National Fettuccine Alfredo Day!)

GROWN-UP MAC AND CHEESE

½ cup (1 stick) unsalted butter

2 tablespoons all-purpose flour

2 cups heavy whipping cream

1 (8-ounce) bag shredded Parmesan cheese (about 2 cups)

2 ounces cream cheese

¼ teaspoon nutmeg

¼ teaspoon garlic powder

1 tablespoon onion flakes

½ teaspoon crushed red pepper flakes

1 tablespoon lemon juice

¼ teaspoon salt

1 (1-pound) box fettuccine

1 (15-ounce) can sweet peas, drained and rinsed

1 (15-ounce) can cannellini beans, drained and rinsed

In a pot over medium-high heat, melt the butter. Add the flour and whisk until pasty. Add the cream, Parmesan cheese, and cream cheese. Whisk until blended. Add the nutmeg, garlic powder, onion flakes, pepper flakes, lemon juice, and salt. Bring this all to a boil before turning down to a simmer.

While the sauce is thickening, make the fettuccine according to the directions on the box. When the pasta is done, drain it and add it back to the pot it was cooking in. Pour the sauce over the fettuccine and add the peas and the cannellini beans. Toss until everything is combined and the pasta is coated, and serve.

NATIONAL MOLASSES BAR DAY

"The Wine of Truth is not fermented from molasses." —Sri Guru Granth Sahib

"Slowah than molasses goin' uphill in the dead ah' wintah."

Oh, molasses. It's a food item that either invokes smiles and memories of delicious baked goods our grandmothers made during our childhood, or grimaces . . . and memories of our parents reciting the above idiom to us during our childhood when we were forced to do something we weren't particularly interested in as sluggishly as possible. Love it or hate it, the thick, sticky, sometimes pungent syrup has definitely left an impact on everyone who's come into contact with it.

The word *molasses* stems from *melaço*, a Portuguese word that evolved from *mel,* which is the Latin word for "honey." It's produced by extracting the juice from sugarcane, which is then boiled down into sugar. And believe it or not, molasses isn't as sweet as you might think it is. On January 15, 1919, an enormous molasses storage tank in Boston exploded, sending lava-esque molasses coursing through the streets killing twenty-one people.

When molasses isn't causing public damage, it can actually be quite delicious (contained in bar form, that is). And if you really want to celebrate today like a true champ, try eating it outside walking slowly uphill. February is, after all, the dead of winter.

DID YOU KNOW?

Printing presses originally used molasses and glue for their ink rollers.

Today is also National Potato Lover's Day.

FEBRUARY 09 — NATIONAL PIZZA PIE DAY

"Ideas are like pizza dough, made to be tossed around." —Anna Quindlen

I'm not sure why some parts of the world call it pizza pie. Maybe it's just a regional thing like soda versus pop, or maybe it's because pizza is essentially just an open-faced version of a pie. (There's a crust, there's a filling, and then it's baked—makes sense, right?) I've never really put that much thought into it; my grandfather just *always* called it pizza pie.

Whatever you call it, pizza is delicious and versatile and one of our country's favorite foods. Pizza as we know it today comes from Italy (although the concept of the food may have originated elsewhere). The romantic legend goes that when Queen Margherita visited Naples in 1889, she was served pizza by a chef named Raffaele Esposito. The slice of pie featured tomato sauce, mozzarella, and basil, which was representative of the three colors of the Italian flag.

And today we call that style of pizza what? *Margherita.* Brilliant, right?

Today is also National Bagels and Lox Day.

NATIONAL CREAM CHEESE BROWNIE DAY

"Childhood smells of perfume and brownies." —David Leavitt, Territory

So you're craving both a brownie and a piece of cheesecake. Such a conundrum! How does one fix such an epic problem without, oh, I don't know, just eating both and feeling like a fatty later? The answer is easy: Make cream cheese brownies.

Personally, I'm a *huge* fan of the chocolate/cheese flavor combination in just about any form (see National Cheese Ball Day on April 17, page 129), and today's no different. While I'm generally not the world's biggest brownie lover, I do think there's something extra special tasting about the fudgy (not cakey) consistency of a well-made brownie marbled with tangy, sweet cream cheese.

So today I made my own: avocado brownies topped with a citrus and cane sugar-sweetened cream cheese. The best part? Dolloping the cream cheese on top of the brownie batter, grabbing a single chopstick, and swirling it all together madly, like I was a little kid just given permission to scribble all over the wall.

Oh, and eating them wasn't too bad either!

DID YOU KNOW?

Chocolate syrup was used in *Psycho*'s famous blood-swirling-down-the-drain shower scene.

NATIONAL PEPPERMINT PATTY DAY

"Every meal should end with something sweet. Maybe it's jelly on toast at breakfast or a small piece of chocolate at dinner—but it always helps my brain bring a close to the meal." —Robert Irvine

When I was in seventh grade I had short red hair, dark brown freckles that made a "W" across my face (they started at one cheekbone, looped up to the bridge of my nose, then looped over to the other cheekbone), and I wore sandals every day of the year. So my French teacher started calling me Peppermint Patty. I hadn't thought of that in years until today.

Even though I was in a rush to get out of the house because I had to go to work as a Heineken Girl at a ski resort (because nothing sells skunky beer to tired skiers like girls in skimpy black outfits at après–ski parties), I decided to make my own peppermint patties from scratch. I used coconut in the center instead of powdered sugar, and it absolutely changed my mind about the candy that I was a little indifferent to before. They take a little effort, but are so, so worth it!

Trust me on this one, Chuck.

Today is also National Don't Cry Over Spilled Milk Day.

FROZEN COCOMINT PATTIES

Makes 12 patties

2 cups packed, sweetened, shredded coconut

¼ cup corn syrup

4 tablespoons unsalted butter, at room temperature, divided

2 tablespoons coconut milk

2 teaspoons pure peppermint extract

1 (8-ounce) bag chocolate chips (about 2 cups)

1 teaspoon vanilla extract

Line a baking sheet with waxed paper and set aside.

With a wooden spoon, mix together the shredded coconut, corn syrup, 2 tablespoons butter, coconut milk, and peppermint extract. Drop rounded tablespoons onto the baking sheet. Gently flatten each spoonful into a "patty" shape with your hand. Place the baking sheet in the freezer and freeze for 20 minutes.

Toward the end of the freezing time, melt the chocolate chips, remaining 2 tablespoons butter, and vanilla over low heat. Remove the baking sheet from the freezer and, working quickly, dunk each patty into the chocolate to coat each side evenly.

Using a toothpick or fork, gently pull out each patty and place them back on the lined baking sheet. Once you've finished coating all the patties in chocolate, put the baking sheet back in the freezer for another 20 minutes before enjoying. Frozen tastes best!

FEBRUARY 12 — NATIONAL PLUM PUDDING DAY

". . . the art of cooking as practiced by Englishmen does not extend much beyond roast beef and plum pudding." —Pehr Kalm

What contains no plums and is also called Christmas pudding?

If your guess is plum pudding . . . you're right!

This particular dessert was popularized in the seventeenth century when raisins, prunes, and other dried fruits were all referred to as plums. Original ingredients included not only dried fruit but also alcohol and suet (as in straight-up fat from animals like sheep and cows). It was so rich and decadent that the Puritans even banned it because it was "sinful" (read: it was saturated in booze).

It was (and still is in some places) tradition in England to bake small silver charms into the pudding. Wishbones represent good luck; a ring symbolizes marriage; and a coin indicates wealth in the coming year. When I lived in Berkshire, I actually got to partake in this tradition. I did *not* receive the silver coin in my portion of plum pudding. Then again, I had no idea that I was supposed to even be looking for one until one of my friend's girlfriends started squealing in delight when she found it.

I did, however, find the coin when I celebrated today. Then again, I was the only person partaking in my super whiskey-soaked slice of pudding. I wonder if that still means there's wealth in my future. After all, eating the year is not the cheapest hobby!

FEBRUARY 13 — NATIONAL TORTELLINI DAY

"Life is a combination of magic and pasta." —Federico Fellini

Somewhere hidden among the many arched passageways in Bologna, Italy, there's a group of serious foodies who call themselves *Dotta Confraternita del Tortellino*. (In English: the Learned Order of the Tortellini—sounds a lot more impressive in Italian, doesn't it?) This large-in-number "brotherhood" serves one very important purpose: the preservation of the beloved and traditional pasta that is said to have originated in their fair city.

Sign me up!

They take their pasta seriously, too. On December 7, 1974, they, along with the Accademia Italiana della Cucina, registered what they considered the one true, authentic tortellini recipe with the Chamber of Commerce in Bologna. The ingredients include pork loin, mortadella, and prosciutto crudo.

Pig three ways, eh? Guess I'm forced to resign early. I'll just stick to my cheese-filled belly button-looking pasta, thanks.

Today may have been my favorite food holiday to date, because *someone else did the cooking*. My mom (whose name is Dell, thus the play on words in the recipe's title), who has discovered a serious passion for Italian cuisine, was eager to use today as an opportunity to show me her newest dish. All I had to do was show up and eat.

Good food, good company . . . who needs a brotherhood?

Today is also National Crab Rangoon Day.

DELL-IZIOSO TORTELLINI CON MOLTI INGREDIENTI

Makes 4 servings

10 to 12 ounces tortellini

¼ cup olive oil

1 teaspoon crushed red pepper flakes

1 (28-ounce) can whole plum tomatoes

1 (10-ounce) jar green olives with pimientos

½ cup sliced Bella mushrooms

½ (8-ounce) block Parmesan cheese, grated
   (about 1 cup)

Prepare the tortellini according to package directions.

While the tortellini is cooking, put the olive oil and pepper flakes into a large skillet on medium heat. Drain the tomatoes, cut them into chunks, and add them to the skillet *gently*, as the oil will be hot. Drain the olives, chop them, and add them and the mushrooms to the skillet. Gently stir all the ingredients together in the skillet to heat everything through, about 1 minute; turn off the heat and leave the skillet on the burner.

When the tortellini is cooked, use a slotted spoon to gently transfer the pasta directly from the water to the skillet, one spoonful at a time. When all the tortellini is in the skillet, gently stir everything together until all the ingredients are combined.

Spoon the pasta into four bowls or onto four plates, top each with ¼ cup of the grated Parmesan cheese and serve.

NATIONAL CREAM-FILLED CHOCOLATES DAY

"Chemically speaking, chocolate really is the world's perfect food." —Michael Levine

How appropriate (and cliché) it is that today's food holiday is cream-filled chocolates. Is it National Dozen Red Roses Day, too? National Sparkly Jewelry Day? National Expensive Dinner Out Day? National Forced Sentiments on a Three-Dollar Greeting Card Day?

I'm not bitter. I'm just terrified. This is what nervous energy looks like. You see, when you decide to eat cream-filled chocolates—especially the ones that come in a big heart-shaped box with no map on the inside cover to tell you what's hiding inside each little piece—you take your life into your own hands. When you finally decide on a piece to eat, it's never filled with what you want it to be filled with, like orange or rum-flavored crème. No. Instead, it's filled with something like rock-hard molasses that gets stuck on your front teeth. (Friends don't let friends walk around with stuff in their teeth, by the way.)

Instead of playing games (which today *so* isn't about), I spent my evening with a love I can trust. I got dressed up in my finest sweats, poured myself a glass of wine, turned on a reality TV show about finding love, and ate an entire package of Oreos. Which are what?

Cream-filled chocolates!

(If you're trying to celebrate these food holidays as literally as possible, it's gonna be a very, very long year my friends.)

DID YOU KNOW?

Casanova ate chocolate to help enhance his . . . um . . . libido.

NATIONAL GUMDROP DAY

"No! Not the buttons! Not my gumdrop buttons!" —Gingerbread Man, **Shrek**

I have a confession to make: When I was younger and played Candy Land, I always rigged the deck of cards so that I could land on Queen Frostine's square because she was pretty and wore an awesome dress. (Although she confused me; what candy was she representing exactly? I never understood.) I always thought that she and Mr. Mint should be together. But they couldn't be, because Jolly and the stupid Gumdrop Mountains were always in the way. And I imagine traveling through the Gumdrop Mountains is incredibly difficult and sticky. All I can picture is poor Mr. Mint taking a step into very deep red goo and his long, gangly leg getting stuck before being sucked down into it, eaten alive by this incline of sugar and gelatin.

It's horrifying, right?

Today, you can find gumdrops in all sorts of different flavor options like licorice, spearmint, orange, cherry, grape, lemon, cinnamon, vanilla, mango, grapefruit, and even fruit punch.

Here's to a happy National Gumdrop Day!

(Unless you're part of the star-crossed lover duo of Mr. Mint and Queen Frostine, that is.)

DID YOU KNOW?

The Apollo 9 Command Module
was nicknamed Gumdrop.

NATIONAL ALMOND DAY

"I said to the almond tree: 'Speak to me of God,' and the almond tree blossomed."
—Nikos Kazantzakis, The Fratricides

Almonds are full of really great nutrients like Vitamin E, magnesium, protein, and fiber. People have eaten and respected the nut almost nearly forever—the almond's actually mentioned in the Bible on several occasions. The first time, in Genesis 43:11, as being one of "the best products of land" (New American Standard).

To pay homage to these little nuts that have been such a significant source of food and symbolism for many different cultures throughout the ages, I wanted to do more than just stuff my face with the lovely tear-shaped nuts. So I attempted to make my first batch of glazed, roasted almonds. How difficult could it be, right? After coating the nuts in a delicious spicy, brown sugary glaze, I put them in the oven to bake at 350°F. The process seemed to be taking too long for my liking, so I turned my oven up to 400°.

Ten minutes later, smoke was pouring out of my oven, quickly filling my entire apartment. The almonds had burned completely black. Frantically, I grabbed the baking sheet the nuts were on with a towel and threw the entire thing outside into the snow. I ripped open all my windows, jumped up on my kitchen chair, and began vigorously waving a magazine in front of my screeching fire alarm in hopes of silencing it (the whole building did not need to know what a failure I was).

It was one of the only food holidays all year I wished I could have had a do-over on.

Next year? Pre-roasted almonds for this girl.

MONTANA BEAR POOP, AKA MAINE MOOSE DROPPINGS

Makes 36 cookies

1 (8-ounce) bag chocolate chips (about 2 cups)
½ cup heavy whipping cream
1¼ cups almond butter
3 cups quick oats
1 cup tamari almonds

Line a baking sheet with waxed paper and set aside.

In a medium-size pot on medium heat, melt the chocolate chips with the cream. Stir in the almond butter to melt.

Using a wooden spoon, add the oats and tamari almonds, stirring until everything is combined. Make one-inch-size balls and place them on the baking sheet. Place the baking sheet in the fridge to cool for at least 1 hour, until the cookies have set. Enjoy with a nice cup of coffee!

Tip! The more nut butter you add, the better the oats will stick (with the result more like a granola bar).

FEBRUARY 17 — NATIONAL CABBAGE DAY

"At middle age the soul should be opening up like a rose, not closing up like a cabbage." —John Andrew Holmes

I have this crazy obsession with food smells. When I was younger, I used to pack an extra shirt with me if I went out to eat because I couldn't stand smelling like the restaurant afterward. It's a bizarre quirk, I know.

When I moved into my own apartment, I became really neurotic about the way it smelled after I cooked. So I would go out of my way to find the most potent candles that I could to light while cooking in hopes that it would mask the smell of the food. One day I found an awesome recipe for sauerkraut and told my sister about it. She took me by the shoulders, looked me dead in the eye, and said, "Do you know what cabbage smells like when it's cooking? Like a big, giant fart."

Even though the sauerkraut was delicious, she was absolutely right. My house reeked of flatulence for days afterward.

Cabbage is considered a national food of Russia; it was also my grandmother's pet name for my sister and me growing up; she called us her *chouchou*, or her "little cabbages." The veg is related to broccoli, cauliflower, kohlrabi, and kale, and is a great source of potassium, Vitamin K, and fiber (it's considered an excellent food for intestinal health).

This makes me wonder if maybe my house didn't smell like farts because I had *cooked* cabbage. Hmm.

Today is also National Café au Lait Day and National Indian Pudding Day.

CABBAGE ROLLS IN BOWLS

Makes 4 to 6 servings

8 ounces ground chicken or 1 (1-pound) package tempeh, crumbled

4 tablespoons olive oil, divided

½ large Vidalia onion, chopped (about 1 cup)

2 garlic cloves, minced

1 small cabbage, shredded (about 3 cups)

1 (15-ounce) can stewed tomatoes (about 2 cups)

½ cup brown rice, cooked

2½ tablespoons tomato paste

2 teaspoons granulated sugar

½ teaspoon dried oregano

¼ teaspoon dried basil

¼ teaspoon cumin

¾ teaspoon salt

½ teaspoon black pepper

1 cup cherry tomatoes, quartered

In a large pot, cook the ground chicken or sauté the tempeh in two tablespoons of the olive oil until cooked through and golden-brown, about 5 to 7 minutes. Using a slotted spoon, transfer your choice of protein from the pot to a bowl and set it aside.

Add the other 2 tablespoons of olive oil to the pot and sauté the onions until translucent, about 3 to 5 minutes. Add the garlic and cook until fragrant, another 2 to 3 minutes. Add the cabbage, stewed tomatoes, rice, tomato paste, sugar, oregano, basil, cumin, salt, and pepper. Simmer on medium-low heat for about 15 minutes, stirring occasionally.

Add the cherry tomatoes and cook for another 5 minutes. Serve immediately.

Tip! This dish freezes really well.

NATIONAL DRINK WINE DAY

"Wine cheers the sad, revives the old, inspires the young, makes weariness forget his toil." —Lord Byron

In the sixth grade, I wrote a report about wine. Luckily for me, and apropos for today, I still have that research paper! What's more charming than a twelve-year-old attempting to explain the wine-making process?

"It doesn't take a rocket scientist to figure out how to make wine," I wrote. "All it takes is a little luck and a lot of hard work. . . . People also think that white wine must be made with white grapes and red wine with red grapes, which is completely untrue. White wine can be made with white, pink, green, and even red grapes. Red wine can be made with red, black, and blue grapes. Blush (pink) wines can be made with just about any color grapes.

Making wine is fairly easy. When the grapes are ready, they have to be picked in clusters, which can either be loose or tight. After picking the grapes, they need to be washed. But only the ones that are being used immediately need washing. Now you must crush the grapes,

either by jumping up and down on them with bare feet or by blending them in a blender.

Once the grapes have been picked, washed, and squashed, they go into a fermenting machine (a large container with a lid) and are left to set. After the grapes have set for some time, the yeasty liquid on the top is scooped off and the rest is compressed to get rid of any whole grapes. What's left has to set for a few more days, but this has to be stirred occasionally. A few days later the wine is ready to drink!"

Couldn't have said it better myself.

DID YOU KNOW?

Oenophobia is the intense fear, or even hatred, of wine. What's the opposite of that? 'Cause that's what I have.

Today is also National Crab-Stuffed Flounder Day.

NATIONAL CHOCOLATE MINT DAY

"It is the destiny of mint to be crushed." —Waverley Lewis Root

The chocolate and mint duo reminds me of that kind of couple other people are inspired by because they seem so perfect for each other, not in spite of, but because of their differences. "Chocolate and mint? Their relationship is so honest, sincere, refreshing, and comfortable. I just love those two together!"

Am I the only one who thinks of food this way?

I associate the end of a meal with some kind of dessert. And I associate the end of my day with a good teeth brushing before I climb into bed. Weird as it may seem, I'm a fan of the chocolate-mint flavor combination. It seems like the perfect gastronomical *and* psychological way to end dinner, which is also at the end of the day. It's sort of like the very last period at the end of a chapter. You know there's more to come, but in that moment you revel in what you just read (or ate).

There are so many delicious ways to celebrate today—ice cream, martinis, those little mints you get after a meal, or even with the actual herb—but I decided to go with a package of chocolate peppermint break-apart-and-bake cookies. Only I didn't bake them.

Love is best raw anyway.

DID YOU KNOW?

Ever wonder why chocolate melts in your mouth? It's because chocolate's melting point is very close to our own body temperature.

NATIONAL CHERRY PIE DAY

"So we grow together, Like to a double cherry, seeming parted, But yet an union in partition." —Shakespeare, A Midsummer Night's Dream

Cherry pie, like its cousin the apple pie, is considered both a staple and classic American dessert. The fruit was originally brought over by early European settlers sometime in the seventeenth century. Currently, most of the tart cherries grown in the U.S. actually come from Michigan. And Traverse City, Michigan, even calls itself the Cherry Capital of the World, hosting an annual festival in early July.

The placement of many food holidays makes no sense, so it's best not to overanalyze why Cherry Pie Day—or Cherry Month in general—falls in the midst of winter. Maybe it's because February is the month of love . . . red is the color associated with

love . . . and cherries are red. Is that too much of a stretch? Maybe it's Cherry Pie Day and Cherry Month because our country's original fearless leader, Mr. George Washington, has a birthday in two days and will forever be associated with hacking down a cherry tree.

Whatever the reason, instead of celebrating our first president's birthday with a slice of cake, honor him this year with a big ol' slice of cherry pie!

DID YOU KNOW?

The Cherry Pit Spitting Capital of the World is in Eau Claire, Michigan.

NATIONAL STICKY BUN DAY

FEBRUARY 21

"Life, within doors, has few pleasanter prospects than a neatly arranged and well-provisioned breakfast table." —Nathaniel Hawthorne, The House of the Seven Gables

If you're attempting to eat the year, do make sure you're actually celebrating today with a sticky bun and not a cinnamon roll. I hate to get technical, but because there's *both* a National Sticky Bun Day *and* a National Cinnamon Rolls Day (October 4, page 318), it's important to know the difference.

Cinnamon rolls are filled with cinnamon and sugar before being rolled up, sliced evenly, and baked. After which they're topped with icing or cream cheese. (Team Icing all the way!) Sticky buns are filled with anything from cinnamon and sugar, espresso powder and sugar, pumpkin pie spice, apple pie spice, nuts, raisins, you name it. They're rolled up, sliced evenly, and placed in a baking dish that has a layer of caramel sauce on the bottom. After the buns are baked, they're flipped upside down out of the dish so the caramel goo can further drown the layers of the roll. This sweet treat comes from the German settlers in Pennsylvania and was originally called *schnecken*, which is German for "snails."

Before I dove headfirst into making sticky buns for the first time, I thought it'd be smart to call my pastry chef friend back up for her advice. "However tempting it might seem," she started, "do *not* eat the remaining sticky caramel mixture out from the bottom of the pan. You will want to, but I'm telling you right now it will be very, *very* hot. Okay?" Seemed like common sense to me, yet I feel the need to tell you. . . .

Don't do it. Trust me on this one. You will not feel your fingertip for weeks after.

Today is also National Biscuits and Gravy Day.

NATIONAL MARGARITA DAY

"That's the problem with drinking, I thought, as I poured myself a drink. If something bad happens you drink in an attempt to forget; if something good happens you drink in order to celebrate; and if nothing happens you drink to make something happen." —Charles Bukowski, Women

I spent most of my twenties working as an alcohol spokesmodel. It was an incredibly fun job that I was really good at. I made everyone around me feel comfortable despite the fact that I was usually wearing little to no clothing and rudely interrupting their conversations or dinners to promote alcohol. I was courteous to the personnel at the restaurants and stores we were sent to, and after every promotion I always thanked every single person (from the bouncers to the bartenders to the waiters to the patrons) who played along with us. I know I was a rock star at my job.

Some of my favorite promos were the tequila ones we did at locally owned Mexican restaurants. Not only did the promo girls have sweet giveaways like tank tops for the ladies and shirts for the guys in *all* sizes (whereas usually we only ever had L's and XL's men's shirts), the bar's special was usually something like "buy a margarita for $5 and keep the glass it comes in." That was an *awesome* deal. The glasses they came in were worth at least as

much. So folks were walking out with anywhere from $20 to $40 worth of merchandise for a fiver! All for enjoying a libation (or four).

So how do you margarita? Me? On ice with extra rock salt.

Today is also National Cook a Sweet Potato Day.

FEBRUARY 23 — NATIONAL BANANA BREAD DAY

"Good bread is the most fundamentally satisfying of all foods; good bread with fresh butter, the greatest of feasts!" —James Beard

If you've frequented a farm stand in the past couple of years, you may have noticed little signs near the bananas that compare the fruit's ripeness to the three colors of a stoplight. Green means go, orange means slow down, and red means stop in the traffic world; however, that's inverted when it comes to bananas: Green means stop, yellow means go, and spotty yellow means *go go go!*

But what about the fourth dimension of the banana world? Well, friends, today is *not* the day to consider it "bin it brown," but rather "*bake* it brown." Even if bananas and their phloem bundles (those stringy bits attached to the fruit—yes, they actually have a name!) aren't your favorite, you have to admit: There are few things quite as lovely as a piece of freshly baked banana chocolate chip bread slathered with melting butter on a cold wintry morning.

I'm drooling just thinking about it.

FEBRUARY 24 — NATIONAL TORTILLA CHIP DAY

"A falta de pan, tortillas." (In the absence of bread, tortillas will do.) —Mexican proverb

I'm addicted to red tortilla chips.

I don't know what it is about them—it's not like they taste any different—but I'm obsessed. So much so, that if I'm at a restaurant that serves all three colors, I'll attempt to either (A) get our waiter to only give me red ones, or (B) trade off my white and blue tortilla chips with anyone around me willing to do so.

Tortilla chips didn't start off red. For that matter, they didn't even start in Mexico. Tortilla chips were originally made by Rebecca Webb Carranza in Los Angeles, California. Sometime in the late 1940s she took the misshapen tortillas from the machines of her family's El Zarape Tortilla Factory and instead of throwing them away, she cut them in triangles, fried them, and sold them in baggies for ten cents apiece. They became very, very popular, which is kind of an understatement given that today is a food holiday entirely devoted to them!

I love tortilla chips all ways: with salsa, with guacamole, with a chili-cheese dip (one can of chili plus one tub of cream cheese plus a couple minutes in the microwave equals total mouthgasm), or even with all three at once! Today, no one can judge you. (Even if you do have weird tortilla color preferences.)

JOSH'S "HELLA GOOD" HANGOVER FOOD

Makes 2 servings

1½ pounds tomatillos, peeled, washed, and dried
½ large Vidalia onion, cut into one-inch chunks
½ teaspoon salt, divided
¼ teaspoon black pepper
1½ tablespoons olive oil
2 or 3 Japones chile peppers
1 cup boiling water
2 garlic cloves
1 (8-ounce) bag tortilla chips
1 cup queso freso (or feta cheese if you're in a bind)
6 eggs, fried
Crema, crème fraiche, or sour cream, to taste

Preheat the oven to 350°F. Grease a baking sheet and set it aside.

Cut the tomatillos into quarters. Place the tomatillos and onions on the baking sheet, sprinkle with ¼ teaspoon of salt and the pepper, drizzle with olive oil, and roast in the oven until the tomatillos and onions are browned and the juices are running out, about 40 to 50 minutes.

Twenty minutes before the oven roasting is done, toast the Japones peppers in a hot, ungreased pan for about 10 seconds on each side; they should begin to develop a darker skin. Move the peppers to a small bowl, add the remaining salt, cover them with boiling water, and let them soak for 15 to 20 minutes.

To make salsa verde:

Remove the baking sheet from the oven. Scrape the tomatillos, onions, and their juices, and the garlic into a food processor. Remove the Japones peppers from the water, saving the water in case it's needed later for thinning, and add them to the food processor. Pulse everything until it's puréed to a textured consistency—not too chunky; not too runny (add some Japones pepper water if too thick).

To build:

Place 4 ounces of tortilla chips on a plate. Top with ¾ cup salsa verde, ½ cup queso freso, three fried eggs, and crema to taste. Make a second serving with the rest of the ingredients.

FEBRUARY 25

NATIONAL CLAM CHOWDER DAY

"Chowder breathes reassurance. It steams consolation." —Clementine Paddleford

Didn't we just celebrate this holiday? Oh, wait, no—that was National *New England* Clam Chowder Day on January 21st (page 30). Totally different (no, seriously).

Chowder, which has been around for hundreds and hundreds of years, was originally considered to be a poor man's food (might seem crazy, but remember: Lobster was once considered only good enough for prisoners and peasants to eat!) because it was a relatively simple and unimpressive dish made from stewed fish and/or vegetables.

Over the years, though, it's evolved into something much more hearty and complex, with different regions of the world boasting that theirs is the best.

We already know that New England clam chowder is usually made from cream, clams, potatoes, and onions (and should be topped with oyster crackers, too!). Stateside, there are two other primary options: Manhattan clam chowder, which is made from tomatoes in more of a stewlike fashion, and Rhode Island clam chowder, which usually has a clear clam broth. Another lesser known version perhaps is Minorcan clam chowder—from St. Augustine, Florida—which is similar to Manhattan's version, but with the addition of locally grown datil peppers (anywhere from 100,000 to 300,000 SHU).

So basically your options are: creamy, tomato-y, extra clammy, or hot. Which will you go for?

Today is also National Chocolate Covered Peanuts Day.

FEBRUARY 26 — NATIONAL PISTACHIO DAY

"Pistachio nuts, the red ones, cure any problem." —Paula Danziger, The Pistachio Prescription

I don't usually like having to fight with my food before eating it, but I don't mind wrestling with a pistachio or two hundred. They're delicious! And fun to look at—they naturally split open when they mature in a manner that has led them to be called both the "smiling nut" and "the happy nut" in regions of both the Middle East and China, respectively.

Pistachios were brought to the States sometime in the latter half of the nineteenth century. More importantly, a gentleman by the name of James Parkinson from Philadelphia is credited with creating pistachio ice cream. This actually helped propel their popularity! The little greenish nut is chock-a-block-full of fiber, copper, and Vitamin B6.

After the drama of National Almond Day (page 59), I decided it would be best to just eat my pistachios raw. But feel free not to play it as safe. There are loads of delicious ways to enjoy pistachios—in biscotti, baklava, as a butter, or even in pesto!

NATIONAL KAHLÚA DAY

"Someone is putting brandy in your bonbons, Grand Marnier in your breakfast jam, Kahlúa in your ice cream, Scotch in your mustard, and Wild Turkey in your cake." —Marian Burros

Kahlúa is a coffee-based liqueur made from 100 percent Arabica coffee beans, sugar cane spirits, caramel, and vanilla. It's been handcrafted in Veracruz, Mexico, since 1936. While many suggest the name *Kahlúa* comes from the old Nahuatl language for "House of the Acolhua people," the company itself says the name comes from the Arabic slang word for coffee (*kahwa*).

I'm no stranger to coffee-based liqueurs. I once spent an entire summer consuming a locally made version mixed with whole milk in a drink named a Sombrero. (Or, for those of you who are more familiar than you'd like to be with this drink, you'll

know it's also appropriately called Lard in a Jar because of the weight you may gain in your derriere from enjoying one too many of them.)

I thought it would be best just to drink my Kahlúa on the rocks today. If you're not eating the year, and are a little less concerned with your caloric intake, try mixing it with vodka and Irish crème to make a Mudslide, or with amaretto and cream or milk for a Toasted Almond!

Today is also National Strawberry Day and National Chocolate Cake Day.

NATIONAL CHOCOLATE SOUFFLÉ DAY

"You can't make a soufflé rise twice." —Alice Roosevelt Longworth

When I think of chocolate soufflés, I think of very experienced, classically trained pastry chefs. Because of the delicate nature of a soufflé—the way it has a tendency to collapse quickly upon removal from the oven if not absolutely perfectly created and managed (after all, *souffler* in French means "to puff up" or "blow up")—I wasn't particularly interested in attempting to make this in the traditional sense.

It seemed to me that the major difference between chocolate cake and chocolate soufflé was that the latter was much lighter and airier. So I got to thinking. . . .

A long time ago I drank a shot made from one part Frangelico and one part vanilla-flavored vodka. It was served with a slice of lemon coated in sugar.

After shooting the drink and sucking on the lemon, it tasted *exactly* like a bite of chocolate cake. Since there are so many chocolate-based food holidays throughout the year, I decided to celebrate today by making a chocolate soufflé shot, which is the same thing as a chocolate cake shot, but with the addition of a splash of vanilla seltzer. The idea is that the carbonation gives it the same airier feel that chocolate soufflé has over chocolate cake.

Let me tell you this: Alcohol that tastes like a fancy French dessert? *Dangerous.*

DID YOU KNOW?

Chocolate isn't a direct cause of acne. A diet high in fatty and sugary foods, however, is.

NATIONAL SURF AND TURF DAY

"Food should be fun." —Thomas Keller

You didn't think I'd leave out Leap Day, did you? It's a day too, y'know! Since today only comes around once every four years (which is a good thing if you're trying to eat the year on a budget or as a vegetarian), it only makes sense to celebrate one of the most decadent, indulgent, expensive dishes there is . . .

Surf and Turf (which is also called Beef and Reef or Pier and Steer in other regions of the world) features equal portions of both seafood and meat, usually lobster and a big old slab of steak. Where the term originated is unclear, but it seems to have become prevalent sometime during the 1960s.

Oysters and sausage. Filet and lobster. Scallops and bacon. Shrimp and ribs.

How will you get your ocean and land eats on today?

MARCH IS...

MARCH IS ALSO...

International Hamburger and Pickle Month
National Caffeine Awareness Month
National Celery Month
National Flour Month
National Frozen Food Month
National Noodle Month
National Nutrition Month
National Peanut Month
National Sauce Month

. . .

*1st Saturday of NCAA Men's Division 1 Basketball
    Tournament*—National Corn Dog Day
Shrove Tuesday—Pancake Day
Good Friday—National Hot Cross Bun Day
Easter—National Baked Ham with Pineapple Day

NATIONAL PEANUT BUTTER LOVER'S DAY

"No man in the world has more courage than the man who can stop after eating one peanut." —Channing Pollock

After living in Ireland as an au pair for a couple weeks, I realized I never saw peanut butter at the grocery store. So one day, I meticulously went through every single shelf of every single aisle until I finally found it—in the ethnic foods section—and it was very, *very* expensive (about the equivalent of $10 at the time). Having grown up in a home that *always* had a jar of both crunchy and creamy peanut butter on hand at all times, I found this amusing and called my mom to tell her so.

A week later, a care package from home arrived from my friendly postman, Noel. Inside was a jar of Reese's peanut butter with a note from my grandfather: *No girl should be without her peanut butter!* After that, every care package always had a jar from him.

Erika, the Spanish woman I was au pairing for, had never tried peanut butter until she met me. I made tea and toast with peanut butter one morning for breakfast for us. She lifted the piece of toast to her nose and sniffed the melting brown goo before hesitantly taking a bite.

From that moment on, our home on Briarwood Park *always* had a jar in the cupboard. (Even now—years later—every now and then Erika randomly sends me photos of her enjoying some peanut butter.)

Today—and every day—is the perfect time to spread the (peanut buttery) love!

Today is also National Fruit Compote Day.

NATIONAL BANANA CREAM PIE DAY

"When life lands a hammer blow in your face, do your best to respond to the hammer as if it had been a cream pie." —Dean Koontz, Seize the Night

When I think about banana pie, I think about school lunches. Every now and then there would be a misleading-looking mound of pale yellow pudding plopped on our plastic, blue trays. I always hoped, and assumed, it was lemon-flavored. So I dove in, scooping a huge spoonful into my mouth only to discover that it was banana-flavored every single time.

Gross. (Can you believe banana cream pie was named the U.S. Armed Forces' favorite dessert in 1951?)

So instead of making a pie filled with that off-putting pudding, I decided to let my inner Brit out to play in the kitchen and whipped together a banoffee pie. Truly, it's one of the sexiest-tasting desserts I've ever had. Toffee, fresh bananas, and whipped cream chilled in a piecrust made of graham crackers? It's the kind of thing you think about late at night when you're lonely . . . maybe a little hungry. . . .

Was that a happy shudder? Sure was!

A FIT AMERICAN BIRD MAKES BANOFFEE PIE (THE EASY WAY)

Makes one 9-inch pie

1 cup dark brown sugar, packed

½ cup plus 1 tablespoon heavy whipping cream, divided

½ cup (1 stick) unsalted butter

1 tablespoon cornstarch

2½ medium-size bananas

1 (9-inch) premade graham cracker piecrust

6 ounces whipped cream or Cool Whip

Cocoa powder, for dusting

Cinnamon, for dusting

Melt the sugar, ½ cup of cream, and butter in a medium saucepan over low heat. Whisk gently until the mixture comes to a rolling boil, about 10 minutes.

In a small bowl, make a paste with the remaining 1 tablespoon of cream and cornstarch. Add the paste to the sugar mixture and whisk gently for another

10 minutes. Turn off the heat, whisk for 1 more minute, and then let the pan sit on the counter for 5 minutes, during which time the toffee mixture will begin to thicken.

Slice the bananas and layer them along the bottom of the piecrust. Pour the toffee mixture slowly over the bananas. Refrigerate for *at least* 1 hour, or until settled. Top the pie with your whipped topping of choice and dust with cocoa powder and cinnamon prior to serving.

NATIONAL MULLED WINE DAY

MARCH 03

"Mulled wine, heavy on the cinnamon and light on the cloves. Off with you, me lad, and be lively!" —Clarence the Angel, It's a Wonderful Life

I think cooks of all ages would agree that sometimes the best culinary treats happen entirely accidentally. After polishing off a jug of home-made sangria with dinner, my friend and I decided to open a second bottle of wine and dump it into the citrus-fruit laden pitcher. But we never got to it because we fell asleep watching TV (too much sangria and a full belly of good food will do that to the best of us). The next day it was bitter cold and snowing outside, so I dumped the contents of the new sangria into my slow cooker with a few other ingredients I had on hand. An hour later it became mulled wine.

Mulled just refers to something that's both heated and spiced. (Remember this: National Hot Mulled Cider Day happens on September 30, page 311.) Mulled wine (also known as *vin chaud*, *gløgg*, or *Glühwein*, among other names) is commonly consumed in cold-weather climates, because warm drinks, well, they literally warm your insides. So after a glass—or three—of mulled wine, don't be surprised if you find yourself feeling all delightfully cozy and sleepy again! Hopefully you'll have nowhere you need to be and can just enjoy the falling snow from a comfy couch indoors.

Today is also National Cold Cuts Day.

NATIONAL POUND CAKE DAY

"We never repent of having eaten too little." —Thomas Jefferson, Cannons of Conduct

The pound cake may be one of the most approximately named foods in the culinary kingdom. The sweet treat, created in the 1700s, was originally made from one pound of butter, one pound of sugar, one pound of eggs, and one pound of flour.

That sounds like a whole lotta cake to me. Over the years the recipe was scaled down a wee bit to fit an individual family's needs.

Personally, I'm not a huge fan of pound cake. In my opinion—even with all that butter—it's still a little drab. But, to its credit, it can be *the perfect* vessel for tasty toppings like the strawberries I picked in July, smashed with sugar, and frozen for an occasion to invoke the spirit of summer during drab winter days. Today is that day.

What do you top your pound cake with?

NATIONAL CHEESE DOODLE DAY

"Food that consumers used to think of as junk food is being reinvented as health food." —Nathan Coyle

I'm no cheese doodle connoisseur, but my younger sister, Cari, is. When I asked her why people seemed more interested in National Cheese Doodle Day than National Absinthe Day, she wisely responded:

There's absinthe art work, absinthe culture with the Bohemians in Paris, Oscar Wilde, Ernest Hemingway—all of it is pretentious! I've had both Italian and French absinthe (which is significantly better, by the way), but the real crap isn't what these young, trendy kids are going for. So screw

absinthe! It's not even something you get introduced to until you're old or European. Unlike cheese doodles, which are a universal food. And people have been eating them since they were so little they couldn't even reach to the bottom of the bag. And I think that's the appeal: Doodles span ages. There are lots of options, too. When you say doodle, do you mean the condensed billy club kind or the puffed up ones? They're both appealing. The poufy ones are great because you can suck on 'em until they completely melt away in your mouth. And the billy club ones, with their undeniable scent of foot and cheese, are disgusting and you get fake orange crap all over you, but still . . . they're amazing. Even crappy knock-off companies make a cheese doodle variant. Why? Because people will eat them. People will always choose cheese doodles over absinthe every time. That's *the truth.*

DID YOU KNOW?

A man by the name of Morrie Yohai created the Cheez Doodle.

Today is also National Absinthe Day.

MARCH 06 — NATIONAL FROZEN FOOD DAY

"How to thaw a frozen turkey: Blow in its ear." —Johnny Carson

When I was a teenager, my family unceremoniously volunteered me to clean out my grandparents' freezer—a task no one could remember ever having done before—because of my pseudo-OCD with food safety and cleanliness. That's the day I made my grandmother cry. I threw away spaghetti sauce she had made in the 1960s (not a joke) as well as, what I'm pretty sure was, one of the very first bricks of frozen peas ever invented. Clarence Birdseye himself may have actually been the one to pack it (maybe a joke . . . maybe).

Although overwhelmingly full (seriously, it's like a terrifying game of Jenga in there), you'll find no questionable leftovers in my freezer! Mine is usually filled with a delicious and fun plethora of goodies—pints of ice cream, bags of onion rings, interesting mock meat products, and a variety of homemade soups and stews made from the fresh veggies I receive during my annual summer farm share.

Have you gone treasure hunting in your freezer lately? Maybe today's the day to see what kind of delicious gems you have hiding back there!

MARCH 07

NATIONAL CEREAL DAY

"Like religion, politics, and family planning, cereal is not a topic to be brought up in public. It's too controversial." —Erma Bombeck

Once upon a time, there was this group of people called Americans. Each morning they would greet the day with a hearty breakfast of eggs, bacon, sausage, chicken, beef . . . whatever animal they could get their hands on, really. Sound familiar? It's actually sort of the way cereal got its start back in the nineteenth century. The long and short of it goes like this: Striving to come up with a healthier, vegetarian breakfast alternative, Dr. James Caleb Jackson created Granula (yes, *ula* not *ola* . . . yet!), the first "cereal" made from bran nuggets, which had to be soaked overnight before eaten. Fast-forward a couple decades, and a pair of brothers named John Harvey and Will Kellogg (sound familiar?) also jumped into the cereal-making game and eventually created the first commercial cereal flake.

From day one of my journey eating the year, I knew what I wanted my National Cereal Day picture to be—me, naked, in a bathtub full of milk and cereal. Sounds sexy, right? The picture absolutely is, but the process was a total disaster. The fruity ringed cereal became gummy and stuck to my hair, it cemented itself to the walls of the bathtub, and the longer it sat in the milk, the more swollen it became—the cereal eventually clogged my drain. And the milk? It took hours of scrubbing to get the smell of old dairy out of the bathroom.

But it certainly made my National Cereal Day a memorable one!

MARCH 08

NATIONAL PEANUT CLUSTER DAY

"Those big-shot writers could never dig the fact that there are more salted peanuts consumed than caviar." —Mickey Spillane

For the first time all year, people thought I was making up today's food holiday. (Because National Curried Chicken Day on January 12 seemed so much more legit, right?)

Peanut clusters are real, and they're pretty basic sweets that satiate a chocolate and salt craving. Take some melted chocolate, mix in some peanuts, form into little "clusters," and let them harden on waxed paper. Variations include the addition of mini marshmallows, butterscotch chips, peanut butter chips, peanut butter, coconut, instant coffee, dried cranberries. . . . Really, it's one of those recipes that you can do just about anything to and call it a peanut cluster.

Just don't get too crazy with ingredients. If you do, you might end up with a serious Charlie Foxtrot on your hands, if you know what I mean.

NATIONAL CRABMEAT DAY

"Have you ever watched a crab on the shore crawling backward in search of the Atlantic Ocean, and missing? That's the way the mind of man operates."
—Henry Louis Mencken

I like crabs. And so do both Maryland and Oregon—the blue crab has been Maryland's official state crustacean since 1989, while Oregon began touting the Dungeness crab starting in 2009.

When I visited Seattle for the first time, on my list of things to do while there was to eat crab (which is the equivalent of people coming to my state to eat lobster, I suppose). So after a day of sightseeing, my boyfriend at the time took me to Athenian Seafood Restaurant and Bar located in Pike Place Market for a giant platter of crab legs. And yes, I sat on the same stool that Tom Hanks sat on when he filmed *Sleepless in Seattle*. After all, if you're gonna be cliché, you might as well go all the way, right?

I couldn't exactly get 3,200 miles across the country for dinner, so I celebrated a tad more tame—vegan crab cakes served with four separate dipping sauces on the side (a remoulade, a tartar, a lemon aïoli, and a horseradish mayo) placed on a salad of avocado, cherry tomatoes, and sweet corn with a drizzle of olive oil, white wine vinegar, and salt.

I did say just *a tad more* tame, didn't I?

DID YOU KNOW?

While crabs do not have teeth, they do have teethlike structures inside their stomachs.

Today is also National Meatball Day.

NATIONAL BLUEBERRY POPOVER DAY

"Blueberries is one of the great forces o'good in the world." —James A. Owen, Here, There Be Dragons

Until today's food holiday, I was convinced that a popover was a turnover. While I usually planned out each food holiday days in advance, I didn't bother for today because I *absolutely knew* the natural foods store in town carried popovers—I had even tried both the pumpkin and lemon varieties before. My plan was to just pick one up and call it good—an easy day for me! But as I rifled through the box of flavors, repeatedly seeing the word *turnover* on the labels, that's when I began to wonder if perhaps turnovers and popovers were actually two different things.

A quick search on my phone revealed that my sudden fear was correct. Turnovers are folded puff pastries filled with something sweet (like pumpkin or lemon). A popover, on the other hand, is actually much more similar to a Yorkshire pudding—a small, circular, airy-on-the-inside, crispy-on-the-outside, roll of sorts.

Despite the rushing around I had to do to get these bad boys baked, photo'd, and eaten (my favorite part), I was thrilled to learn the difference. After all, there are two more popover days to celebrate this year!

DID YOU KNOW?

Native Americans called blueberries "star berries," because the blossom of the berry formed a perfect five-pointed star shape.

Today is also National Pack Your Lunch Day.

NATIONAL EAT YOUR NOODLES DAY

"We are noodle folk. Broth runs through our veins." —Mr. Ping, Kung Fu Panda

For many college students, today's food holiday might be one of the most unremarkable ones of the year. Ho, there, collegiate friend. Did you know that the instant noodle bowl you're eating every day (sometimes multiple times a day, I know, I've been there)—which was first developed by Momofuku Ando in the late 1950s—comes to you from generations and generations of noodle-crafting expertise?

While many different regions of the world try and lay claim to the "invention" of the noodle, it was most likely the Chinese who were the masterminds behind the beloved food. In 2005, a 4,000-year-old bowl of noodles was discovered in Lajia, an archaeological site located in China's northwest Qinghai province.

It's no wonder noodles symbolize longevity in Chinese culture!

So buck up, noodle-slurping scholars: While eating noodles may or may not give you a long life, you're certainly ahead of the game as far as celebrating today's food holiday goes!

Today is also National Oatmeal Nut Waffles Day.

CHICKEN NOODLE CASSEROLE

Makes 4 to 6 servings

2 (10- or 11-ounce) cans condensed cream of
   chicken soup
1 (8-ounce) container sour cream
½ cup whole milk
¼ teaspoon black pepper
¼ teaspoon salt
2 medium boneless, skinless chicken breasts,
   cooked and cut into cubes

2 cups egg noodles, cooked and drained
3 large hard-cooked eggs, shelled and chopped
1 (3- to 5-ounce) bag regular potato chips, crushed

Preheat the oven to 350°F.

In a 2-quart oven-proof casserole dish, mix the soup, sour cream, milk, pepper, and salt together. Fold in the chicken, noodles, and eggs. Top with the crushed chips. Bake uncovered for 1 hour. Serve hot.

NATIONAL BAKED SCALLOPS DAY

"Scallops are expensive, so they should be treated with some class. But then, I suppose that every creature that gives his life for our table should be treated with class." —Jeff Smith, The Frugal Gourmet

If you've ever watched a reality TV show featuring Gordon Ramsey, you'll know that he's quite difficult to please, especially when it comes to cooking scallops. Contestants just can't seem to find the middle ground of that elusive golden sear that exists somewhere between undercooked and raw or overcooked and rubbery. Luckily for you, there's a good chance Ramsey isn't going to be popping into your kitchen to call you a donkey or anything else today!

Scallops are bivalve mollusks, and many people enjoy eating the sweet, fleshy, white-colored muscle that opens and closes the shell. Today, however, can actually be interpreted one of two ways. So if scallops aren't your thing, or you're adverse to eating seafood in general, take heart. The term "scalloped" has, over the years, also come to refer to dishes that are baked in a cream sauce, like scalloped potatoes.

So what will it be today? Mollusk or spud?

RI-DANG-DICULOUSLY GOOD SCALLOPS WITH BROCCOLI

Makes 2 servings

2 pounds broccoli, cut into florets

3 to 4 tablespoons olive oil

2 tablespoons lemon juice

½ teaspoon lemon pepper

4 tablespoons salted butter, melted

½ pound medium-size sea scallops, patted dry

Salt and pepper, to taste

Preheat the oven to 375°F.

In a large bowl, mix together the broccoli, olive oil, lemon juice, and lemon pepper, making sure the broccoli is coated evenly. Pour into an 8 x 8- or 9 x 9-inch baking dish and roast for 25 to 30 minutes, or until the tops of the broccoli have started to brown.

While the broccoli is roasting, brush the melted butter on both sides of the scallops, and season with salt and pepper to taste. Place the scallops in a foil-lined 8 x 8- or 9 x 9-inch baking dish.

Halfway through the broccoli's roasting time, and in order for the broccoli and the scallops to be ready at the same time, put the scallops in the oven next to the broccoli for 12 to 15 minutes, or until they are slightly white in color and firm to the touch. Serve the scallops on top of the broccoli. *Yum!*

- -

MARCH 13 — NATIONAL COCONUT TORTE DAY

"The coconut trees, lithe and graceful, crowd the beach like a minuet of slender elderly virgins adopting flippant poses." —William Manchester

In my experience, today has been one of the food holidays met with the most delightful and honest surprise. "Coconut Torte Day?" People repeated when I told them, warm smiles lighting up their faces. "Really? That sounds wonderful!"

Which was immediately followed with, "What's a torte, again? Isn't it some kind of cake?"

Actually, it is, although it can be very confusing telling the two apart. As a general rule of thumb, cake is less dense than a torte because it's made using flour (meaning it's also, usually, taller in height). *Tortes*—the German word for "cake," by the way—use little to no flour but add ground nut meal, sometimes even breadcrumbs, to achieve that aforementioned density (and, as a result, are usually shorter in height).

Don't let the details of today confound you! Lots of people across the country use the two terms interchangeably, so if you happen to accidentally eat a slice of coconut cake instead, don't worry—I won't tell on you. Promise!

DID YOU KNOW?

Coconut water is a universal donor, because it's identical to human blood plasma.

NATIONAL POTATO CHIP DAY

"It is easy to halve the potato where there is love." —Irish proverb

Chips, chippies, crisps, crackers.

Ribbed, rippled, ruffled, wavy.

Thin-cut, thick-cut, waffle-cut, crinkle-cut.

Extra salt, sea salt, lightly salted, unsalted.

Baked, fried, old-fashioned, home style.

Scoops, stackers, sticks, shoestring.

Even these lists of potato chip names, styles, cuts, salt, cook, or shape preferences don't begin to scratch the surface of this internationally known and loved snack food.

Whom do we owe thanks to for bringing to life our favorite flavors—dill pickle, jalapeño, barbeque, ranch—in small, crunchy bite-size form? Credit—and the traditional tale of these tubers—is usually given to a man by the name of George Crum, who worked as a chef at a fancy schmancy restaurant in Saratoga Springs, New York. During the summer of 1853, a customer sent back his fried potatoes because they were too thick and soggy for his liking. So Crum, in an attempt to send an overly dramatic message, sent back potatoes that were much thinner and crispier. However, they were more than just a little well-received, and ended up becoming a staple item—called Saratoga Chips—on the menu.

And a staple item in our foodie hearts forever after. N'aww!

With so many options, there's absolutely no excuse for not celebrating with a bag or four today!

DID YOU KNOW?

Think ketchup or oyster is an interesting potato chip flavor? There's also prawn cocktail, roast ox, Cajun squirrel, firecracker lobster, and crispy duck with hoisin (and all of those come to us from the U.K.).

Today is also National Pi(e) Day.

NATIONAL PEARS HÉLÈNE DAY

"If you want to know the taste of a pear, you must change the pear by eating it yourself." —Mao Tse-Tung, On Practice

What?! What's this?! French chef Auguste Escoffier made *another* fancy dessert inspired by *another* lovely woman? Peach Melba (celebrated back on January 13, page 21) for Australian opera singer Dame Nellie Melba just wasn't enough was it, Monsieur Escoffier? So now, who is this *Helen you're making pears for!?* How jealous do you have to make me? And did I not already demand that an eligible bachelor come impress *me* with food like Escoffier did to the ladies of the mid- to late nineteenth century. (Listen, at this point you don't even need to try, guys—just show up with a package of Halloween Oreos, and we'll call it good.)

Escoffier, in the mid-1860s, named his dish—more elegantly known in French as *Poire belle Hélène—after* the operetta *La bell Hélène* (*The Beautiful Helen*) by Jacques Offenbach, which was about the elopement of Helen of Troy and Paris.

The dessert itself is actually quite lovely and easy to make: It's simply peeled and cored pears poached in sugar water, drained, and then topped with vanilla ice cream and chocolate syrup.

Et voilà!

Today is also National Peanut Lover's Day.

NATIONAL ARTICHOKE HEARTS DAY

"After all the trouble you go to, you get about as much actual 'food' out of eating an artichoke as you would from licking thirty or forty postage stamps."
—Miss Piggy

Like anything worth fighting for, artichokes make you work to get to the heart of things. Literally. Technically speaking, the artichoke is a thistle (that comes from the sunflower family), and after peeling back layers and layers of leaves, the bud of the flower—the heart—is what's left and eaten.

Artichokes come from the Mediterranean. Here in the States, they're primarily grown in California. As a matter of fact, Castroville, CA, calls itself the Artichoke Center of the World. And every year they host an annual festival where they crown an Artichoke Queen. The first one? A woman by the name of Norma Jean, aka Marilyn Monroe.

As if that weren't cool enough, artichokes are tied to the Mafia, too! In the 1920s, Mafia man Ciro Terranova, dubbed the Artichoke King, started the artichoke wars when he began purchasing all the artichokes being shipped from California to New York on the cheap only to turn around and sell them at a huge margin. And those who didn't play along? They had their fields destroyed in the middle of the night. The mayor of NYC at the time, Fiorello La Guardia, ended up banning the sale and possession of artichokes in the city; it only lasted for a week, though, as La Guardia loved him some artichokes!

I told you: artichokes, worth fighting for.

NATIONAL GREEN BEER DAY

"An Irishman is never drunk as long as he can hold onto one blade of grass to keep from falling off the Earth." —Old Irish saying

It's St. Patrick's Day! Today is *all about* green *everything*—even the city of Chicago celebrates by pouring pounds and pounds of biodegradable food coloring into its river every year to turn it the same brilliant shade of the rolling hills of the Emerald Isle itself.

Wearing a green, white, and orange feather boa, my then beau and I took to the streets to celebrate today's "food" holiday. We found a place in town serving $2.50 green Bud Light draughts. I muscled my way up to the bar, but the bartender kept overlooking me—this happens when you're 5'2." Some tall guy next to me leaned in and screamed in my ear, "You wanna shot?!" "No thanks, man, I just want a green beer," I responded. "How about a green beer *and* a shot?" he suggested, pulling out a wad of cash, reaching over the bar, and throwing it at the bartender to get his attention.

As two Jäger bombs and a green beer appeared in front of us, my beau finally pushed through the crowd. "Who's this?" the tall guy asked. "It's my boyfriend. Thanks for the beer!" I replied, grabbing my Solo cup off the counter. The guy looked at my boyfriend, shrugged, and pushed the drink toward him. "I've never bought a drink for a dude before. First time for everything, I suppose," he yelled over the music, picking up his shot, and saluting my boyfriend in what had to be the most awkward-looking toast I had ever seen in my life.

It was an unforgettable way to celebrate today. So here's to your night being filled with as much good craic as mine was!

Sláinte!

DID YOU KNOW?

Originally, blue was the color associated with St. Patrick's Day.

Today is also National Corned Beef and Cabbage Day.

NATIONAL LACY OATMEAL COOKIE DAY

"Think what a better world it would be if we all, the whole world, had cookies and milk about three o'clock every afternoon and then lay down on our blankets for a nap." —Robert Fulghum

Talk about specific: Today isn't just a celebration of oatmeal cookies; it's a day to honor more specifically, the *lacy* oatmeal cookie. Wondering what the difference is? Don't worry—I've got you covered!

An oatmeal cookie is generally soft and thick in texture. It's considered a drop cookie because the dough is dropped by the spoonful on a baking sheet, and it doesn't spread out too much during the baking process.

Lacy oatmeal cookies are crispier and more delicate in nature. They have a much looser batter. When baked they usually spread out, so much so that when they're done, they're so thin that they may have holes here and there looking similar to lace. They can be partially dipped in chocolate, rolled up and filled with cream and fruit, or even used in sandwich cookie form.

Now go forth and celebrate your holiday as a more informed foodie!

NATIONAL POULTRY DAY

"An election is coming. Universal peace is declared, and the foxes have a sincere interest in prolonging the lives of the poultry." —George Eliot, Felix Holt, the Radical

Today is not just for chickens.

Poultry are domesticated birds that are raised specifically to be used for their meat and eggs (sometimes their feathers, too). The group includes, but isn't limited to, ducks, emus, geese, guinea fowl, ostriches, pheasants, pigeons, quails, rheas, squabs, and turkeys (which are my personal favorite). When I was three, I was attacked by a giant one. I'm sure it wasn't as gargantuan as I remember it to be, but when you're a little kid *everything* seems way bigger—especially birds that kind of look like dinosaurs and screech "gobble gobble" as they peck at your knees and shoulders.

Did you know there are more chickens on Earth than there are people? Seriously! Don't feel like you have to eat one because if you don't "they might take over the world and start running through our streets"—'cause guess what? They already have, and in some places, they already do! Eating fowl can be downright foul. So if you're an herbivore, don't let today scare you away from celebrating. Use it as an opportunity to honor the birds and educate your family and friends on where their chicken nuggets are most likely coming from.

DID YOU KNOW?

Alektrophobia is the fear of chickens and other feathered flying creatures.

Today is also National Chocolate Caramel Day.

BAKED CHICKEN FUN

Makes 2 servings

½ cup salsa, any flavor, any heat

¼ cup green olives, any size, chopped

2 medium chicken breasts, boneless and skinless

2 slices extra sharp Cheddar cheese

1 (15-ounce) can pinto beans, drained and rinsed

1 avocado, peeled, seeded, and cut into small
   chunks

Preheat the oven to 375°F.

Spray an 8 x 8-inch baking pan with nonstick cooking or baking spray. Set it aside.

Mix the salsa and the green olives in a small bowl and set aside.

Place the chicken in the baking pan and bake for 20 minutes. Remove the pan from the oven and place it onto a heat-proof surface. Spread half the salsa mixture on top of each chicken breast, making sure to keep the salsa *on* the chicken. Return the pan to the oven and bake the chicken for another 20 minutes.

Gently remove the pan from the oven and once again place it on a heat-proof surface. If any of the salsa mixture has fallen off the chicken, spoon it back on. Place one slice of cheese on each chicken breast. Bake for another 10 minutes, or until the cheese is bubbly. Remove the chicken from the oven and let it rest for 5 minutes.

While the chicken is resting, put the beans in a microwave-safe dish. Cook the beans on high for 2 to 3 minutes, stirring once halfway through cooking, until they are heated through.

Divide the beans in half and place each half on two plates. Place one chicken breast on each plate of beans. Top with avocado and serve.

Tip! Wanna make this vegetarian? Use Gardein Crispy Chick'n Filets instead. Cook the chick'n for 15 minutes at 450°F, flipping twice. Remove the chick'n from the oven, top it with salsa and cheese, and stick it back in the oven until the cheese has melted, about 3 to 5 minutes.

NATIONAL RAVIOLI DAY

"Remember, ravioli ravioli, give me the formuloni." —Sheldon J. Plankton,
SpongeBob SquarePants

In the bedroom of pasta, where lasagna noodles are like big comfy duvets, ravioli definitely represent comfortable pillows. Whether you like multiple ones stacked on top of each other, ones with less stuffing, ones with more stuffing, reliable ones you've had for years, or new ones every couple of months—eating ravioli, like choosing pillows, can be a very personal experience.

The oldest record of ravioli comes to us from letters written by a man named Francesco di Marco Datini sometime in the fourteenth century. The original filling he used in the pasta was a mixture of cheese, eggs, and fresh herbs.

To celebrate, I sat outside in the sunshine and ate three bowls of ravioli today: four-cheese ravioli tossed with cherry tomatoes and fresh basil; butternut squash ravioli in a curry sauce; and spinach and ricotta ravioli with sautéed mushrooms and tomato sauce. Every bite was a mouthgasm! My hope for you today: No matter how tempting it might be to just open a can of uninspired rubbery ravioli swimming in red mystery sauce, you, too, can enjoy a mouth full of bliss. Like, have you ever had toasted ravioli before? If they were a woman, they would have sonnets written about them—that's just how epically awesome they are.

And don't you deserve that kind of love affair?

*Today is also National Bock Beer Day,
National (French) Macaron Day, and
Great American Meatout.*

TOASTY RAVS

Makes 2 servings

1 (16-ounce) package fresh ravioli (or about 20 ravioli)

½ cup Italian seasoned breadcrumbs

½ cup panko crumbs

½ teaspoon dried basil

½ teaspoon dried oregano

2 sprigs fresh rosemary, stemmed and diced (about 4 teaspoons)

2 large eggs

¼ cup grated Parmesan cheese

1 cup cherry tomatoes, halved

8 basil leaves, torn into small pieces

Marinara, pesto sauce (page 294), and spinach sauce (page 102), for dipping (optional)

Preheat the oven to 450°F.

Grease a baking sheet and set aside.

Boil the ravioli for *half* of the recommended package directions. (Mine from Trader Joe's took only 2 or 3 minutes.) With a slotted spoon, transfer the raviolis to a plate lined with paper towels so they can dry.

In a shallow bowl, mix together the breadcrumbs, panko crumbs, basil, oregano, and rosemary. Set the bowl aside.

In a second bowl, beat the eggs together.

Dip one ravioli into the egg, letting the excess drip off, and then coat in the breadcrumb mixture. Place the ravioli on the baking sheet. Repeat the process with the remaining ravioli. Bake for 15 minutes, or until golden-brown and crunchy to the touch. Flip them over halfway through the baking process.

To serve, place the ravioli on a plate and sprinkle with Parmesan cheese. Top with the cherry tomatoes and basil. Eat as is or serve with your favorite sauces.

NATIONAL FRENCH BREAD DAY

"How can a nation be called great if its bread tastes like Kleenex?" —Julia Child

When I think about shopping for food at a market, a few particular things come to mind: friendly banter with familiar faces, fresh cheese samples, locally grown produce, and long, slender baguettes sticking out of people's reusable totes. The whole image is romantic to me!

And very French. The baguette—made simply of flour, yeast, water, and salt—has been associated with the country for some time now. In the 1920s, a law passed in France that prevented bakers from working before four a.m. (I was a commercial baker once; I started work between one and two every morning—I couldn't imagine such time constraints!) To be able to produce enough loaves for their customers, the bakers turned to making baguettes, which, because of their thin shape, baked faster.

Personally, I have fond memories of eating crusty baguettes filled with partially melted Brie and cranberry compote—with a side of chips and mayo!—overlooking the sea on the isle of Guernsey. I couldn't think of a more appropriate way to celebrate today than reliving that beloved holiday fare!

DID YOU KNOW?

The concept of the baguette actually comes to us via Vienna.

Today is also National California Strawberry Day.

GUERNSEY SEASIDE SANDWICH

Makes 2 sandwiches

2 cups frozen cranberries

1 tablespoon orange zest

¼ cup orange juice

¼ cup plus 1 tablespoon granulated sugar

1 baguette

3 tablespoons salted butter

2 tablespoons mayonnaise, plus more to serve

5 to 6 ounces Brie, sliced

Julienne french fries, to serve (optional)

Preheat the oven to 375°F.

Place the cranberries, orange zest, orange juice, sugar, and ¼ cup water in a medium saucepan. Cover and turn the heat to medium-high. Cook until the cranberries turn really red and begin to burst, about 10 minutes. Turn the heat down to low and mash the berries to your liking. Turn off the heat and transfer the pan somewhere else to cool to room temperature—it will thicken as it cools.

While the cranberry mixture is cooling, slice the baguette open lengthwise. Spread each open side with half of the butter. Spread the mayonnaise over the butter on just one side of the bread, and then layer the Brie on top of the mayonnaise. Place the open baguette on a baking sheet and bake until the cheese has just begun to melt and the bread begins to warm (but doesn't toast), about 6 to 8 minutes.

Remove the baguette from the oven and drizzle cranberry sauce on top of the melted Brie. Serve with a side of julienne french fries, if desired, and extra mayo as a dipping sauce.

WORLD WATER DAY

"All water has a perfect memory and is forever trying to get back to where it was."
—Toni Morrison

If there's anything first-world inhabitants take for granted, it's definitely water. We fill water bottles up right from the comfort of our own sinks, take long showers, leave the water running while brushing our teeth, and flush the toilet multiple times a day, all without a second thought. Believe it or not, these are luxuries many people in the world don't have.

World Water Day was created by the United Nations General Assembly; it's been held every March 22nd since 1993 as a way to educate the public and bring awareness to the global water crisis we're facing. There's a severe shortage of fresh, clean water available worldwide, and unless we proactively do something to make the sources we *do* have more sustainable and hygienic, the situation is only going to get worse. Consider the following:

- Nearly 800 million people lack access to clean water.
- Today, more people have access to cell phones than they do to toilets.
- When the average American showers, he or she is using more water than the average person in a developing country uses all day.

For more information, check out *Unwater.org* or *Water.org*.

DID YOU KNOW?

Hydrology is the study of the movement, distribution, and quality of water throughout the Earth.

Today is also National Bavarian Crêpes Day, National Coq Au Vin Day, and National We Love Broccoli Day.

NATIONAL CHIP AND DIP DAY

"Dip is defined based on its ability to maintain contact with its transport mechanism over three feet of white carpet." —Alton Brown, Good Eats

Celebrating National Potato Chip Day (page 87) a little over a week ago clearly wasn't enough to satiate our immense craving for the crunchy snack, so today we honor one of the happiest marriages there is in the culinary world: the chip and dip duo.

The possibilities are endless for today. You could celebrate with salsa (page 267), hummus, chutney, tzatziki, spinach and artichoke dip, crab and artichoke dip, fruit dip, onion dip, clam dip, beer and cheese dip, Texas caviar (page 232), guacamole (page 296), or the king of all party dips: the seven-layer Mexican dip—which is what I decided to eat today!

It started off with refried beans on the bottom, then a layer of sour cream mixed with taco seasoning, some mildly spicy nacho cheese sauce on top of that, then a layer of homemade guacamole, topped with jalapeños and sprinkled with some olives, then a layer of shredded lettuce, and I finished it off with fresh diced tomatoes because salsa, in my opinion, makes everything too wet. Wait . . . doesn't that make it an *eight* layer dip?

Who doesn't love one extra layer of awesomeness?!

Today is also National Melba Toast Day.

KICKIN' BACON DIP

Makes 1 bowl of dip

1 (16-ounce) container sour cream
½ (4- to 6-ounce) jar real bacon bits
1 teaspoon crushed red pepper flakes

In a medium-size bowl with an airtight cover, mix the sour cream, bacon bits, and red pepper flakes together. Cover the bowl and place the dip in the refrigerator overnight.

This dip tastes best with ripple chips or pretzel sticks, but if you're in a healthy frame of mind, veggies like carrots, celery, or sliced cucumbers would be just as kickin'!

Tip! This absolutely needs to be chilled overnight for maximum flavor.

NATIONAL CHOCOLATE COVERED RAISINS DAY

"What god awful mess those things are. Chocolate with raisins in it. Yeah, yeah that's what kids want with their chocolate, fruit. Why don't you put sunflowers in the Ding Dongs while you're at it?" —Stewie Griffin, Family Guy

One of the most quintessential movie theater snacks, chocolate covered raisins have been popular for decades. While many companies make them, Nestlé Raisinets are by far the most popular brand.

I've been having a love affair with chocolate covered raisins for years. They're like the yin and yang of the food world: While raisins—sun-dried grapes considered nature's candy—are seen as über healthy, chocolate is a little more on the sinful side. It's like being a good girl with a bad girl streak on the weekends.

Best of both worlds, really.

The raisins and chocolate, that is!

OOEY, GOOEY GOBS OF SUPERFOOD

Makes 15 candies

1 cup golden raisins

1 cup raisins

½ cup sweetened shredded coconut

1 (8-ounce) bag chocolate chips (about 2 cups)

2 tablespoons unsalted butter

1 teaspoon vanilla extract

2 tablespoons heavy whipping cream

Line a baking sheet with waxed paper and set aside.

In a medium bowl, mix together the raisins and coconut. Set aside.

Melt the chocolate, butter, vanilla, and cream in a saucepan on medium heat until creamy. Empty the bowl of raisins and coconut into the chocolate and mix until everything's coated. Drop by tablespoonfuls onto waxed paper and place the baking sheet in a dry area of your kitchen for 30 minutes. Transfer the clusters to the refrigerator to finish hardening.

MARCH 25

INTERNATIONAL WAFFLES DAY

"A waffle is like a pancake with a syrup trap." —Mitch Hedberg

The United States is a country comprised of many different nationalities and cultures. It only makes sense, therefore, to celebrate and incorporate another country's food holidays as part of our own culinary celebrations.

For example, our International Waffle Day is in thanks to Sweden's *Vårfrudagen*, which stands for "Our Lady's Day," or the "Feast of the Annunciation." It honors the day when Gabriel the angel visited Mary nine months before Jesus was born. It's also a time to celebrate the beginning of spring. Because *Vårfrudagen* sounds like *Våffeldagen*—which means

Waffle Day—an extremely important moment in religious history is celebrated by eating waffles. Naturally.

This is not as weird as it may seem. Remember February 2nd? We learned that the French celebrate *La Chandeleur* (in English: Candlemas—the day of Jesus' presentation in the temple and Mary's purification) with crêpes!

However you end up celebrating today, be sure to eat your absolute fill of those delicious breakfast cakes—after all, you will have to wait five long months before the next Waffle Day!

DID YOU KNOW?

Eggo waffles first appeared in supermarkets in 1953.

Today is also National Lobster Newburg Day and National Pecan Day.

MARCH / 101

NATIONAL SPINACH DAY

"What was paradise, but a garden full of vegetables and herbs and pleasure? Nothing there but delights." —William Lawson

You may not instantly have a bodybuilder physique, an anchor tattoo on your forearm, and the ability to punch a shark in the face like Popeye after eating spinach, but this green leafy vegetable is certainly going to make you feel better about yourself than, oh, say, eating chocolate cookies will. Spinach is over-abundantly filled with iron, as well as folic acid, calcium, and a slew of other vitamins and minerals.

In 1937, Crystal City, Texas—dubbed the Spinach Capital of the World—erected a statue of Popeye. The monument pays homage to creator E.C. Segar for promoting and popularizing the humble veg, which dominated the agricultural scene of the city for so long.

Just the sound of the word *spinach*—like Brussels sprouts—tends to turn people off. I don't know what traumatic experience so many people may have had with it in their youth (probably the lack of Popeye's influence in today's culture!), but today you have no excuse. Try it in a salad; use it to make pesto; toss it into a smoothie; or smother it with cheese in lasagna. Your body will love the influx of nutrients!

(Just don't go out and attempt to punch any large wildlife after eating your spinach.)

Today is also National Nougat Day.

SEXY SPINACH CREAM SAUCE

Makes enough for 2 to 4 people

- ½ cup (1 stick) unsalted butter
- 1 large Vidalia onion, diced
- 4 garlic cloves, minced
- 4 tablespoons all-purpose flour
- 1¾ cups warm milk
- 1 teaspoon dried parsley
- Salt, black pepper, crushed red pepper flakes, to taste
- 2 tightly packed cups of fresh spinach

In a large saucepan on medium-low heat, melt the butter. Add the onions and cook until translucent, about 3 to 5 minutes. Add the garlic and cook until fragrant, another 2 to 3 minutes.

Turn the heat up to medium and sprinkle in the flour. Stir together with a wooden spoon until the flour and butter start forming a golden paste. Stir in the warm milk, parsley, salt, pepper, and pepper flakes.

Shred the spinach by hand and add. Cook down until creamy and the spinach is cooked through, about 15 to 20 minutes. Best served over rice balls.

Tip! This sauce goes great on rice, on meat, on toasted ravioli (page 95), or straight out of the pot with a spoon!

MARCH 27

NATIONAL SPANISH PAELLA DAY

"A good meal makes a man feel more charitable toward the whole world than any sermon." —Arthur Pendenys

When I think about my time living in the Canary Islands of Spain, I think about the beautiful weather, people, and food. It seemed to me that time stood still when friends and family came together over a nice meal or what seemed to be never-ending glasses of wine.

They know how to live in the moment.

I have many fond memories of eating paella—a rice dish that originated in Valencia—on Sunday afternoons with the family I was living with. The mother of the house would make an enormous pan of it filled with delicious seafood that was caught off the shores of the island that morning. We'd eat leisurely, laughing and talking truly as if none of us had anywhere else we needed—or wanted—to be.

But one of the most special moments for me was when the man I was teaching English to decided to teach me how to make traditional paella. After going to the market and purchasing fresh squid (*el calamar*), prawns (*de gambas*), and mussels (*el mejillones*), we invited friends over and began cooking. "The first step to *buena* paella is a glass of vino," he told me as he opened a bottle of wine, poured a glass for both of us, and then leaned against the counter to drink it as if there weren't a room full of people waiting to be fed. Then, while making the paella, it was important to drink another glass. "This makes *los sabores* (the flavors) come alive," he explained. And finally, before serving it, it was integral to toast your guests with—yes—another glass of wine.

Now *that's* the way to host a dinner party!

Today is also International Whiskey Day.

PAELLA CON POLLO DE SOL

Makes about 4 servings

 4 tablespoons Spanish olive oil, divided
 1 pound chicken drumsticks
 ½ cup chopped green beans
 ½ large Spanish onion, chopped
 ½ large green pepper, diced
 ½ large red pepper, diced
 2 medium tomatoes, chopped
 1 cup rice
 3 cups water (Note: For every cup of rice, you must add 3 cups of water!)
 1 cup chicken stock
 1 strand saffron

Fry the chicken drumsticks in half of the olive oil in a skillet until golden-brown, about 6 to 8 minutes. Turn the drumsticks over and fry until golden-brown, another 6 to 8 minutes. Put the chicken inside the *pallera* (paella pan or large pot).

In a separate pan, sauté the green beans, onion, green pepper, red pepper, and tomatoes in the remaining olive oil on medium-high heat until browned, about 6 to 8 minutes. When the vegetables are browned and soft, transfer them to the paella pan or large pot. Turn the heat to high. Add the rice with the 3 cups of water and start cooking. Once it comes to a boil, turn the heat down to medium.

In a small saucepan, boil the chicken stock. Add the stock very slowly to the large pot of chicken, vegetables, and rice. Mix everything together, and add the saffron to get a nice orange color. Once the water has reduced, signifying that the rice has cooked, turn the heat to low and cook for about 15 minutes, stirring every few minutes. Serve in large bowls with an accompanying glass of vino!

NATIONAL SOMETHING ON A STICK DAY

"Speak softly and carry a big stick; you will go far." —Theodore Roosevelt

While this holiday may seem vague, it *is* a celebration dedicated entirely to all those delicious, usually sinful foods that can be eaten straight off a stick.

Seems easy enough, right? Yet when this particular food holiday rolled around, I had a complete brain fart about how to celebrate. So just in case you also get stuck today, don't worry. I've got your back!

Here are just a few items that can be eaten off a stick:

- Lollipops
- Popsicles
- Cake balls
- Ice cream novelties
- Kebabs
- Corn dogs
- Cotton candy
- Caramel/candy apples
- Corn on the cob
- Deep-fried candy bars
- Most things at cocktail parties
- Samples at the market or grocery store

And any item eaten with chopsticks, which may be a bit of a stretch, but it still counts!

Today is also National Black Forest Cake Day.

NATIONAL LEMON CHIFFON CAKE DAY

"All the world is birthday cake so take a piece, but not too much." —George Harrison, I, Me, Mine

Imagine holding on to a cake recipe that no one else had, but wanted. Oh, the power! That's how California insurance salesman Harry Baker must have felt in 1927 when he invented what would become known as chiffon cake—a much lighter, airier, and more tender cake that called for vegetable shortening instead of butter or lard, and egg whites that were beaten separately from the yolks before being folded into the batter.

Baker kept his lips sealed about the recipe for twenty years before finally relenting and selling it to General Mills so "Betty Crocker could give the secret to the women of America" (after all, sharing is caring). A year later, in May of 1948, the recipe was printed in a *Better Homes and Gardens* magazine and was advertised as "the first new cake recipe in one hundred years." It was an instant success. So much so that it eventually got its own national food holiday!

Today is specifically all about *lemon* chiffon cake. And really, is there anything dreamier than sweet cake and tangy citrus flavors coming together in such a heavenly dessert?

DID YOU KNOW?

The average lemon contains eight seeds.

NATIONAL TURKEY NECK SOUP DAY

"For the Truth the Turkey is in Comparison a much more respectable Bird, and withal a true original Native of America." —Ben Franklin

Yes, you absolutely read that right: It's National Turkey Neck Soup Day.

I'm not entirely sure why the originator of today's food holiday needed to be so specific, unless she or he was *that* convinced that the meat of the turkey neck—which is dark and tough—really does make a soup that much more flavorful. (My grandmother made turkey soup, so I'm sure she'd agree.) So instead of discarding that baggy full of body parts found in the cavity of your turkey, today is the day to remove the neck (in all seriousness, if you're really planning on making this, you may actually need to call your butcher ahead of time to have him help you), toss it into a pot filled with water, and let it cook for a couple hours until it becomes tender. Then you can add your other soup fixins' like mirepoix (a mixture of chopped celery, onions, and carrots), potatoes, rice—whatever you normally would make a turkey soup with.

And if you can't get your hands around a neck or two today, don't sweat it. Eating a bowl of turkey—or turk'y soup, for those of us who don't even eat meat—is just as good. I promise the turkey neck soup police won't come after you—they'll be too busy eating to notice!

DID YOU KNOW?

Because turkeys have an eye on each side of their head, they can see two things at once (although their depth perception isn't that great as a result).

NATIONAL ORANGES AND LEMONS DAY

"Life without love is like a tree without blossoms or fruit." —Kahlil Gibran, The Prophet

You don't just take two random citrus fruits, pair them together, and call it a national food holiday. Obviously, there *had* to be a reason (because food holidays make oh-so-much-sense) why oranges and lemons were picked for today. Perhaps it comes from the English nursery rhyme of the same name that goes:

"Oranges and lemons"
Say the Bells of St. Clement's
"You owe me five farthings"
Say the Bells of St. Martin's
"When will you pay me?"
Says the Bells of Old Bailey
"When I grow rich"
Say the Bells of Shoreditch

"When will that be?"
Say the Bells of Stepney
"I do not know"
Say the Great Bells of Bow
"Here comes a candle to light you to bed
Here comes a chopper to chop off your head
Chip chop chip chop—the last man's dead."

Why do nursery rhymes always have to be so darn creepy? If I were you, I would just ignore the last few lines and order yourself a St. Clements at your local soda bar—it's one part orange juice and one part lemonade or lemon-flavored soda water!

Today is also National Tater Day and National Clams on the Half Shell Day.

FIZZY FRUIT SALAD

Makes 4 to 6 servings

1 large apple, any kind, cored and chopped into
   small pieces
1 large seedless orange, peeled, segmented, and
   cut into pieces
1 large banana, peeled and sliced
1 medium kiwi, peeled (if preferred) and cut into
   pieces
1 cup seedless grapes, any color, cut into halves
2 tablespoons orange seltzer water
1 tablespoon lemon juice

Place the apple pieces, orange segments, banana slices, kiwi pieces, and halved grapes into a large serving bowl. Add the seltzer water and lemon juice, stirring it all together to make sure all the fruit is coated with liquid. Cover the bowl of fruit and chill it in the refrigerator for at least 1 hour. Stir the contents of the bowl again to make sure everything is mixed. Serve.

APRIL IS...

APRIL IS ALSO...

National BLT Month
National Food Month
National Fresh Florida Tomato Month
National Fresh Celery Month
National Garlic Month
National Grilled Cheese Month
National Pecan Month
National Soft Pretzel Month
National Soyfoods Month

. . .

Good Friday—National Hot Cross Bun Day
Easter—National Baked Ham with Pineapple Day

NATIONAL SOURDOUGH BREAD DAY

APRIL 01

"Ignorance and error are necessary to life, like bread and water." —Anatole France, Pierre Nozière

Sourdough bread begins with a starter—usually a combination of flour and water, maybe a little sugar—and is left to sit at room temperature. Natural wild yeasts present in both the flour and in the air begin to eat the carbohydrates (the natural sugars) in the dough; it begins to ferment and produce lactic acid, which gives the bread its sour smell and flavor. Once you've created a starter, it can actually be used for years and years if properly managed. (Fed equal parts flour and water, that is; if you don't, you might end up with an awfully smelly mess.) And, as it ages, it'll actually get more of a distinct sourness to it, too, as it becomes uniquely yours.

No joke!

Add some starter to flour, water, and salt, and you're on your way to creating a bread that has thousands (and thousands) of years in the making.

DID YOU KNOW?

Sourdough bread has been around since ancient Egyptian times.

APRIL 02
NATIONAL PEANUT BUTTER AND JELLY DAY

"Peanut butter is the pâté of childhood." —Florence Fabricant

I wonder if Montreal native Marcellus Gilmore Edson knew just how popular peanut butter was going to become when he filed his patent in 1884. Obviously he knew he was on to something, but I'm sure he would have laughed if he heard that, before high school graduation, the average student in the United States consumes close to 1,500 peanut butter and jelly sandwiches.

I don't think I'm part of that average (although I might be if we were talking about egg salad on potato bread with lettuce and a ton of black pepper—something I ate for lunch most days . . . yeah, I was *that* kid). I actually stopped eating peanut butter and jelly sandwiches altogether in the second grade. It was at that point that I randomly decided I wanted to become a vegetarian. I remember very distinctly my second grade teacher taking me aside and explaining that I would never again be able to eat chicken nuggets and mashed potatoes with ketchup swirls—my favorite food at the time. And that the only thing vegetarians could eat were peanut butter and jelly sandwiches.

Three days later—after eating nothing but peanut butter and jelly sandwiches—I decided that being a vegetarian at that point in my life wasn't for me, but that I might try it again when I was all grown-up.

Now that I *am* all grown-up I actually super dig the old PB&J. Served on waffles, grilled, and accompanied by a tall glass of chocolate milk was the perfect way to celebrate today, too!

DID YOU KNOW?

Two peanut farmers went on to become U.S. presidents: Thomas Jefferson and Jimmy Carter.

NATIONAL CHOCOLATE MOUSSE DAY

"Chocolate is the first luxury. It has so many things wrapped up in it: deliciousness in the moment, childhood memories, and that grin-inducing feeling of getting a reward for being good." —Mariska Hargitay

What's the difference between pudding and mousse?

Dessert pudding is a thick, creamy dessert made from milk or cream, eggs, sugar, flavoring, and a thickening agent (like cornstarch, flour, or additional eggs). *Mousse*—meaning "foam" in French—is similar to pudding the same way ice cream is similar to gelato; the major difference between the two lies in the fact that mousse is much airier and lighter due to the gentle addition of fresh whipped cream or beaten egg whites that are folded into the mixture.

It's no surprise that chocolate mousse—which I think is the kind of mousse most Americans identify with—has its own national food holiday. Not only does just saying it feel fancy, but the dessert is also incredibly rich, delicious, and decadent!

And shouldn't we all spoil ourselves from time to time?

DID YOU KNOW?

The world's only life-sized moose made entirely of chocolate (1,700 pounds of it!) is located in Scarborough, Maine.

INTERNATIONAL CARROT DAY

"I never worry about diets. The only carrots that interest me are the number you get in a diamond." —Mae West

Believe it or not, rabbits are not behind today's food holiday! It was actually founded by lovers of the veg who, in 2003, declared that April 4th was International Carrot Day—a day to celebrate and promote the traditionally orange vegetable and all its nutritional benefits.

Carrots—which also come in shades of purple, white, yellow, and even red varieties—contain phytonutrients and beta carotene (which, when processed by the body, becomes Vitamin A; and Vitamin A, kiddos, is awesome for eye health!). Although, did you know, eating carrots—or any veg high in Vitamin A—in extreme excess may cause parts of your body, like your palms and the bottom of your feet, to turn a yellowish-orange color?

Which kind of takes "celebrating a food holiday" to a whole other level!

Today is also National Cordon Bleu Day.

VEG SOUP WITH VEG STOCK

Makes 4 to 6 servings

4 tablespoons unsalted butter
1 large Vidalia onion, chopped
¼ cup all-purpose flour
2 cups milk
1 cup heavy whipping cream
3 cups vegetable stock
½ small cabbage, shredded (about 2 cups)
4 medium carrots, chopped (about 2 cups)

1 small head cauliflower, florets chopped
   (about 2 cups)
2 (8-ounce) cans sliced water chestnuts, drained
Salt, black pepper, cayenne pepper, to taste

In a large pot, melt the butter and sauté the onions on medium-low heat until translucent, about 3 to 5 minutes. Sprinkle in the flour and stir while cooking for another minute until pasty. Add the milk, cream, and stock. Whisk everything together to mix well and turn the heat up to high. Bring the liquid to a boil and reduce the heat to low. Add the veggies and the seasonings to taste. Simmer on low for about 50 minutes. Serve with a soft roll and be ready to enjoy a full belly!

- -

APRIL 05 — NATIONAL RAISIN AND SPICE BAR DAY

"Is not birth, beauty, good shape, discourse, manhood, learning, gentleness, virtue, youth, liberality, and such like, the spice and salt that season a man?" —William Shakespeare, Troilus and Cressida

Raisin and spice bars aren't something I grew up with. I feel like this is one of those sweet treats sincere grandmothers make. My maternal grandmother, who usually babysat my sister and me, was far too sassy for this kind of baking. She was more the slip-you-a-fiver-to-go-to-the-store-and-get-a-pint-of-your-favorite-ice-cream kinda gal. Unless you were my sister, then she was a give-you-a-bowl-filled-with-Cool-Whip-topped-with-sprinkles-and-hot-fudge-sauce-but-don't-tell-your-mother-I-let-you-eat-this kinda woman.

I'm not sure I've ever actually sought out raisin and spice bars. For that matter, until today I didn't think *anybody* actually sought them out. But there wouldn't be a national food holiday if someone—a large body of someones—didn't love them. Is there some sort of secret raisin and spice bar baked goods club I don't know about?!

Perhaps there is. These hearty, spicy treats—reminiscent of the smells and flavors of Christmastime—have a little more oomph to them than brownies or cookies do. They're immensely flavorful (think brown sugar, cinnamon, cloves, and ginger), soft, and with just the right balance of natural sweetness from the plump raisins.

They're a good treat to share with someone you love—like your granny or your mom. (When was the last time you called either one of those lovely ladies, eh?!)

Today is also National Caramel Day and National Deep Dish Pizza Day.

NATIONAL FRESH TOMATO DAY

APRIL
06

"It's difficult to think anything but pleasant thoughts while eating a homegrown tomato." —Lewis Grizzard

It's important to eat seasonally; I mean, who really wants to eat anything that was picked with the intention of being ripened *in a truck* during a thousand-plus-mile journey to a grocery store in another part of the world? For some of us, that means today's food holiday may seem out of place or undoable. However, if you're fortunate enough, like I am, you may actually live near greenhouses that sustainably grow tomatoes (or other produce) all year long.

And is there anything that tastes as glorious as fresh, locally grown tomatoes? I think not.

Tomatoes—like potatoes, tomatillos, both sweet and hot peppers, mandrakes, tobacco, and belladonna—belong to the nightshade family, because they all produce alkaloid. In some plants this is edible, and in other plants it's extremely toxic. Fun to know, right?

Tomatoes, though technically a fruit, have been called a vegetable since the late nineteenth century when a U.S. Supreme Court decision (*Nix v. Hedden*) declared them as such for taxation purposes. (Fruit wasn't taxed, and since tomatoes aren't sweet and are more often than not used for savory dishes, they were—and still are—considered a veg.)

Fruit, veg, to-may-to, to-mah-to . . . all I know is this: Sliced on pizza with some shredded basil is a fine, fine way to celebrate today!

Today is also National Caramel Popcorn Day.

APRIL 07 — NATIONAL COFFEE CAKE DAY

"A compromise is the art of dividing a cake in such a way that everyone believes he has the biggest piece." —Ludwig Erhard

Because I was such a well-behaved child, I was frequently allowed to tag along with my mom when she had or hosted coffee dates with friends. Part of the perk, of course, was that I—sitting quietly nearby, no doubt immersed in a good book—was always allowed to partake in the ritual coffee cake that seemed to be ever present at such gatherings. The sweet cake—which evolved from generations of other culture's breads and cakes—was *always* delicious, and it seemed to instantly evoke generosity, goodwill, and hours of good conversation.

It only makes sense, then, that the best way to celebrate this particular food holiday is with no agenda or time constraints and surrounded by friends holding bottomless mugs of good java. There is magic when those things, combined with coffee cake—regardless if it was lovingly made from scratch or (just as lovingly) purchased from the store—meet.

Today is also National Beer Day.

NATIONAL EMPANADA DAY

"Cultivation to the mind is as necessary as food to the body." —Marcus Tullius Cicero

APRIL 08

An *empanada*—which comes from the Spanish word *empanar*, meaning "to cover, wrap, or coat something with bread"—is dough stuffed with meat, seafood, cheese, or veggies that's traditionally folded into a half-moon shape and then baked or fried. Sound familiar? It should! Conceptually, the idea of stuffing dough with a filling of some kind is commonplace in many cultures. It was something that may have originally resulted out of necessity as a way for food to be transported with ease, kept warm, and also kept clean.

And they're darn tasty to boot.

Variations on the theme include the *Cornish pasty* in Great Britain, the *calzone* in Italy, the *samosa* in India, turnovers, or even the "hand pie" as it's called in regions of the U.S. (But c'mon, that just sounds dirty, doesn't it?)

So what's in a name? If it's an empanada, or any of its cousins, then nothing but delicious, delicious fillings!

NATIONAL CHINESE ALMOND COOKIE DAY

"Preach not to others what they should eat, but eat as becomes you and be silent." —Epictetus

APRIL 09

Chinese almond cookies, or *Hang Geen Beng*, are usually eaten around Chinese New Year. They're given to friends and family as gifts because they symbolize coins—and who doesn't want to wish fortune and prosperity onto their loved ones? And, according to traditional Chinese medicine, almonds can suppress muscle cramps while also acting as an anti-inflammatory.

It seems to me that this food holiday is nearly two months later than it should be, given that Chinese New Year typically falls between the end of January and the end of February. Better late than never, right? Or, maybe, today was deemed National Chinese Almond Cookie Day as practice for next year's New Year celebrations. It's something to think about . . . while eating cookies, that is.

Whatever the case may be, here's to wealth and health!

R-RATED ALMOND COOKIES

Makes 1 dozen cookies

½ cup (1 stick) unsalted butter, at room temperature
½ cup granulated sugar
1 teaspoon almond extract
¼ cup amaretto
1 teaspoon baking powder
1 teaspoon baking soda
½ teaspoon salt
1½ cups all-purpose flour
12 almond slivers

Preheat the oven to 375°F.

In a large bowl, cream together the butter, sugar, almond extract, and amaretto.

In a separate bowl, mix together the baking powder, baking soda, salt, and flour. Gradually stir the dry ingredients into the wet ingredients, stirring until well blended.

Drop the dough by spoonfuls onto an ungreased baking sheet. Press a sliver of almond onto the top of each cookie. Bake the cookies for 8 to 10 minutes, or until they begin to color around the edges. Don't be freaked out if the tops stay pale (the bottoms are probably going to brown quite quickly). Enjoy a few with some amaretto on the rocks and drift away on sugar and alcohol!

NATIONAL CINNAMON CRESCENT DAY

"Cinnamon bites and kisses simultaneously." —Vanna Bonta

Crescent. Like the moon? Like the yoga pose? Like the city in California, Florida, or Illinois? Fear not, foodie. You are not required to contort your body in any weird positions at night in any of those states while taking the cinnamon challenge—y'know, where you swallow one tablespoon of ground cinnamon within sixty seconds sans any water?

Today is actually all about crescent-shaped rolls (you know the kind—you can get them premade in a tube) filled with cinnamon and preferably sugar, too. And no, regular old cinnamon buns don't count today, especially considering they have their own day on October 4th. Or a different interpretation of today includes crescent-shaped cinnamon cookies (which, on the other hand, are a totally acceptable way of celebrating today).

However you end up celebrating—doing *anjaneyasana* under the lunar glow, with rolls (not buns), or with cookies—know that cinnamon has *great* health benefits: I take it daily to keep my cholesterol down, and it totally works!

DID YOU KNOW?

Delicious and useful: In addition to a flavoring, cinnamon was used in the ancient Egyptians' embalming process.

Today is also National Farm Animals Day.

BRUNCH-PERFECT CC ROLLS

Makes 8 crescents

1 (8-ounce) can refrigerated crescent rolls

2 ounces cream cheese, at room temperature

1 tablespoon granulated sugar

½ teaspoon cinnamon

½ large green apple, cut into sticks

¼ cup chopped walnuts

2 tablespoons salted butter

1 teaspoon honey or agave syrup

Preheat the oven to 375°F.

Divide the crescent rolls into individual triangles (they should already be perforated) and place them on a greased baking sheet.

In a bowl, combine the cream cheese, sugar, and cinnamon until they are completely smooth and not grainy. Spread a teaspoon of the mixture onto each triangle.

At the wide end of each triangle, place three or four apple sticks and a few walnuts. Repeat this process with the remaining triangles, making sure all the apples and walnuts have been evenly distributed. Roll each triangle up from the wide end to the small end and place them on an ungreased baking sheet.

In a small bowl, melt the butter in the microwave. Whisk in the honey. Brush this mixture onto each crescent roll. Bake according to crescent roll package directions. Serve immediately!

NATIONAL CHEESE FONDUE DAY

"Wine and cheese are ageless companions, like aspirin and aches, or June and moon, or good people and noble ventures." —M.F.K. Fisher

Although fondue is believed to have potentially originated in Switzerland, it stems from the French word *fondre,* which means "to melt." This mixture of cheese, wine or brandy (or beer, which was my alcohol of choice today), flour or cornstarch, and seasonings was first served in a *caquelon,* which was a communal pot that folks dipped their bread into. Sometime in the 1930s, the Swiss Cheese Board declared fondue as the national dish of Switzerland.

I was really hoping to get my hands on a fondue set to celebrate today as authentically as possible. I used to see them at thrift stores all the time, so I thought it would be relatively easy to find one. But it's when you start *actively* looking for something (like a relationship or the remote) that it suddenly isn't available anymore. After hours of searching every store in my area, I ended up settling on a slow cooker instead. And you know what? Everything worked out just fine. The cheese was melty and delicious; I'm sure it would have been that way even if I had just used a saucepan on the stove or done it all in the microwave, too!

The moral of the story: Don't let any shortcomings prevent you from getting your cheese on today! After all: *La fondue crée la bonne humeur* (fondue creates a good mood)!

DID YOU KNOW?

Turophilia is the love of cheese.

NATIONAL GRILLED CHEESE DAY

"Who do you think would win in a fight between a grilled cheese sandwich and a taco?" —Andy Samberg, Hot Rod

My non-French-Canadian grandmother liked to make my sister and me a pedestrian version of croque monsieurs when we were little. She called them "yumbos"—it was ham and cheese on white bread that she would microwave. It wasn't until decades later that I realized she was just recreating (quite accurately actually) a really terrible Burger King sandwich from the 1980s and not the French version at all.

When I lived in England, every day for lunch I would eat a cheese toastie (there are lots of variations of this, by the way). The way it was made for me was with two pieces of bread toasted *really* well, each slathered with butter. Then a layer of sliced cheese would go on one of the buttered pieces before the other piece was placed on top,

butter-side down. It was given a firm press with both hands (I think that this transferred some of the heat from the toast to the cheese slices, which made them soften *more* than room temperature, but not melt) before being served with a cuppa tea.

The point is: Today, of all food holidays, you could line up one hundred people and you may very well get one hundred different answers about how they would celebrate the day. So whether you're a traditionalist (butter, bread, cheese, frying pan, *voilà*!) or an innovative spirit (a grilled sandwich of cashew cheeze with apples, agave, and walnuts sounds delicious), today the possibilities are absolutely endless!

Today is also National Licorice Day.

STEFF'S STRONG AND BEAUTIFUL GRILLED CHEESE

Makes 1 sandwich

2 slices sourdough bread

2 tablespoons maple syrup

3 tablespoons goat cheese

2 rounded tablespoons chopped candied walnuts

½ average-sized pear, cut into 4 slices

3 slices Swiss cheese

Heat your George Foreman grill or a skillet on medium-high heat.

Spread 1 tablespoon of the maple syrup evenly across one side of each of the two slices of bread. On one slice of bread, spread the goat cheese on top of the maple syrup. Top the goat cheese with the walnuts, pear slices, and Swiss cheese. Add the second piece of sourdough bread—maple syrup-side down—to close the sandwich. Grill until the bread is toasty and the cheese is melty.

APRIL
13

NATIONAL PEACH COBBLER DAY

"The ripest peach is highest on the tree." —James Whitcomb Riley, "The Ripest Peach"

Depending on where you're geographically located, a cobbler can be made in a variety of ways. Generally, it's thought of as a dessert with a bottom layer of fruit that's then topped with piecrust, streusel or crumbs, or most traditionally drop biscuit dough (which may be where the name *cobbler* comes from—visually, the lumps of dough on the surface resemble a cobblestoned street) before being baked. Variations include a "dump"—which is when a basic yellow cake mixture is spread over a layer of canned fruit and then baked; or, similarly, a "buckle"—which is when a basic yellow cake batter is mixed with fruit and then topped with streusel before it's baked.

Regardless of where you come from or how you choose to celebrate, today is the perfect day to invoke that Southern feeling with a bowl of warm, naturally sweet peach cobbler topped with a scoop of creamy vanilla ice cream!

APRIL 14 — NATIONAL PECAN DAY

"God gives the nuts, but he does not crack them." —Franz Kafka

Every year during the holidays when I was younger, my parents had a big centerpiece on our kitchen table of walnuts, hazelnuts, almonds, Brazil nuts, and pecans in their shells. For some strange reason—maybe it was because of their smooth, shiny surface—our two cats just loved to scoop out the pecans and bat them around all over our linoleum floor. We would always find the nuts scattered throughout the house months after the holiday season had come and gone!

Pecans are the only truly native nut tree naturally growing in North America. The name comes from the Native American Algonquin word for "a nut requiring a stone to crack." And pecans are naturally full of protein, fiber, and unsaturated fats, making them a heart-healthy snack!

Since our country *loves* the pecan (there are quite a few national food holidays associated with the buttery-flavored nut), try to celebrate today with a savory instead of sweet recipe!

Today is also National Grits Day.

MUSHROOM AND NUT STUFFING

Makes 6 to 10 side servings

- 3 cups vegetable stock, divided
- 1 (14-ounce) bag cubed stuffing
- 1 large yellow onion, chopped
- 4 tablespoons olive oil
- ½ cup walnuts, chopped
- ½ cup pecans, chopped
- 1½ pounds mushrooms (Crimini, Shiitake, Oyster, or a combination of any or all), sliced
- ½ teaspoon grated nutmeg
- ½ teaspoon black pepper
- ½ teaspoon salt

In a large pot, heat 2 cups of the stock on medium heat. Add the stuffing cubes and stir, and let this heat through for 3 minutes. Turn the heat off.

In a large skillet, brown the onions in the olive oil on medium heat until translucent, about 3 to 5 minutes. Stir in the walnuts and pecans, cooking until the nuts are warmed through, about 3 minutes. Reduce the heat to medium-low. Add the mushrooms, nutmeg, pepper, and salt, stirring often, until the mushrooms have cooked down (they will be smaller, soft, and the smell will be lovely and earthy).

Add the mushroom and onion mixture to the pot of stuffing. Turn the heat back to medium and add the remaining 1 cup of stock, stirring until everything is combined and heated through. Serve.

APRIL
15

NATIONAL GLAZED SPIRAL HAM DAY

"I do not like them here or there. I do not like them anywhere. I do not like green eggs and ham. I do not like them, Sam-I-am." —Dr. Seuss, Green Eggs and Ham

My speculation is that National Glazed Spiral Ham Day falls in April because it's close to Easter. And many families associate a succulent, glistening ham with their Easter dinner, like they do a golden-brown, mouthwatering turkey with Thanksgiving dinner.

Unless you're my family, that is. Our Easter dinner

for six years running once was pizza, because none of us particularly liked ham. What we did enjoy was the maple syrup, brown sugar, pineapple, and cherries that made up the glaze part of it! Give any of us a spoon and a big ol' bowl of just that and we'd be happier than a pig in . . . well, than a pig being eaten today, I guess.

If you're burned out on spiral ham off the bone, or are just not sure you're up for the challenge of baking an entire ham, no worries! It's completely acceptable to celebrate today with a glazed ham sandwich. Technically speaking, sliced ham comes in a circular shape like the meat off a spiraled ham does, so it still counts!

DID YOU KNOW?

Pigs don't have sweat glands. They roll around in the mud as a way to cool down.

NATIONAL DAY OF THE MUSHROOM

"Falling in love is like eating mushrooms, you never know if it's the real thing until it's too late." —Bill Balance

Here's how you're *not* going to celebrate today: by taking a stroll in the woods and eating some wild mushrooms that look appealing to you. It will not make you power up; it will not give you an extra life. Mario was lying. It will, most likely, make you very sick—and who wants to celebrate a national food holiday ill?

So here's how you *are* going to celebrate today: by shaking off the mindset that boring white button mushrooms dredged through ranch dressing are the only way to celebrate this fungus. There's an entire world of delicious (and safe) mushrooms that can be eaten! Like Crimini mushrooms, which are similar to the traditional white mushroom most people are comfortable and familiar with. It's brown in color and has more of a buttery and nutty flavor profile. Portabella mushrooms are earthy-smelling and naturally very meaty in texture. Shiitake mushrooms are spongy—they have both a woodsy and smoky flavor to them. Oyster mushrooms visually resemble oyster shells—they're soft and have a very mild and pleasant taste to them.

Or if you're feeling more adventurous (but, again, not in the "let's go outside and eat random growing things" way), you could try a lobster, lion's mane, chicken, or hedgehog mushroom! All are commercially harvested edible varieties!

Today is also National Eggs Benedict Day.

LIFE-UP MUSHROOMS

Makes 12 to 15 mushrooms (depending on how many are in the package)

½ large white onion, diced

1 garlic clove, minced

4 tablespoons unsalted butter

1 (12-ounce) package whole white mushrooms

1 cup frozen broccoli florets, thawed

½ cup panko crumbs

½ cup shredded sharp Cheddar cheese

¼ teaspoon salt

Preheat the oven to 350°F.

Line a baking sheet with aluminum foil and set it aside.

In a large pot, begin to sauté the onion and garlic in butter on low heat.

While that's cooking, wash and dry the mushrooms before gently removing the stems, being careful not to break the caps during this process. Chop the stems (after slicing off and discarding the ends) and add them to the sautéing onions and garlic. Roughly chop the broccoli and add it to the sauté pan. Stir everything to combine.

Hollow out the mushroom caps gently with a spoon and place them hollow-side up on the baking sheet.

Remove the vegetable sauté from the stove and transfer it to a bowl. Add the panko crumbs, cheese, and salt, and mix everything together to combine. Stuff the mushrooms (it's encouraged to mound them up!) with the mixture.

Bake for 15 minutes, or until golden on top. Let cool for 5 minutes before stuffing your mouth!

NATIONAL CHEESE BALL DAY

"Bachelor's fare: bread, cheese, and kisses." —Jonathan Swift

Was today borne because snackers just couldn't get enough of the neon-orange, puffed balls that always seem to come in industrial-size tubs? Is it due to the love our country inherently has for all things deep-fried that today we celebrate with orb-shaped versions of mozzarella sticks? Or is it a nod of appreciation to the yellow, sometimes pinkish, tinted balls of tangy cheese covered in nuts and served with crackers at parties?

Whichever way, I would say today is win-win-win!

Cheese balls—the spreadable kind, and how I celebrated today's food holiday—have definitely evolved from the uninspired party fare of yesteryear. They're completely customizable and with a little creativity they can feature just about any flavor your palate desires, whether that's beer and pretzels, seafood, BLTs, or bleu cheese and blueberry!

Today is also Malbec World Day.

CHEESE BALLIN' SPUMONI-STYLE

Makes 1 large cheese ball (about the size of a softball)

- ¼ cup chopped pistachios
- ¼ cup chopped dried cherries or cherry-flavored Craisins
- 2 tablespoons dark chocolate chips, finely chopped
- 2 cups shredded sharp Cheddar cheese
- 4 ounces plain cream cheese
- 2 teaspoons lemon juice

Mix the pistachios, dried cherries, and chocolate chips together on a dinner plate. Spread the mix flatly out across the plate and set it aside.

In a medium bowl, mix the cheese, cream cheese, and lemon juice together until everything is combined. Using your hands, form the mixture into a ball (or balls). Gently roll the cheese ball(s) around on the plate of coatings until they are completely covered. If there is extra coating, gently press your thumb into the center of the ball(s), fill the hole(s) with the rest of the coating, and gently press the hole(s) closed.

Refrigerate for 1 hour. When ready to eat, serve with crackers of choice and a glass of wine!

NATIONAL ANIMAL CRACKERS DAY

"One morning I shot an elephant in my pajamas. How he got in my pajamas, I'll never know." —Groucho Marx, Animal Crackers

Inspired by animal-shaped digestive-like biscuits from the mother country we tried so hard to disassociate ourselves with, animal crackers were made Stateside in the latter half of the nineteenth century by Stauffer's Biscuit Company, located in York, Pennsylvania. Other bakeries followed suit, and NABISCO—known as the National Biscuit Company back in the day—released their Barnum's Animal Crackers in 1902. Current animal shapes include the giraffe, lion, bear, elephant, monkey, camel, hippo, and seal, just to name a few.

I only have one gripe with animal crackers. They're incredibly difficult to prop upright, aren't they?

Maybe the next wave of the little cookies can be made thicker on the bottom so they naturally stand up without having to be leaned against anything. That would certainly make it easier to line them up in parade fashion! And let's face it—regardless of age—we all play with our animal cookies before chomping their little heads off!

DID YOU KNOW?

Ever notice the string on a box of animal crackers? It was originally there to hang on a Christmas tree as an ornament.

NATIONAL GARLIC DAY

APRIL
19

"What garlic is to salad, insanity is to art." —Augustus Saint-Gaudens,
The Reminiscences of Augustus Saint-Gaudens

It's a good thing today is not also International Kissing Day (which falls on July 6, in case you were wondering)!

Garlic, known as "the stinking rose," is considered both an herb and a vegetable. Among its medicinal uses, garlic has been known to help reduce cholesterol and lower blood pressure; it's good for you when you have a cold; and, most importantly, it wards off both vampires and bad dates from making the move on you (especially if your date has alliumphobia—or the fear of garlic).

Whether you're celebrating garlic in ice cream (no, seriously: Gilroy, California—the "Garlic Capitol of the World"—has garlic-flavored ice cream at their annual festival), in bruschetta, infused in vodka, or by covering an entire head in olive oil before roasting it until creamy, here's hoping your day is spent with people who *really* love you despite the way you might smell afterward!

Today is also National Amaretto Day and National Rice Ball Day.

TARA'S HAPPY ACCIDENT BEANS

Makes 4 to 6 servings

Note: This recipe needs to cook for 5 hours.

- 2 (15-ounce) cans pinto beans, drained and rinsed
- 2 (15-ounce) cans dark red kidney beans, drained and rinsed
- 1 large Vidalia onion, diced (about 2 cups)
- 4 garlic cloves, minced
- 1½ cups dark molasses
- ⅓ cup stone-ground mustard
- 3 tablespoons Worcestershire sauce
- 1 teaspoon cumin

Preheat the oven to 200°F.

Mix all the ingredients together in a large casserole dish. Cover and bake for 4 hours.

After 4 hours, remove the cover from the casserole dish, raise the oven temperature to 300, and bake for 1 more hour, or until the top is crusty. Serve in a bowl with a side of cornbread, if desired.

NATIONAL PINEAPPLE UPSIDE DOWN CAKE DAY

"A bad review is like baking a cake with all the best ingredients and having someone sit on it." —Danielle Steel

Historically, the pineapple has been a symbol of hospitality. So bust out your cake pans, canned pineapple rings, and bright red maraschino cherries and get to baking—you've got people to invite over today!

Pineapple upside down cake is my culinary kryptonite. Every time I make it, something goes horribly wrong. For example, the first time I attempted it was a couple years back when a friend sweet-talked me into making one for her. "My oven isn't calibrated right," I tried to explain to her, knowing it wouldn't bake evenly. "Don't worry. We'll just work around that little detail," she said all too convincingly. *Unsurprisingly*, the cake didn't cook through.

"We can probably just use the microwave to finish it," she encouraged me. "It'll be delicious."

So we did.

And it was not.

Still, I encourage you today—and every food holiday—to face your foodie fears head-on. Just make sure you have a Plan B (like a grocery store nearby) in case whatever you make ends disastrously!

DID YOU KNOW?

Pineapple juice was once used to induce labor.

Today is also National Lima Bean Respect Day.

APRIL 21 NATIONAL CHOCOLATE COVERED CASHEWS DAY

"Unanimously, worldwide, nobody I know of dislikes cashews." —George Paulose

Ever wonder why you can buy most every other nut in their shell, but never the kidney-shaped cashew? It's because the raw nut has two shells protecting it, between which is a very caustic oil. (This Cashew Nutshell Liquid, or CNSL, can be used to make things like brake fluid and insecticides.) The shells are removed through a burning and roasting process.

While cashews themselves naturally grow in tropical climates, chocolate covered cashews are a favorite treat in many candy shops and with chocolatiers around the world. There's just something entirely sensual about the marriage of melt-in-your-mouth chocolate and the creamy consistency of a cashew. Whoever first decided to pair the two knew *exactly* what he or she was doing. (And if it was to impress somebody, I have no doubt that it worked favorably for them!)

They say the way to someone's heart is through the belly, so win over someone today by making your own chocolate covered cashews!

NATIONAL JELLY BEAN DAY

"You can tell a lot about a fellow's character by his way of eating jelly beans."
—Ronald Regan

Another food associated with Easter (because of their egglike shape), today is all about those brightly colored—sometimes deceiving—little candies: the jelly bean! Thought to have been based off both the Turkish Delight and the Jordan almond, the jelly bean has certainly come a long way over the course of just the past century.

I was addicted to Jelly Belly jelly beans when I was younger. Like crayon names, I was intrigued with the incredibly specific flavors the creators came up with. And it was mind-boggling to me that they could so perfectly capture the flavor of beverages, desserts, and fruits in tiny pieces of candy. It didn't matter whether you were craving root beer, bubblegum, buttered popcorn, chocolate pudding, pear, strawberry cheesecake, margaritas (my favorite), toasted marshmallow, or grapefruit. There was

a jelly bean to satisfy your every whim! Then, thanks to the incredibly inventive folks at Jelly Belly, and with the introduction of *Harry Potter,* people were able to taste new flavors (like dirt, earthworm, soap, pencil shavings, canned dog food, centipede, and skunk spray) they never even knew they wanted to taste.

So whether you have a hankering for a banana split or ear wax, today is the perfect day to satiate those cravings with a jelly bean or two!

DID YOU KNOW?

Jelly Belly developed their blueberry flavor specifically for Ronald Reagan's presidential inauguration in 1981.

APRIL 23 · NATIONAL PICNIC DAY

"We hope that, when the insects take over the world, they will remember with gratitude how we took them along on all our picnics." —Bill Vaughan

Whether it's hunter-gatherers cooking a day's find over an open fire on the plains of Africa, or the elusive *Dîner en Blanc* ("dinner in white")—the spontaneous, yet perfectly synchronized, elaborate pop-up dining events—people have always, and probably always will, enjoy eating outside. There's something so spiritual and fulfilling about combining the elements of the outdoors with good, thoughtfully crafted food and excellent company to share it all with.

Alternatively, my little sister and I used to love when our mom would let us have picnics in the living room. Not only was it the ultimate treat to be able to eat sprawled out on the floor or couch while watching a movie, but I think it also made us both have this major sense of responsibility because we were being trusted not to spill anything, to clean up after ourselves, and, y'know, not chuck food at each other (which has always been a temptation regardless of where we were or how old we are)!

So I thought it would be appropriate today to spread out a blanket on my living room floor and recreate those Saturday afternoons as a kid. Besides, it—of course—rained when I first celebrated today, so I didn't really have a choice!

Today is also National Cherry Cheesecake Day.

PA AMB TOMÀQUET

Makes 1 serving

- 2 slices French bread
- 1 garlic clove, cut in half
- 1 small tomato, cut in half
- 2 teaspoons olive oil (this also tastes *outstanding* with grape seed oil)
- ½ teaspoon sea salt
- 4 thin slices deli ham

Toast the two slices of bread really well. Rub one side of each piece vigorously with the garlic, using half a clove for each piece. Rub half of the tomato vigorously over the garlic rubbed toast, and then squeeze the tomato's insides onto each piece of toast. Drizzle each piece of toast with half of the olive oil and sprinkle each piece with half the sea salt. Finish by topping each piece of toast with two slices of the ham.

APRIL 24

NATIONAL PIGS-IN-A-BLANKET DAY

"I am fond of pigs. Dogs look up to us. Cats look down on us. Pigs treat us as equals." —Sir Winston Churchill

The concept of taking a pork product (the "pig") and wrapping it in dough (the "blanket") is one that's familiar worldwide. For example, in Germany, *Würstchen im Schlafrock* (or sausage in a nightgown) is a sausage sometimes wrapped in bacon and then wrapped in dough (or pancakes). Meanwhile, in Israel, *Moshe Ba'Teiva* (or Moses in the Ark)—a dish loved by kids—adds ketchup in, on, or under the dough before being cooked.

Today is the perfect day to take a trip down memory lane and recreate the pigs-in-a-blanket—no doubt one of the most awesome finger foods there is—you had as a child. Whether that's hot dogs wrapped in puff pastry, or something a little more nontraditional like sausages wrapped in pancakes, or for vegetarians, a soy dog and some vegan cream cheese wrapped in crescent roll dough!

NATIONAL ZUCCHINI BREAD DAY

"Bread deals with living things, with giving life, with growth, with the seed, the grain that nurtures. It is not coincidence that we say bread is the staff of life."
—Lionel Poilane

Zucchini bread was one of the very first things I learned how to make. I was fortunate enough to take a class in high school called International Foods. Not to brag, but I ended up finishing with a grade of 116—my teacher actually asked me to stop showing up the last couple of weeks because my grade was so high. A few years later, when my sister took the course, she got a twenty-three. And now? She's a better cook than I am!

Before submerging us in the world of fried rice, curries, and chiles rellenos, we were taught a slew of basic foods like cookies and quick breads. Playing with yeast and learning to proof dough can be intimidating, so quick breads are a great way to introduce a novice to the world of baking because of their simplicity in both ingredients and directions.

So the way I learned how to make zucchini bread was with an orange glaze and *not* with chocolate chips or nuts. Call me a purist, but when I cut into zucchini bread all I want to see are the green shreds of the vegetable—this also helps fool me into believing that I'm actually doing something good for my body by eating the bread. After all, when you're eating the year, you gotta get those servings of F&V in where you can!

'CCHINI 'CCHINI BREAD

Makes 1 loaf

Bread:

2 cups all-purpose flour
¾ cup granulated sugar
1 teaspoon salt
1 tablespoon cinnamon
2 teaspoons baking powder
1 teaspoon baking soda
¼ cup vegetable oil
½ cup orange juice
1 tablespoon grated orange zest
1 large zucchini, grated (about 1½ packed cups)
1 teaspoon vanilla extract

Glaze:

1 cup confectioners' sugar
2 tablespoons orange juice

Preheat the oven to 350°F.

Grease a 9-inch loaf pan and set it aside.

In a medium bowl, mix together the flour, sugar, salt, cinnamon, baking powder, and baking soda.

In a large bowl, mix together the vegetable oil, orange juice, orange zest, zucchini, and vanilla. Add the dry ingredients to the wet ingredients and stir until they are just combined.

Spread the batter evenly in the pan and bake for 55 to 60 minutes, or until a toothpick inserted in the center comes out clean. Let the bread cool for 30 minutes.

Whisk together the confectioners' sugar and orange juice. Drizzle the glaze across the top of the bread. As the bread continues to cool completely, the glaze will solidify. You could also use the glaze as a spread on a slice of the warm bread!

APRIL 26 — NATIONAL PRETZEL DAY

"Yeah, okay. So the thing is, I think that maybe I might have feelings. Like weird, weird feelings for . . . pretzels." —Parker, Leverage

I quite like pretzels. I always have. They remind me of my childhood, of my German ancestry, and of baseball games.

I never realized, though, that the pretzel had such heavy religious meaning. It's commonly believed that they were first created in Europe by a monk in the seventh century who gave out the pretzels as rewards to those children who learned their prayers. He called them *Pretiola* (which is Latin for "little reward"); the folded strips of dough were supposed to resemble the crossing of one's arms over her chest in prayer. There's also belief that the three holes in a pretzel may represent the Father, Son, and Holy Spirit.

And, unlike other food holidays, National Pretzel Day actually has an origin! In 2003, Pennsylvania's then governor, Ed Rendell, declared it a day of celebration because of the food's importance to both their economy and history.

So now that you know all that, the most important decision you need to make today is going to be whether you dredge your pretzel through mustard, onion dip, peanut butter, Sriracha, or cheese.

APRIL 27 — NATIONAL PRIME RIB DAY

"A good cook is like a sorceress who dispenses happiness." —Elsa Schiaparelli

Today is definitely not an ideal day to be a vegetarian or a cow!

Prime rib, more appropriately called *standing rib roast* (partially because when it's cooked, it's naturally propped up by bones), comes from the—you guessed it!—rib region of a cow, between the chuck and short loin. It's called prime rib not because it comes from the top USDA grade of beef there is (if it was, it would have the USDA label in front of it to specifically denote its quality), but because it comes from one of the eight choice primal cuts of a cow. A rib eye steak or roast, by the way, comes from the prime rib cut, but both the bones and fat will have been removed.

What's your perfect side to prime rib? Whether it's mashed potatoes and gravy, creamed spinach, Yorkshire pudding, or asparagus with hollandaise sauce and a sunny side up egg, if you're celebrating today's food holiday, you'll definitely be doing it in style!

DID YOU KNOW?

Cows have thirty-two teeth.

- -

APRIL 28 — NATIONAL BLUEBERRY PIE DAY

"Men may come and men may go . . . but pie goes on forever." —George Augustus Sala

As cliché as it sounds as a Mainer, today is one of my favorite food holidays all year long. How could I be blue on a day when my state's official dessert is being celebrated?

I grew up enamored with hot blueberry pie topped with cold vanilla ice cream. The flavor, texture, and temperature combinations are a sensation like no other I've ever experienced (though I may be

140 / EAT THE YEAR

biased because of the state I'm from)! Plus, blueberries really do grow in abundance here. The beach of my family's summer home had bushes of the tiny little berries randomly growing among the rocks, and as I write this, the elderly couple next door to me has a big blueberry tree they are *very* protective of!

What made today even more wonderful for me was that my younger sister was home to help me honor this food holiday—and any day that you can spend time eating pie with someone you love is cause for celebration! A few years back, neither she nor I were very good when it came to cooking (eating, on the other hand, is something we've always excelled at). But over the course of time, each of us has come into our own. She's a pro at making pies now, so today *she* did all the cooking while *I* did all the eating.

What bliss!

APRIL 29 — NATIONAL SHRIMP SCAMPI DAY

"I shall be but a shrimp of an author." —Thomas Gray, "Letter to Horace Walpole"

Shrimp scampi: an elegant dish? Sure. A time-consuming one? No, not really. A confusing one to folks outside of the U.S. or "connoisseurs"? Potentially!

Scampi is a term used Stateside for an Italian-American dish that involves shrimp served in a garlicky-butter, lemon juice, and white wine sauce over a bed of pasta like linguine. Outside of the states, scampi are actually a kind of small, edible lobster—also known as Dublin Bay prawns—that are popular throughout parts of Europe. To make things a little more confusing, even the word *scampi* itself refers to shrimp served in garlicky-butter sauce. So "shrimp scampi"—if we're being technical—is actually redundant as it basically means "shrimp shrimp."

I don't know about you, but as long as it's *good good* then I'm not sure I care what it's called!

NATIONAL OATMEAL COOKIE DAY

"Oats. A grain, which in England is generally given to horses, but in Scotland supports the people." —Samuel Johnson, A Dictionary of the English Language

When I lived in England, I discovered Nairn's Oatcakes. They were unlike any other "cracker" I had ever had before. The best way to describe them, if you've never had the pleasure of eating one, is that they're kind of like a large, circular, flat, very dense, very compact oatmeal cookie minus the sweetness. My family calls them oak cakes, because (A) they misheard me the first time I tried explaining them to my mom over the phone, and (B) they can be a little hard and bland probably like oak bark is.

But I love them. I ate them every day I lived abroad. What I didn't know then was that they're probably really similar to the precursor of the oatmeal cookie as we know it today. Oatmeal cakes originated in Scotland —they were thin like a pancake and crunchy. The Scots used to carry them around for an energy boost during attacks or while traveling. (Nairn's still advertises them as being "naturally energizing.") It wasn't until the late nineteenth century/early twentieth century that the modern version of the oatmeal cookie was created as an attempt at making a healthier dessert option.

If you're not a huge oatmeal cookie fan, you should try oatcakes today instead! They can be eaten as is or topped with a variety of wonderful things like jam, cheese, or even a scoop of chicken salad!

Today is also National Raisin Day.

MAY IS...

MAY IS ALSO...

National Artisan Gelato Month
National Asparagus Month
National BBQ Month
National Beef Month
National Chocolate Custard Month
National Egg Month
National Gazpacho Aficionado Month
National Hamburger Month
National Herb Month
National Mediterranean Diet Month
National Salad Month
National Salsa Month
National Strawberry Month
National Vinegar Month

. . .

1st Saturday—National Homebrew Day
3rd Thursday—National Hummus Day
3rd Friday—National Pizza Party Day
3rd Saturday—World Whisky Day
3rd Sunday—World Baking Day
Memorial Day—National BBQ Day

MAY 01 NATIONAL CHOCOLATE PARFAIT DAY

"You know what else everybody likes? Parfaits! Have you ever met a person, you say, 'Let's get some parfait,' they say, 'Hell no! I don't like no parfait'? Parfaits are delicious!" —Donkey, Shrek

Ever stop to consider the differences between a parfait and a sundae? While similar, they *are* different, and it's important to know what those differences are so you can celebrate today in appropriate style!

Parfait, meaning "perfect" in French, was originally used to describe certain frozen desserts made from layered sugar syrups, eggs, and creams starting in the late nineteenth century. Stateside, we think we've really perfected the parfait . . . or is that *perfected* the *perfect* . . . *parfaited* the *parfait*? Our versions can include anything from ice cream to frozen custard, to pudding, to mousse, to sponge cake with layers of fresh fruit, nuts, whipped cream, and sometimes even liqueur, all served in a tall, clear glass.

Still sound like a sundae? The key is that sundaes are usually always made with ice cream and aren't generally layered, are they? Instead, you get a couple scoops of hard serve *topped* with syrups and the like. I don't know about you, but I prefer even distribution—a layer of ice cream, a layer of chocolate syrup, another layer of ice cream, and another layer of chocolate syrup sounds absolutely divine to this chocoholic today!

MAY

02

NATIONAL TRUFFLE DAY

"Truffle isn't exactly aphrodisiac but under certain circumstances it tends to make women more tender and men more likable." —J.A. Brillat-Savarin

Sweet or savory? Today, you have options!

Savory truffles are a type of edible fungus that grows underground near the root systems of specific trees. These aromatic, valuable delicacies are found using trained pigs or dogs that sniff them out. Because they're difficult to find and are becoming rarer in the natural world, they can be *very* expensive. If the path of today's choose-your-own-adventure leads you down the savory trail, it may end up breaking the bank. Luckily, many places that now boast of making gourmet french fries and dips usually offer truffle oil ketchup. Do yourself a favor and try some. It is *epically* good.

Sweet truffles, on the other hand, are delicious little chocolate balls that are usually made from a ganache (though they might also include caramel or flavored creams) and are coated in cocoa powder, nuts, powdered sugar, or more chocolate! Unlike their savory counterpart, they're incredibly easy to find (you can get mass-manufactured ones with a shelf life of like eight years from the grocery store). They're also easy to make. As in, if everyone knew how easy, we'd all be fatty-fatty two-by-fours.

Y'know what? Bring on the two-by-four, boys.

NATIONAL RASPBERRY TART DAY

"A gourmet who thinks of calories is like a tart who looks at her watch." —James Beard

There's nothing sour or promiscuous about today's food holiday. It's all about the sweet desserts made from a flaky pastry base, a creamy filling, and fresh fruit—like raspberries!

Tarts date back to the Middle Ages and consisted of basically an open-topped pie shell traditionally filled with some kind of meat product. Even today, savory tarts are super fashionable—you can find them in a variety of flavors like caramelized onion and goat cheese, egg and sun-dried tomato, and mushroom and feta. Eventually, chefs made a spin-off dessert version using custard and fruit, which is what we're celebrating today.

While raspberries aren't quite in season yet, today serves as a reminder that summer is steamrolling toward us. You still have plenty of time to work on getting that perfect beach bod, though, so embrace today and indulge on a tart or two made with just raspberries or with custard, ganache, white chocolate, or a sweet mascarpone filling, too!

Today is also National Chocolate Custard Day and National Raspberry Popover Day.

NATIONAL ORANGE JUICE DAY

"Orange is the happiest color." —Frank Sinatra

Besides chicken soup, orange juice might be the ultimate go-to when people feel under the weather. When I was little and would get sick, my mom used to make me a special drink that she called a bomb—one-third OJ and two-thirds ginger ale—and it had serious healing properties! After all, orange juice is loaded with Vitamin C, which is important for a healthy immune system. It also aids tissue repair in the body and helps prevent scurvy. (Scurvy Awareness Day was May 2nd, by the way—it's really no wonder National Orange Juice Day is held just a couple days later.)

Orange juice comes in all shapes and sizes these days. There's OJ with no pulp, some pulp, or extra pulp; OJ with extra antioxidants, calcium, or omega 3; organic OJ; frozen OJ; fresh squeezed OJ; OJ with pineapple juice, mango juice, honey—there really is something for everyone!

So celebrate today with a glass of orange juice first thing in the morning, as a midafternoon pick-me-up, or with a brownie for dessert tonight (seriously, OJ and chocolate anything is a magical combo).

DID YOU KNOW?

Approximately 80 percent of America's orange juice comes from Florida-grown oranges.

Today is also National Candied Orange Peel Day.

NATIONAL ENCHILADA DAY

"If God dwells inside us like some people say, I sure hope He likes enchiladas, because that's what He's getting." —Jack Handy, Deep Thoughts

Today you get the whole enchilada: a food holiday and a real holiday—Cinco de Mayo—that actually complement each other! Really, it only makes sense to celebrate Mexican culture, heritage, and history with delicious food and refreshing drinks. (I mean, isn't that essentially how we celebrate *all* holidays now, regardless of how or why they originated?) And a platter of enchiladas and a pitcher of margaritas sound like the perfect way to celebrate, doesn't it?

Enchilada comes from the Spanish word *enchilar,* which means "to season with chile." Corn tortillas rolled around a filling have been a staple food in the Mexican diet for centuries; perhaps even the Aztecs were munching on a primitive version of them. How they're prepared, though, can differ depending on where in the world you're located. The kind many of us are familiar with are made with chicken, beef, seafood, veggies, or beans wrapped in a tortilla that's smothered in either a red or green sauce and cheese before being baked. The uniqueness of the enchilada doesn't stop there; enchiladas can come stacked, with a béchamel-like cream sauce, or even with mole.

Which means, if you are a diehard foodie, you can eat a different version for breakfast, lunch, and dinner today. Margaritas at each meal are optional!

Today is also National Hoagie Day, National Chocolate Custard Day, National Oyster Day, and Totally Chipotle Day.

TASTY 'CHILADAS

1 boil-in-bag of brown rice, boiled according to package directions

1 (16- to 20-ounce) can black beans, drained and rinsed

1 (16-ounce) can refried beans

1 (4-ounce) can chopped green chilies, drained and rinsed

1 (10- to 12-ounce) can green enchilada sauce, divided

1 (8-ounce) bag sharp Cheddar cheese, divided

6 large, soft tortillas, any flavor

6 toothpicks (any size)

Sour cream, chopped avocados, chopped tomatoes, chopped onions (optional)

Preheat the oven to 350°F.

Spray the bottom of a 9 x 13-inch baking pan with nonstick cooking spray. Set aside.

In a large bowl, combine the rice, black beans, refried beans, and the green chilies. Stir in half of the enchilada sauce and half of the cheese. Divide the mixture equally down the middle of the six tortillas. Roll each tortilla up, secure with a toothpick, and place them in the baking pan, toothpick-side up. Pour the remaining enchilada sauce evenly across the tops of the 'chiladas, and then sprinkle the rest of the cheese evenly across the tops. Remove and discard the toothpicks. Bake for 45 minutes.

Remove the enchiladas from the oven and let them sit for 5 minutes. Serve the enchiladas as is or with sour cream, chopped avocados, chopped tomatoes, or chopped onions.

Tip! If you want, you can add 12 ounces of cooked soy meat crumbles or 1 pound of cooked, drained, and crumbled ground beef by mixing either into the bowl after adding the green chilies. Just know, this will make these already enormous enchiladas even bigger!

INTERNATIONAL NO DIET DAY

"If nature had intended our skeletons to be visible, it would have put them on the outside of our bodies." —Elmer Rice

I don't have a perfect body—and I'm okay with that. But it was something that took me a really long time to accept. God gave me curves, and no matter how hard I limited my caloric intake, no matter how many miles I ran, there were certain things about my body and about my bone structure, like these hips, that were just *never* going to change. So why waste any more energy than I needed to on worrying or punishing myself (because that's what dieting is) when I could be using it to do something so much more productive?

And that's what today is all about—acceptance, forgiveness, and making peace with the body you have and the hunger you feel. International No Diet Day was started by a British woman named Mary Evans Young in 1992 after she herself had suffered from anorexia and image issues; a light blue ribbon symbolizes the cause to eliminate prejudice toward people of all body shapes and to promote a more sustainable lifestyle choice than dieting.

Trust me, life is much easier when you eat what you want in moderation (and remember to move that booty around a few times a week, too)!

Today is also National Crêpe Suzette Day and National Beverage Day.

THE NYC DREAM BAGEL SANDWICH

Note: Part of this recipe needs to chill for 2 hours prior to eating.

1 (8-ounce) tub cream cheese

¼ cup jarred jalapeños, chopped, juice reserved

¼ cup shredded sharp Cheddar cheese

3 tablespoons olive oil, divided

¼ cup all-purpose flour

1 teaspoon cumin

¼ teaspoon salt

¼ cup milk

½ cup panko crumbs

2 medium green tomatoes (tomatillos), sliced

4 eggs

4 large bagels, sliced

1 avocado, peeled, seeded, sliced

In a bowl, mix together the cream cheese, jalapeños and juice, and cheese. Refrigerate for 2 hours to let flavors blend.

When the cream cheese spread has chilled, place 2 tablespoons of the olive oil in a skillet and turn the heat to medium.

While the oil is heating, mix together the flour, cumin, and salt in a small bowl. In a second small bowl, add the milk. In a third small bowl, place the panko crumbs. Dredge each slice of green tomato through the flour mix, then the milk, and then the panko crumbs. Gently place each coated tomato slice into the hot oil and cook for 3 minutes on each side, or until golden-brown. If the tomatoes get too brown too fast, lower the heat. Remove the fried green tomatoes and place them on a plate lined with 2 or 3 paper towels to remove any excess oil.

Fry the eggs in the remaining oil.

Toast the bagels. Spread all eight bagel halves with some of the cream cheese spread. On four bagel halves, place a fried egg, fried green tomato slices, and some avocado. Top those four halves with the other four halves to create sandwiches.

NATIONAL ROAST LEG OF LAMB DAY

"What do you mean he don't eat no meat? Oh, that's okay. I make lamb."—Aunt Voula, My Big Fat Greek Wedding

I think it's safe to assume that for the average person in modern day America, lamb isn't something that's often on the home menu rotation. It can be labor intensive to make, expensive, and since many of us are unfamiliar with the taste, we simply avoid it—unless it's Easter or National Roast Leg of Lamb Day, of course! It is, however, a cut of meat that has been eaten for thousands and thousands of years, and it is still consumed in many different parts of the world.

Lamb in the culinary world refers to the moist, tender meat that comes from sheep that are less than one year old. (When you eat mutton you're technically eating adult sheep.) And roast leg of lamb is exactly what it sounds like—a cut of meat from the leg of a young sheep that's roasted.

Easy enough, right? But how will you marinate it? Perhaps with a simple garlic, rosemary, lemon, and olive oil mixture? And will you serve it with a mint jelly or a red wine sauce? What about your side dishes? Will you go with roasted potatoes, seasonal veggies, rice pilaf, creamed Brussels sprouts, or braised Swiss chard? So many things to think about!

Let's hope when you celebrate today it falls on a weekend.

DID YOU KNOW?

The first animal to ever be cloned was a sheep named Dolly in 1996.

NATIONAL COCONUT CREAM PIE DAY

"There is sweet water inside a tender coconut. Who poured the water inside the coconut? Was it the work of any man? No. Only the Divine can do such a thing."
—*Sri Sathya Sai Baba*

Coconut has a very specific flavor to it, doesn't it? I tend to think that people are put off by it because of the way so many companies artificially enhance its very pleasant, very mellow natural taste. This is especially true when it comes to coconut cream pie, so I'm asking you—if you're not a fan of coconut—to go into today with an open mind. There are other ways to celebrate than with a traditional coconut-flavored custard topped with a mountain of dull whipped cream and cloyingly sweet shreds of toasted coconut.

Have you ever tried *fried* coconut cream pie? It's melt-in-your-mouth fried dough filled with a velvety, rich coconut cream. Sinfully good.

Have you ever tried *vegan* coconut cream pie? I was fortunate enough to receive five five-bite mini vegan coconut cream pies to celebrate today with. Twenty-five bites later and there was nothing left but crumbs and (metaphorical) tears—it was unexpectedly one of the best foods I had eaten during this year-long project of face stuffing. The pie dough was flaky and the coconut cream filling was both silky smooth and stunningly flavorful. What I didn't know then was that I would think about these delicious pies for the rest of the year—that's how exceptional they were.

Even now there's a pang in my heart like I'm writing about some long lost lover. Don't you love it when food moves you like that?

DID YOU KNOW?

There are over 425 calories in an average-size piece of pie.

Today is also National Have a Coke Day and National Empanada Day.

NATIONAL MOSCATO DAY

"It is the hour to be drunken. To escape being martyred slaves of time, be cease-lessly drunk. On wine, on poetry, or on virtue, as you wish." —Charles Baudelaire

In 2012, Gallo Family Vineyards established May 9th as National Moscato Day. Food bloggers and wine aficionados everywhere jumped at the chance to promote and be a part of a new food holiday right from its inception (which is a treat for those of us who follow the food calendar, since most of the days' origins are a complete mystery to us)!

And while there are several wine-based holidays, why *not* dedicate a day to a specific kind? Especially a varietal that isn't as mainstream as Merlot and Chardonnay seem to be. Moscato has gained popularity in recent memory; probably because it's a great wine to introduce to (or convert) non-wine drinkers. It's traditionally a white wine that's light, crisp, fruity (think peaches, melon, and citrus), and has just the right balance of sweetness. A basic Moscato goes really well with cheeses of all kinds and most desserts, but it's especially delicious chilled on its own, making it an ideal wine to drink as the weather gets hotter.

So pour yourself a glass, sit back, put your feet up, and relax. Eating—or drinking—the year doesn't get much easier than this!

DID YOU KNOW?

The Muscat grape is one of the oldest known varieties (for one of the oldest known fruits!) there is.

Today is also National Butterscotch Brownie Day.

NATIONAL SHRIMP DAY

"Civilization as it is known today could not have evolved, nor can it survive, without an adequate food supply." —Norman Borlaug

Bubba Gump would tell you today that " . . . shrimp is the fruit of the sea. You can barbecue it, boil it, broil it, bake it, sauté it. There's, um, shrimp kebabs, shrimp Creole, shrimp gumbo, pan fried, deep-fried, stir-fried. There's pineapple shrimp, lemon shrimp, coconut shrimp, pepper shrimp, shrimp soup, shrimp stew, shrimp salad, shrimp and potatoes, shrimp burger, shrimp sandwich . . . that's about it."

I loved shrimp when I was younger. Their curly, pink bodies were delicious dredged through cocktail sauce or, better yet, deep-fried. I admit, unashamedly, that at weddings or Chinese food buffets when popcorn or coconut shrimp was an option, I was the person taking far more than her fair share and holding up the line as I loaded mountain-size piles of the goodies onto my plate. But then something terrible happened: I grew up. And I realized that there was a crappy side to eating shrimp . . . literally. After peeling them, you have to devein the little crustaceans, i.e., take the black, ropy digestive tube out of its body. If you don't, you might get a mouthful of . . . grit.

If you know what I'm sayin'.

DID YOU KNOW?

Many shrimp that start their lives as males end their lives as females.

NATIONAL EAT WHAT YOU WANT DAY

"Part of the secret of success in life is to eat what you like and let the food fight it out inside." —Mark Twain

Today epitomizes the proverbial "oasis in the desert" metaphor. It's National Eat What You Want Day, which means you can actually eat *whatever* you want. For those of you attempting to eat the year, today is a glorious, refreshing break from having to eat or drink whatever the calendar dictates. Even if you're not, use today as an excuse to stuff your face full of all those sinful once-in-a-while treats you've been thinking about! Calories don't count today!

Okay, they do, but suspended disbelief is so much more fun than a guilt trip after a giant slab of peanut butter cream pie, am I right?

National Eat What You Want Day was created by Thomas and Ruth Roy of *WellCat.com* (also the creators of Sneak a Zucchini on Your Neighbor's Porch Day on August 8th and Cook Something Bold and Pungent Day on November 8th, among other fun days).

Today is a perfect day to be authentically you! If you love Greek yogurt with honey, eat Greek yogurt with honey. If you crave cannolis, eat cannolis. If you can't stop thinking about spinach and mushroom quesadillas, go right on ahead and eat a spinach and mushroom quesadilla. Today, *anything* goes. So take the opportunity to *eat what you want*—because tomorrow? Tomorrow we go back to our strict food calendar diet!

Today is also National Mocha Torte Day.

PANKOCADO

Makes 2 servings

Chili Lime Crema:

¾ cup sour cream
1 tablespoon lime juice
2 teaspoons lime zest
1 teaspoon chili powder
¼ teaspoon Sriracha or hot sauce
Pinch of salt (optional)

Pankocados:

1 cup all-purpose flour
1 cup milk
1 cup panko crumbs
1 teaspoon cumin
½ teaspoon salt
2 avocados
½ cup pico de gallo or salsa
½ cup sharp Cheddar cheese

Preheat the oven to 400°F.

In a bowl, mix together the sour cream, lime juice, lime zest, chili powder, Sriracha, and salt. Refrigerate the chili lime crema until ready to use.

Using three bowls, place the flour in one, the milk in the second, and the panko crumbs, cumin, and salt in the third.

Carefully slice and skin the avocados and remove the pits so that you have four halves. Place half of an avocado in the bowl of flour and cover it completely. Remove it from the flour and quickly submerge it into the bowl of milk. Remove the avocado from the milk and place it in the bowl of panko crumbs, covering it completely. Place the avocado on a baking sheet, sliced-side up. Repeat the coating process with the other three avocado halves. Bake for 30 minutes, or until the outsides have browned and become crispy.

Remove the baking sheet from the oven and turn the oven to broil. Fill the holes of each avocado half with two tablespoons of pico de gallo or salsa, and then two tablespoons of cheese. Broil for 5 to 7 minutes, or until the cheese has melted and become slightly brown.

Serve immediately with a dollop or drizzle of the chili lime crema.

MAY 12

NATIONAL NUTTY FUDGE DAY

"Fudge is a noun, a verb, an interjection, and delicious!" —Terri Guillemets

Many people think of fudge as a holiday treat. It's time to shake off that mindset—today is just one of *several* fudge-related food holidays we're about to celebrate together! May 12 is specifically all about *nutty* fudge, and I suppose that could be interpreted one of two ways: as a zany or unique flavor of the candy or, in a more literal sense, as fudge that actually contains nuts.

Either way, fudge is insanely decadent, isn't it? It's kind of like brownies on steroids: richer, denser, and creamier than their innocent counterpart, for sure. It's also much trickier to make, because fudge is a crystalline candy (which means its texture actually comes from the formation of crystals). If you don't get the temperature *just right* during the process, you could end up with something very runny (like mine) or very grainy! No one would blame you if you decided to forgo making your own today in lieu of something made by a professional!

MAY 13

NATIONAL APPLE PIE DAY

"If you wish to make an apple pie from scratch, you must first invent the Universe." —Carl Sagan, Cosmos

Today's food holiday was obviously created by someone like me—an apple addict—who just couldn't wait until autumn to celebrate the beloved fruit. It's like whoever decided National Apple Pie Day should be placed in the middle of May was saying, "Fall, *you* are my favorite. This pie represents both my love and acknowledgment of you year-round. Now please forgive me as I have a small love affair with summer."

Apple pie didn't originate in the U.S.; it was most likely a dessert brought over with the European colonists (as were their favorite apple trees since the only native ones to the States were crab apples). It certainly evolved into a dish that we embraced as our own, though, as it has become a quintessentially American symbol.

There's no question how much we love apple pie. So the only thing left to ask is how do *you* enjoy your slice? Whether it's topped with whipped cream, a scoop of ice cream, a slice of sharp Cheddar cheese, or as is, there's really no wrong answer!

DID YOU KNOW?

A "mock" apple pie isn't made with apples, but with crackers, lemon, butter, and spices. It was popular during the Great Depression, when apples were crazy expensive.

Today is also National Fruit Cocktail Day.

MAY 14 NATIONAL BUTTERMILK BISCUIT DAY

"Poetry is the synthesis of hyacinths and biscuits." —Carl Sandburg

Biscuits carry a great responsibility. It's their duty to be a sturdy, reliable foundation for things like butter, honey, jam, molasses, and gravy to be safely transported from our plates to our mouths with minimum spillage. Not just any baked product could handle such an important task, but tender, flaky, buttery biscuits do. And they do it well.

Not only are biscuits historically cheaper and easier to make than their cousins with yeast, they also store better. Obviously they've come a long way, as they're now a commonplace item on many fast food chains' menus!

Today is all about, specifically, the buttermilk biscuit (which some people believe is the superior type of biscuit). Buttermilk is the sour, leftover liquid after butter has been churned from milk or cream. It can also be made at home by introducing an ingredient that curdles milk (like lemon juice or white vinegar)!

B15CU17 R3DUX

Makes 8 to 10 biscuits

1 cup minus 1 tablespoon milk

1 tablespoon lemon juice

3 cups all-purpose flour

3 tablespoons granulated sugar

4 teaspoons baking powder

1 teaspoon cream of tartar

½ teaspoon cornstarch

½ teaspoon salt

1 cup (2 sticks) unsalted butter, at room temperature

Preheat the oven to 425°F.

Grease a baking sheet and set aside.

In a small bowl, whisk together the milk and lemon juice and set it aside. Let it sit for 5 to 10 minutes (I like to wait until there's a yellowish tinge around the sides).

In a large bowl, mix together the flour, sugar, baking powder, cream of tartar, cornstarch, and salt. Cut in the butter—I find it's easiest to use hands—and mix until *just* combined. Slowly pour the wet ingredients in and gently mix it all together. *Do not overmix.* You want everything to just barely come together.

Gather the dough together and gently pat it out on a floured surface to a ¾-inch thickness. You won't need a rolling pin because the dough will be thick and easy to pat down. Using a cookie cutter or the open end of a pint glass, cut eight to ten biscuits out of the dough. Place the biscuits on the baking sheet, sides touching. Bake 18 to 20 minutes, or until golden-brown.

NATIONAL CHOCOLATE CHIP DAY

"Number one, I absolutely love making chocolate chip cookies. I mean, it's fun. It's exciting. Beyond the fact that I love making them, I love eating them." —Debbi Fields

Oh, chocolate chips. We had quite the romance in culinary school, didn't we? Whenever the instructor wasn't looking, my friends and I would fill up plastic cups with chocolate chips from the industrial-size boxes in the refrigerator. And we'd just spend all day eating them as discreetly as possible since we weren't technically allowed to use any ingredients in the kitchen for our own personal use or consumption (weird rule, right?).

Don't make the same mistake I did! When I first celebrated today's food holiday, I was under the impression it was National Chocolate Chip *Cookie* Day. It's not. It's just National Chocolate Chip Day. (If I had known that, I might have just recreated my collegiate years!) Meaning you could celebrate by eating chocolate chip pancakes, waffles, muffins, breads, cheesecake, or ice cream; you could melt them down and make hot chocolate, or a sauce to dip fruits or nuts in—or you could even use them as an ingredient in your chili!

And *this* is why the delicious, tear-shaped chunks of chocolate have not just one, but two food holidays dedicated to them. They're so much more darn versatile than people think they are.

DID YOU KNOW?

The official state cookie of Massachusetts is chocolate chip.

NATIONAL COQUILLES ST. JACQUES DAY

"Maybe scallops'll fly out of me pants!" —Mr. Krabs, SpongeBob SquarePants

I know what you're thinking: Today sounds like a fancy, made-up holiday to honor the patron saint of cockles. If you *are*, you're actually not too far off the mark!

Coquilles St. Jacques, which translates roughly to "St. James' Scallops," is a classic French dish of scallops and mushrooms served in a wine and cream sauce that's topped with bread crumbs and Gruyère before baked. It's then served back inside cleaned scallop shells. The dish was named after the apostle Saint James the Great, who, legend says, rescued—although he may have just witnessed—a knight—or was it a horse, or maybe a knight on a horse?—who had fallen into the sea, and when he emerged from the murky depths was covered in scallop shells. As a result, the scallop shell became the emblem of the Order of Saint James during the Crusades.

My dad was a recreational scallop diver. After hunting around to find a bed of them, he could usually get four or five buckets of unshucked scallops per two thirty-minute tanks of air. He doesn't do it anymore, but I imagine seafood *that* fresh can be a breath-taking experience.

Much like seeing a knight . . . or a horse . . . or a knight on a horse emerging from the ocean decorated in seashells would be!

DID YOU KNOW?

Unlike other bivalves like mussels and clams, most scallops are free-swimming.

NATIONAL CHERRY COBBLER DAY

"If the only way we judged hunger was how full the stomach is, no one would ever have dessert." —Mark Friedman

If it's true that cobblers—deep-dish fruit desserts topped with piecrust or drop-biscuit dough—were most likely invented by early American settlers traveling west during the late 1800s, then only one thing should come to mind today: The Oregon Trail, which is possibly the coolest game that ever existed (with *Where in the World Is Carmen San Diego?* a close second).

While immersed in the world of *Oregon Trail*, everyone I knew usually died of a broken leg, exhaustion, or dysentery, and all of my ox

constantly drowned every time I attempted to ford a river, regardless of whether it was three feet or thirty feet deep. I don't remember any scenes during the game when I sat around the fire with my family drinking lemonade and eating a Dutch oven cobbler made from whatever fruits I could collect while the men went hunting for rabbits and squirrels. Even though it wasn't displayed in glorious eight-bit pixilation detail, it did most likely happen in real life.

Kind of makes this food holiday that much cooler, am I right?

Today is also National Walnut Day and International Sauvignon Blanc Day.

NATIONAL CHEESE SOUFFLÉ DAY

"When I was a small boy, my father told me never to recommend a church or a woman to anyone. And I have found it wise never to recommend a restaurant either. Something always goes wrong with the cheese soufflé." —Edmund G. Love

It seems only fair, since we celebrate both National Chocolate Fondue Day (February 5, page 45) and National Cheese Fondue Day (April 11, page 122) that we also celebrate *the same* sweet and savory pair of the soufflé world, too!

Back on February 28 (page 72), we paid homage to the chocolate version and learned that *souffler* in French means "to blow or puff up." This, of course, refers to the way the cake expands and inflates during the baking process because soufflés—most likely first created in eighteenth-century France—when properly baked, should be fluffy and light. Unfortunately, they have the tendency to collapse—not because you spoke too loudly or walked too hard near the oven—but most likely because there's either been too much or not enough air incorporated into the egg whites (a staple ingredient in the dish).

Will today be a touch more difficult than knocking back a jigger of whiskey or dialing your local restaurant to have a large pepperoni pie delivered? Yes! But if you've chosen to eat the year the whole way through, then you're used to challenges by now! So sing at the top of your lungs, do a hundred jumping jacks in your kitchen, and try your hands at making a cheese soufflé!

NATIONAL DEVIL'S FOOD CAKE DAY

"If one swallows a cup of chocolate only three hours after a copious lunch, everything will be perfectly digested, and there will still be room for dinner."
—Jean-Anthelme Brillat-Savarin

Devil's food cake is sinfully dark and rich; it's the opposite of the innocently light and airy angel's food cake. I don't know about you, but I'd take red horns and chocolate over wings and vanilla *any* day of the week.

But what makes it different from just a regular old chocolate cake? I always thought what set it apart was the addition of blood, fire, and brimstone. In actuality, it's because of one of several more realistic (read: boring) reasons: (A) Generally it contains more chocolate; (B) The use of baking soda brings out the reddish hue in cocoa powder, which is traditionally used over just melted chocolate; (C) In

the past, devil's food cake was made with shredded beets, which helped give its distinct red color; or (D) food dye. (Duh, right?)

Slipping vegetables into a chocolate cake without anyone noticing? How *devilishly* smart!

If you're anything like me, when you order a slice of devil's food cake it's not because of the how and why of it, it's because you have a mission to overdose on chocolate. So let the dark side win one today and give into evil temptations. You can always absolve your gastronomical sins in October on National Angel Food Cake Day (page 325)!

NATIONAL QUICHE LORRAINE DAY

"I am convinced that I am the one who introduced quiche to America."
—James Beard

Quiche is an egg and custard dish usually baked in an open-faced crust. Quiche Lorraine—named for a northeastern region in France—typically also includes the addition of cheese and bacon. (That's right, I just said the magical "B" word; you may now commence drooling!)

My first encounter with quiche Lorraine was when I was fourteen. I had traveled several hours to visit cousins I hadn't spent much time with growing up. When I arrived at their *very* nice home in Connecticut, they had brunch waiting for me. It included bowls of fruit salad and beautifully prepared quiches, a dish I had never tried before. I knew it would be rude not to eat some, so I tried a small piece. I'm not sure what I was expecting, but it tasted like the best omelet I ever had set in a flaky, buttery tart shell. So I tried a less small piece. And, just to be sure it was as delicious as it seemed to be, I tried an enormous piece.

It was truly love at first bite.

DID YOU KNOW?

The word *quiche* actually originates from the German word for "cake," *kuchen*.

Today is also National Pick Strawberries Day.

NATIONAL STRAWBERRIES AND CREAM DAY

"Doubtless God could have made a better berry, but doubtless God never did."
—William Allen Butler

Strawberries are a magnificent-tasting fruit. They seem to have mastered the art of being sweet, but not too sweet; tart, but not too tart; juicy, but not too juicy. It's no wonder they're prominently featured throughout the year in several different national food holidays.

Strawberries and cream could be defined in any number of delicious ways. You could celebrate today with a cake, a piece of strawberry cheesecake, a fruit trifle, crêpes stuffed with both the berry and a cream cheese sauce, strawberries topped with balsamic vinegar and *crème fraîche*, or you could play it safe and just dredge whole strawberries through a giant bowl of whipped cream—there's nothing wrong with that!

And, hey, don't let the fact that it's still a little early to be enjoying locally grown strawberries in many places across the United States, or that Wimbledon is still a month or so away (strawberries and cream has been the signature dish of the event since the late 1800s), prevent you from enjoying today's sweet treat. Think of it as pre-gaming!

Today is also National Waiters and Waitresses Day.

HEAVENLY STRAWBERRIES AND CREAM SMOOTHIE

Makes 2 to 4 smoothies

2 cups fresh strawberries, chopped
1 cup granulated sugar
1 cup milk
12 ice cubes
1½ cups whipped topping, plus more for garnish

Put the strawberries, sugar, milk, ice cubes, and whipped topping in a blender and blend until creamy and dreamy. Garnish with more whipped topping if so desired!

MAY 22 — NATIONAL VANILLA PUDDING DAY

"One asks of a pudding, not if the cook who offers it is a good woman, but if the pudding itself is good." —Henry Louis Mencken

There are just as many vanilla lovers in the world as there are chocolate fanatics. If that weren't true, there wouldn't be so many food holidays dedicated to the luscious, aromatic, blissfully simple, and universally adored flavor!

Besides (and this is coming from a bona fide chocoholic), a really thick, flavorful vanilla pudding—the kind that sticks to your spoon and has visible specs of bean scattered throughout—can be an extraordinary and very sensual experience. It satiates the soul's craving for something sweet while satisfyingly cleansing the palate. It's not something you just down either; every bite allows you the opportunity to breathe in its deliriously hypnotizing scent, which can be both calming and flood you with a sense of contentment.

Bet you never thought vanilla pudding could create such a pleasurable experience!

DID YOU KNOW?

The vanilla plant is the only edible plant in the orchid family.

NATIONAL TAFFY DAY

"Candy is dandy, but liquor is quicker." —Ogden Nash, Hard Lines

Salt water taffy is believed to have originated after a particularly bad storm hit the Atlantic City boardwalk in the late 1800s. Waves damaged several of the vendor's stalls, including the stall of candy seller David Bradley. Shortly after, when a customer came in looking for taffy, Bradley jokingly offered her salt water taffy. She bought some. Loved it. And, despite the fact that there's no salt water in the ingredients, the name of the candy just stuck.

My grandmother *loved* salt water taffy. And she would always get a box of the brightly colored candy during the summer. I remember being so confused every time she let me try a piece because of how misleading the name was. I think I would have been a bigger fan of it if when I bit down, just once, my mouth was flooded with the flavors of caramel, strawberry, or vanilla . . . and actual salt water. Much to my dismay, this has never happened.

Until I find salt water–flavored salt water taffy, I think I'll stick to the other kind of taffy—the soft, caramel kind that's perfect for dunking apples in! Today—both count!

NATIONAL ESCARGOT DAY

"Escargot is French for 'fat crawling bag of phlegm.'" —Dave Barry

Escargot is a French term that refers to (edible) land snails. This gastropod is considered a delicacy in France and in other parts of the world, while Stateside we tend to view the dish with trepidation. After all, who wants to eat something so slimy and that carries its home on its back?

I grew up humming to the snails my sister and I found at the ocean. It never ceased to delight us that by doing so they would stick their little bodies out of their shells to investigate the vibrations. Even now, whenever I'm at the beach I like to find snails that seem particularly lonely to me—the ones that aren't stuck to any rocks or walls with a community of other snails—and hum to them until enough of their body is poking out that I can stick them near their friends!

Not sure you're ready to eat these little creatures? (I know I wasn't!) No worries! Vegetarian versions usually use mushrooms, because the consistency is relatively close to properly cooked escargot (which actually isn't slimy when prepared correctly!).

DID YOU KNOW?

Heliculture is the science and occupation of growing snails for food.

NATIONAL WINE DAY

"Compromises are for relationships, not wine." —Sir Robert Scott Caywood

I love wine, but sometimes I wonder what exactly goes into making it since the labels—which are filled with great information about the region the grapes come from, the best foods to pair it with, and sometimes whimsical statements about the company— seem to be pretty ingredient- and nutritional information-free. You may be startled to find out exactly what's in that glass of Pinot you're drinking!

Some of the ingredients used during the production process of wine (specifically to filter particles out so your wine has exceptional clarity and flavor) include: gelatin (animal bones); casein (milk proteins); isinglass (fish bladders); chitosan (exoskeleton of crustaceans), and albumin (egg whites).

Kinda gross, right? Don't panic! Not all wines include these ingredients. Some wineries actually let the sediment in their product settle out naturally; others use a clay mineral to clarify it; and some proudly advertise the fact that their wine is entirely unfiltered.

So how do you tell if wine (beer or hard liquor) is free of all the gunk mentioned above?

I suggest visiting *Barnivore.com*. With well over 16,000+ entries that have been checked (and frequently double- and triple-checked) by writing directly to companies for information direct from the source, they're the leading online alcohol directory for those of us who would rather avoid a little fish gut in our vino.

Today is also National Brown Bag-It Day.

NATIONAL BLUEBERRY CHEESECAKE DAY

"Have blueberries whenever you are low—destiny will change and you will be high."
—Adam Voichester

The combination of fruit and cheese in any form is a beautiful thing. I'm always impressed with just how harmoniously the creaminess from cheese and the sweet notes from fruit seem to effortlessly play so well off each other. And with so many varieties of both, there are options for truly every craving and mood.

When it comes to cheesecake, my preferred fruit is blueberries. Because American cheesecake typically tends to be made with cream cheese—which is very dense, heavy, and slightly tangy—it needs a fruit that's going to complement it. Something too sweet or too sour muddles the flavors and makes the entire experience overwhelming; whereas, a fruit that's much more subtle in flavor—like the blueberry—accentuates the cheesecake while still holding its own.

Plus, blueberries are full of antioxidants, so every bite of blueberry cheesecake you eat helps fight off those free radicals in your body. It's a win for your belly and a win for your immune system.

Today is also National Cherry Dessert Day.

MAY 27

NATIONAL GRAPE POPSICLE DAY

"I require a popsicle every fifteen minutes; you obviously did not read the memo."
—Meatwad, Aqua Teen Hunger Force

Show me your tongue! If it's not purple today, you're doing something wrong.

When I was little, I used to love snow cones. Whenever the ice cream truck (or boat, for those of us who lived on a lake in the summer) rolled up (motored up), I *always* got one. And it was a total love affair when I would first start eating it. But at some point, usually about halfway through, it always seemed to melt into one flavor/color: grape/purple. Every single time. How does strawberry (red), lime (green), and orange (um . . . orange) turn into grape (purple)? What kind of mad science is behind that?!

Popsicles of any kind are an ideal treat as the weather starts to heat up. However, if you feel like celebrating today a little more on the R-rated side, you could always make an adult grape popsicle drink: Pour some ginger ale, grape vodka, and grape juice or (my preference) grape-flavored sports drink into a chilled glass. Enjoy the same tasting treat as your kids sans the purple mouth!

- -

MAY 28

NATIONAL HAMBURGER DAY

"There are no ideas in the South, just barbecue." —Pat Conroy, The Prince of Tides

Let me tell you a little story called The McDonald's Incident of 1984.

In 1984, folks collected game pieces from their McDonald's items. The pieces listed an Olympic event, like Polo or 4x400 Relay. If the U.S. won gold in the event you had a piece for, you would win a Big Mac. If the U.S. won silver, you would win french fries; a bronze won you a Coke. Because of some political unrest, in the eleventh hour—far too late for McDonald's to pull the plug on their game—Russia and others boycotted the Olympics.

All of a sudden, the U.S. won more medals than ever before. (Side note: That year, the U.S. won eighty-three gold medals, sixty-one silver medals, and thirty bronze medals for a total of 174 medals.) My mom—who told me this story—explained that she would have some pieces worth a Big Mac, a french fry, *and* a Coke when the U.S. would sweep an event!

"The very first piece I got was for Greco-Roman Wrestling. And I almost threw it away because I assumed McDonald's had printed like eleventy billion of them, knowing that the U.S. could never win that event," she said. But then Steve Fraser came through and got her the first of many Big Macs. Carl Lewis (track and field) got her a Big Mac. Greg Louganis (diving) got her a Big Mac. Mary Lou Retton (gymnastics) got her a Big Mac, and Rowdy Gains (swimming) got her a Big Mac.

In the end, she won twenty-eight Big Macs—and wouldn't let my father eat a single one.

Now that's a tale for National Hamburger Day at the end of National Hamburger Month!

Today is also National Brisket Day.

MOLDY CURRY BURGERS

Makes 4 hamburgers

1 pound ground chicken, pork, or beef
1 small Vidalia onion, diced
3 garlic cloves, minced
1½ teaspoons curry powder
2 tablespoons Worcestershire sauce
4 rounded tablespoons Stilton cheese
2 tablespoons salted butter

Preheat the oven to 350°F.

Line a baking sheet with aluminum foil and set aside.

In a bowl, mix together the meat, onion, garlic, curry powder, and Worcestershire. The best way to do this is with your hands. Divide the mixture into eight equal portions and flatten each portion to create a patty. Press an indent with your thumb in the middle of four of the patties and fill each of the four indents with one rounded tablespoon of cheese. Take the four patties without indents, lay each one over one of the cheese-filled patties, and gently press the edges together, creating four cheese-filled burgers.

Melt the butter in a skillet on medium heat. Add the burgers and cook for 3 to 5 minutes on each side, until golden-brown. Gently transfer the burgers to the baking sheet. Place the baking sheet in the oven and bake for 12 minutes. Gently flip the burgers over and bake for another 12 to 13 minutes. Serve with whatever condiments you like best!

Tip! Wanna make these veg-friendly? Use a beef substitute like Lightlife's Gimme Lean Beef. Use just one twelve-ounce roll of it instead of the meat, and *don't* change anything else in the recipe.

MAY 29

NATIONAL COQ AU VIN DAY

"I thought coq au vin *was love in a lorry." —Victoria Wood*

While today's food sounds positively filthy, it's actually French for "rooster with wine." It's a classic French dish made from slow-braising chicken in a (usually red) wine sauce with bacon or salt pork, mushrooms, garlic, and herbs. Originally, it was considered food for peasants (and we know lobsters were once viewed this way, too!) because it was made from whatever folks had on hand. And they'd use the rooster as their protein once it was past its prime and no longer makin' whoopee with the lady chickens.

Kind of a rough life for the poor bird if you ask me—at least it was forever immortalized in the title of a dish!

Before it gets too hot outside and you no longer want to get anywhere near your oven, try making your own coq au vin. It might seem like an elaborate and time-consuming meal, but it's actually pretty straightforward and easy to pull together.

But the person you're spoiling with this dish doesn't have to know that!

Today is also National Biscuit Day.

NATIONAL MINT JULEP DAY

"They say that you may always know the grave of a Virginian as, from the quantity of julep he has drunk, mint invariably springs up where he has been buried."
—Frederick Marryat

The mint julep became the official drink of the Kentucky Derby in 1938. Every year, over 100,000 are sold at the event. It's made with Early Times Whiskey (which, if you want to get all technical, isn't even a bourbon, by the way—it's a Kentucky whiskey) and served in commemorative pewter glasses folks get to keep. However, for a few bucks more (like $1,000), you can purchase a gold-plated cup filled with an extremely high-end mint julep using Woodford Reserve that's a different Derby-related theme every year.

Unfortunately, mint juleps aren't exactly a popular drink where I'm from. So I headed out to a local Mexican restaurant and asked if they could just make me one. "What's in it?" the waitress asked. So I told her: bourbon, water, sugar, mint leaves, and ice. "Yeah, we can do that," she assured me heading to the bar to confirm this.

Now, if a mint julep is made just right, according to Kentucky legend, you can actually hear angels sing. Let me tell you: Angels weren't just singing, they were raucously yodeling in merriment. That's because the "mint julep" I was given was basically a pint glass filled with whiskey and garnished with a couple mint leaves.

Of course I had to drink the entire thing. All in the name of eating the year, of course!

NATIONAL MACAROON DAY

"Once in a young lifetime one should be allowed to have as much sweetness as one can possibly want and hold." —Judith Olney

Who knew the addition of a single vowel could entirely change the meaning of a word?

Today is *macaroon* day, not to be confused with *macaron* day (which is held on March 20). *Macaroons*—the focus of today—are flourless, dense, chewy cookie-esque confections usually made from shredded coconut, almond, and/or chocolate. (Ever had chocolate-dipped coconut and cherry macaroons before? Bliss!)

On the other hand, *macarons*, which are incredibly popular in France, consist of two colorful meringue cookies—made from egg whites, sugar, and almond flour—sandwiching a ganache, buttercream, and/or jam filling. Flavors can include chocolate, caramel, rose, pistachio, lavender, green tea, s'mores, and espresso, just to name a few of the incredibly creative options available in this light, airy pastry.

While there's a clear distinction between the two sweets—fortunately for us today—many people across the U.S. use the terms interchangeably. So no matter how you celebrate today, to someone somewhere you're probably doing it right!

JUNE IS...

JUNE IS ALSO...

National Beef Steak Month
National Candy Month
National Country Cooking Month
National Dairy Month
National Dairy Alternatives Month
National Frozen Yogurt Month
National Fruits and Vegetables Month
National Hunger Awareness Month
National Iced Tea Month
National Papaya Month
National Seafood Month
National Soul Food Month
National Steakhouse Month
National Turkey Lover's Month

. . .

1st Friday—National Doughnut Day
First day of summer—National Lambrusco Day
2nd or 3rd Saturday (TBD in late winter each year)—
    World Gin Day
3rd Saturday—Día Nacional de Chicharron (Day of Pork
    Rinds in Peru)
Last Saturday—National Vegan Pizza Day

JUNE 01

WORLD MILK DAY

"He who distributes the milk of human kindness cannot help but spill a little on himself." —James Matthew Barrie

World Milk Day was created in 2001 by the Food and Agriculture Organization of the United Nations to globally promote the nutritional importance of milk for our health, and the dairy industry's economical role worldwide. June 1st was originally chosen because it seemed many countries were already celebrating milk around this time. Participating nations have included Argentina, Thailand, Spain, South Africa, Canada, Australia, Ecuador, China, Germany, India, and the U.S., just to name a few!

Don't drink cow, sheep, goat, llama, reindeer, camel, or buffalo milk? Since today is focused on celebrating *all* aspects of "milk," don't count out dairy alternatives that can have equally as awesome health benefits as the animal-based stuff. With a much lower carbon footprint, not only is nondairy milk the more sustainable and compassionate option, but depending on the kind you choose (soy, almond, rice, oat, hemp, hazelnut, coconut, cashew, etc.), it can also be filled with protein, fiber, and vitamins while being low in both carbs and sugar.

All of this makes today a holiday everyone can raise a glass to!

Today is also National Hazelnut Cake Day.

JUNE 02 — NATIONAL ROCKY ROAD DAY

"Chocolate is not cheating! After a salty meal, you need a little bit of sweet. This is living, not cheating." —Ali Landry

It's widely believed that rocky road ice cream was created during the Great Depression by William Dreyer (sound familiar? It should!) after he chopped up nuts and marshmallows and mixed them into a bowl full of chocolate ice cream. He gave it the name he did because it coincided with the difficult economic times people were having, and he hoped it would uplift their spirits.

When people ask me what the most difficult food holiday to celebrate was, I think they expect me to say National Filet Mignon Day (August 13, page 258) or National Escargot Day (May 24, page 170). But no, for me it was today. And it was nearly the downfall of my entire project to eat the year. I assumed that either the candy or cupcake stores in town would have something rocky road–flavored, but they didn't. Shockingly enough, even the grocery and convenience stores in town seem to be devoid of rocky road ice cream. It wasn't until 11:50 p.m.—with only ten minutes left of National Rocky Road Day—that I finally found a pint of the stuff. Ice cream is never supposed to be that stressful!

Then again, I would have expected nothing less from a day that celebrates a food named in honor of trying times.

NATIONAL EGG DAY

"Love and eggs are best when they are fresh." —Russian proverb

Bird, reptile, fish, or Cadbury, today is all about the incredible, edible egg.

I think most people are probably going to celebrate today with the tried-and-true chicken egg. It's high in protein, low in calories, and *incredibly* versatile. After all, it can be fried, basted, poached, baked, steamed, soft-boiled, medium-boiled, microwaved, or—my childhood favorite—scrambled.

Growing up, every Sunday morning my parents would cook an enormous breakfast for the family. They would make platters of fried potatoes, bacon, Canadian bacon, sausage, toast slathered with butter *and* peanut butter, English muffins, fruit salad, the cheesiest scrambled eggs you've ever had in your life, and every condiment known to man. We would sit around the table with mugs of coffee or glasses of brightly colored juice, and just spend hours eating and talking. After everything had been cleaned, the smell of the delicious meal would linger in the house for the rest of the day. It was a weekly tradition for us.

Not a fan of scrambled eggs? Don't worry, today the sky's the limit (don't tell Chicken Little that, though). You can celebrate by making deviled eggs, an omelet, a quiche, fried rice, a frittata, egg salad, egg drop soup, eggnog, custard, eggs Benedict, huevos rancheros, a breakfast burrito, breakfast pizza, breakfast sushi, toad in a hole, pasta . . . the options are endless!

Today is also National Chocolate Macaroon Day.

MY FIRST SCRAMBLE

Makes 2 to 4 servings

1 (1-pound) block extra firm tofu, drained

½ (8-ounce) bag shredded vegan pepper jack cheese (about 1 cup)

1 teaspoon turmeric

¼ teaspoon garlic powder

½ teaspoon salt

1 teaspoon cumin

1 teaspoon lime zest

1 teaspoon lime juice

¼ teaspoon black pepper

¼ teaspoon crushed red pepper flakes

½ large sweet onion, diced (about 1 cup)

2 garlic cloves, minced

2 tablespoons olive oil

1 small green pepper, thinly chopped (about 1 cup)

1 (8-ounce) package sliced mushrooms (about 2 cups)

2 medium tomatoes, chopped

1 (4.25-ounce) can diced green chilies

Mash the tofu in a bowl with the cheese, turmeric, garlic powder, salt, cumin, lime zest, lime juice, black pepper, and pepper flakes until everything is crumbly and resembles scrambled eggs. Set the scramble aside.

Sauté the onions and garlic in the olive oil in a skillet on medium heat for 3 to 5 minutes, or until translucent and fragrant. Add the green peppers and cook for another 2 minutes. Stir in the mushrooms and cook for another 5 minutes. Add the scrambled tofu, turn the heat to high, and cook for 10 minutes, making sure to stir constantly so nothing sticks to the bottom of the pan. Add the tomatoes and green chilies. Cook for another 10 minutes, or until the tofu starts to brown and firm up slightly. Serve.

NATIONAL CHEESE DAY

JUNE 04

"When my brain begins to reel from my literary labors, I make an occasional cheese dip." —John Kennedy Toole

I don't think the universal language is love.

I'm pretty sure it's cheese.

Think about it!

Cheese can be a breakfast, lunch, or dinner item. It spans all courses as an appetizer, entrée, and/or dessert. It complements foods of all kinds including, but not limited to, fruit, vegetables, crackers, nuts, noodles, meat, seafood, and tofu. It pairs exceptionally well with wines, beers, and hard liquors of all sorts. There's a variety for every preference, whether for something soft and sweet (like ricotta), hard and tangy (Romano), or nut-based for vegans. And cheese—in one form or another—can be found in many different cuisines like American, Italian, Mexican, French, Spanish, Indian, Greek, Icelandic, Swedish, Swiss, Dutch, Argentinean, and British, just to name a handful.

So move over *love* (sex, money, power, rock 'n' roll, etc.) because I think the real language we all understand is cheese, glorious cheese!

Today is also National Cognac Day and National Frozen Yogurt Day.

NATIONAL KETCHUP DAY

You know, you really can't beat a household commodity—the ketchup bottle on the kitchen table." —Adlai E. Stevenson

It's National Ketchup Day!

We squeeze it all over our onion rings, chicken fingers, hot dogs, and even mashed potatoes—but where does ketchup come from? Can you believe it actually started as pickled, spiced fish entrails and soybean sauce called "ge-thcup" or "koe-cheup," which first appeared in southern China in 300 B.C.? It spread throughout trade routes in Asia, and eventually British traders brought it back to England, where they changed the recipe.

Don't know about you, but I'm kinda glad they did!

It's funny how particular people can be about certain brands; sometimes it's because they support what a company stands for; sometimes it's because they simply love the taste of the product. For example, growing up I was absolutely obsessed with Heinz. My love for them grew when one day I was at the grocery store and saw a label that didn't say "Heinz Tomato Ketchup," but instead, "Are your french fries lonely?"

I remember looking around to see if I was on camera or something. Why would one solitary bottle of Heinz say that? I told my family that ketchup was talking to me; they ignored my weirdness until one day ketchup was talking to them (and apparently everyone else in the States), too. Labels started appearing that said all kinds of things like: *Warning: Slow moving condiment*, or *Comforts burnt hot dogs*, or *Instructions: Put on food*, or *Quiet, please. Tomatoes meeting inside.*

Who knew ketchup could be so sassy?

Today is also National Gingerbread Day.

NATIONAL APPLESAUCE CAKE DAY

"It is remarkable how closely the history of the apple tree is connected with that of man." —Henry David Thoreau, Wild Apples

While it might seem to be a very random, very particular food holiday, I know lots of folks who would disagree. During the first half of the twentieth century—when sugar, eggs, and butter were more expensive and being rationed during times of war—applesauce was a great substitute in cakes. And, in the plant-based diet communities, using applesauce in lieu of eggs or butter in baking is commonplace because it's moist and acts as a binding agent!

Personally, I'm always a fan of cakes that can be legitimately eaten for either dessert *or* breakfast.

Applesauce cake definitely falls under the umbrella of acceptable breakfast foods! After all, not only does it have fruit, but it's also usually much lower in fat and calories than other cakes, making it a healthy option to start your day (okay, maybe *that's* a stretch).

DID YOU KNOW?

Pomology is the science of apple growing.

JUNE 07
NATIONAL CHOCOLATE ICE CREAM DAY

"I want everyone to throw sugar and cream at each other, then lie about it. I want to attend an ice cream antisocial." —Benson Bruno

While it's baffling to me that chocolate is not the number-one most popular ice cream flavor in the world (vanilla holds that title), I know it's the champion of other more important life categories, like Number-One Ice Cream to Eat After Getting Dumped.

After my Great Heartbreak (everybody has one), I spent a tremendous amount of time trying to heal. In the end only three things helped:

1. Going for long runs late at night through snow.
2. Listening and crying to the same sad song (especially during said epic runs) over and over again on repeat for at least a month ("Woods" by Bon Iver, in case you were curious).
3. Eating my weight in soy-based chocolate ice cream.

And somehow, they always made me feel much better afterward.

This could be because (A) exercising vigorously releases endorphins, (B) crying releases endorphins, and (C) eating chocolate increases—can you guess? That's right!—endorphins. And endorphins are the hormones that create a feeling of euphoria, (i.e., they make us feel better).

So if you're suffering from your Great Heartbreak this National Chocolate Ice Cream Day, my advice is simply this: Work out, have yourself a good cry, and eat some chocolate ice cream. It will do wonders for your body, mind, and soul.

DID YOU KNOW?

Upon arriving in the United States, immigrants at Ellis Island were served ice cream with their first meal.

JUNE
08

WORLD OCEANS DAY

"You must not lose faith in humanity. Humanity is like an ocean; if a few drops of the ocean are dirty, the ocean does not become dirty." —Mahatma Gandhi

The United Nations General Assembly passed a resolution in 2009 that recognized June 8th as World Oceans Day. The purpose of this is to raise global awareness about the importance our oceans (which cover 71 percent of the Earth's surface, and contain 97 percent of the planet's water) play not only on our climates but also in our individual economies, while also advocating change for pollution and overfishing/overconsumption of sea life.

There are lots of things you can do to help, like participate in a beach clean-up effort or donate money to ocean-based causes. Gastronomically speaking, there's no better time than now to promote or educate your community on sustainably harvested seafood options. Or you can always choose to forgo eating seafood altogether in lieu of plant-based substitutes that there are plenty of in this day and age!

For more ideas on what you can do to make a difference, please check out *WorldOceansDay.org*.

Today is also National Jelly-Filled Doughnut Day.

NATIONAL STRAWBERRY RHUBARB PIE DAY

"Nothing would be more tiresome than eating and drinking if God had not made them a pleasure as well as a necessity." —Voltaire

Sugar or salt?

How do you take your rhubarb?

My grandparents used to have a huge rhubarb plant. After our *pépère* would help us cut off beautiful, thick red stalks of it, my *mémé* would give my sister and me a plastic bag filled with salt and a plastic bag filled with sugar to dip our rhubarb in since we could never remember which we liked more. The bag of salt was always abandoned quickly once we remembered that sugar plus, well, anything is always the better option!

The very first pie I remember eating was my mom's homemade strawberry rhubarb. We would wake up very early and go strawberry picking. The first rays of the summer sunlight warmed the berries, which sat heavy and ripe on the plants just waiting to be picked. Or eaten then and there. Swatting away the lazy bees, we would pick a tremendous amount in a very short time. After a quick stop at pépère's to grab a few stalks of the "pie plant," we'd head home so she could make a pie filled with what would become, post-baking, that distinct, unique, delicious pink strawberry rhubarb goo.

Truly, it's the start of another glorious summer season!

DID YOU KNOW?

A strawberry contains (on average) about 200 seeds on its exterior.

JUNE 10 — NATIONAL ICED TEA DAY

"Ecstasy is a glassful of tea and a piece of sugar in the mouth." —Alexander Pushkin

If National Iced Tea Day hadn't fallen during the warmer months of the year, I would have been seriously disappointed in my fellow man. Nobody I know wants to sip *iced* tea when it's thirty below outside, just like nobody wants to sip *hot* tea when it's 103 degrees outside.

Nowadays there are lots of different ways to drink iced tea: sweetened or unsweetened, with a slice of lemon, a sprig of mint, some freshly grated ginger, a dash of vodka, mixed with lemonade, or even stirred with fruit, like peaches and raspberries.

Really, iced tea—like many foods and drinks we consume—is an entirely personal experience. For example, I used to freeze mine . . . and then drink it slowly throughout the day as it melted.

However you like yours, I think we can all agree that the very best way to drink it is always sitting outside enjoying the sun (and if you can do it with friends or family, then even better)!

Today is also National Black Cow Day and National Herbs and Spices Day.

GREEN SUN TEA

Makes about 4 glasses

- 4 green tea teabags
- 4 sprigs fresh rosemary
- 4 sprigs fresh lemon balm
- 4 sprigs fresh mint
- 32 ounces water
- ¼ cup honey or agave syrup

Place the teabags, rosemary, lemon balm, and mint in a large pitcher. Cover everything with water and stir gently for 1 minute. Set the pitcher in direct sunlight for 3 to 4 hours, or until the water has changed color and looks like tea. When the sun tea is ready, stir in the honey. Strain the sun tea over glasses of ice and enjoy. Remember to discard any leftover tea.

Tip! Bacteria can grow in sun tea, so it's best to only make what you're going to drink that day. Use filtered water, if possible, and also be sure to use a really sanitized glass pitcher or very large, well-cleaned jar.

NATIONAL CORN ON THE COB DAY

I have no hostility to nature, but a child's love to it. I expand and live in the warm day like corn and melons." —Ralph Waldo Emerson

There's a whole lotta corn in our country. But most of it becomes ethanol, fodder for animals, or is turned into high fructose corn syrup. Not enough of the beautiful, fresh ears actually make their way onto our plates. Which is a real shame, considering corn is low in calories and cholesterol and contains fiber.

And it's delicious.

Growing up, I looked forward to those few weeks each summer when my parents would bring home bags and bags of locally grown corn on the cob. It was always my duty to shuck the ears. They'd set me up outside with a trash bag for the husk and silk and a clean bowl for the corn itself. With my little fingers, I would slowly and meticulously peel back each layer of green until only the clean, sweet, yellow flesh was left. Within hours, we'd be happily feasting on mountains and mountains of corn that my mom had boiled in water with a little sugar.

Really, not much has changed over the years except maybe how I prepare it (though I've become a big fan of grilling my corn!). In a couple weeks the corn on the cob will be ready locally. I'll buy a big bag of it, come home, and sit outside in the sunshine to carefully and diligently remove each husk. Nothing screams summer to me more!

Today is also National German Chocolate Cake Day and National Cotton Candy Day.

CANARIAN POTATO SALAD

Makes 4 dinner servings or 8 side servings

Note: This recipe tastes best after being chilled 2 hours or overnight.

4 large russet potatoes, peeled and quartered

1 (15-ounce) jar Manzanilla olives, drained and halved

1 (15-ounce) can sweet kernel corn, drained and rinsed

1 (5-ounce) can tuna in oil, partially drained and shredded

¼ cup olive oil

½ teaspoon salt

In a large pot of water, boil the potatoes until they are cooked but not mushy. (Tip: Insert a fork into the potatoes periodically. When the fork yields a bit but goes through the potatoes, the potatoes are ready!) When the potatoes are cooked, drain them, place them in a large bowl, and put the bowl in the refrigerator to cool for 30 to 45 minutes.

When the potatoes have cooled, cut them into bite-size chunks and return them to the bowl. Add the olives, corn, tuna, olive oil, and salt. Mix until everything is combined. Cover the bowl and refrigerate for 2 hours; however, this dish tastes bests if it's chilled overnight.

Tip! Wanna make this veg-friendly? Ditch the tuna and increase the olive oil by another 2 to 4 tablespoons.

JUNE 12 — NATIONAL PEANUT BUTTER COOKIE DAY

"Dear Lord: The gods have been good to me. For the first time in my life, everything is absolutely perfect just the way it is. So here's the deal: You freeze everything the way it is, and I won't ask for anything more. If that is OK, please give me absolutely no sign. OK, deal. In gratitude, I present you this offering of cookies and milk. If you want me to eat them for you, give me no sign. Thy will be done." —Homer, The Simpsons

It seems that the peanut butter cookies I grew up with were always either (A) made with a Hershey Kiss pressed in the center, or (B) "decorated" with fork tine marks.

This first one, I think we can all agree, makes total sense. Chocolate and peanut butter is one of the best flavor combinations in the culinary kingdom. The first person to come up with the idea of pushing a piece of chocolate candy into a mound of peanut butter dough is a total genius!

The second one is actually done for any number of reasons; as a matter of fact, if you've ever speculated as to why, whatever answer you came up with was probably correct. It could just be tradition—people have been doing it since the first half of the twentieth century.

Another reason could be for a more even bake; after all, peanut butter cookie dough tends to be stiffer than other cookie doughs.

Or maybe over time, since those crosshatch marks are specifically associated with peanut butter cookies, they've become a great way for people with nut allergies (or severe *ihatepeanutbutteritis* like my sister has) to tell the cookies apart.

Fork tine marks or no, chocolate or no, peanut butter cookies still rock!

Today is also International Cachaça Day and National Jerky Day.

PEANUT BUTTER "TO THE THIRD POWER" COOKIES

Makes 1 dozen cookies

Cookies:

1 cup unsalted chunky peanut butter
1 cup granulated sugar
1 large egg
½ teaspoon salt
2 teaspoons vanilla extract
1 cup Reese's Pieces candies

Icing:

4 ounces peanut butter chips (about 1 cup)
1 tablespoon unsalted butter
1 tablespoon milk

Preheat the oven to 350°F.

In a bowl, cream together the peanut butter and sugar. Set it aside.

In another bowl, beat together the egg, salt, and vanilla. Add the peanut butter-sugar mixture and stir until everything is well combined. Mix in the Reese's Pieces.

Using your hands, roll the dough into twelve small equal-size balls. Arrange the balls into three rows of four on a baking sheet. Gently flatten each cookie and use a fork to make crosshatch marks on the top of each one. Bake the cookies for 14 to 18 minutes, or until golden-brown. Remove the cookies from the oven.

As the cookies begin to cool, melt the peanut butter chips, butter, and milk together in a pan or in the microwave. Drizzle the icing over the cookies. Let the cookies cool and the icing harden before eating.

JUNE 13 — NATIONAL KITCHEN KLUTZES OF AMERICA DAY

"Who's gonna take you in? You're messy. You're a klutz, you spill everything. And you leave the volume on the TV way too loud." —Jim Halpert, The Office

Everybody knows somebody who just wasn't meant to be in the kitchen. Maybe this person loves cooking and his heart's in the right place, but he's just a complete disaster when he tries to get his cook on. Today is the day to celebrate those clumsier friends and family members, who perhaps are most helpful when they're either washing dishes or shouting recipe directions at us from another room.

One of my best friends means well, but every time he picks up a knife it soon looks like a slasher flick is being filmed in my kitchen. He's baked things but has forgotten to turn the oven on in the process. He once decided to open the espresso machine while it was still running—there were coffee grounds on every single wall of my kitchen that afternoon. And he hasn't quite figured out that if you don't turn the handle of the pot you're using inward, there's a *really* good chance you're going to knock it over (and before you know it your pet bunny will be stomping through puddles of fallen food, not that I know this from firsthand experience or anything).

But my friend loves eating, and he tries really hard. So today I honor him and all the other Kitchen Klutzes of America.

And hopefully they can return the favor by staying far, far away from our cutting boards and ovens!

BLUFETANUT SALAD

- 3 cups packed arugula
- 1 cup candied walnuts, chopped
- ¾ cup blueberries
- ½ cup crumbled feta cheese
- 1 tablespoon olive oil
- 1 tablespoon balsamic vinegar
- 1 teaspoon lemon juice

In a large serving bowl, place the arugula, walnuts, blueberries, and feta.

In a small bowl, whisk together the olive oil, balsamic vinegar, and lemon juice until combined. Drizzle the dressing over the salad and then mix so that everything is evenly coated. Serve as is or divide evenly onto two plates or as four side salads.

Tip! This makes two huge servings of salad and then some. You'll notice that—even after the amounts listed above—you'll still have leftover arugula, walnuts, blueberries, and feta, which means that lunch for the next couple of days is taken care of as well.

JUNE 14

NATIONAL STRAWBERRY SHORTCAKE DAY

"This special feeling towards fruit, its glory and abundance, is I would say universal. . . . We respond to strawberry fields or cherry orchards with a delight that a cabbage patch or even an elegant vegetable garden cannot provoke." —Jane Grigson

When it comes to your strawberry shortcake, do you prefer a hearty biscuit, corn bread, a scone, a slice of angel's food cake, a wedge of pound cake, or those yellow, circular sponge cakes that seem to soak up every drop of liquid? There is no wrong answer, of course, but I find that people are *very* particular about the baked vessel they use—if they use one at all—to support their strawberries and whipped cream.

(I'm Team Biscuit all the way!)

From the strawberries I pick each July, after making pies and setting aside some fresh berries for cereal, I always make two batches of strawberry shortcake "goo" (which is obviously a super technical term for mashed strawberries with sugar). I usually eat one batch right away and freeze the other batch so that sometime during winter I can have a taste of, well, summer!

DID YOU KNOW?

Native Americans called strawberries heart-seed berries.

Today is also National Bourbon Day.

NATIONAL LOBSTER DAY

"All of us are born with a set of instinctive fears—of falling, of the dark, of lobsters, of falling on lobsters in the dark, or speaking before a Rotary Club, and of the words 'Some Assembly Required.'" —Dave Barry

There are loads of rumors about Maine lobsters. Like, there are so many of the crustacean they freely roam our streets (not real). Or that folks who call Vacationland home eat the bottom dwelling sea bug for every meal (not real). Or every now and then activists have been known to purchase all the lobsters from a grocery store or restaurant to then release the critters back into the sea (I can neither confirm nor deny this). Or that you can actually drive through our McDonald's in the summer to get a lobster roll (real).

As a Mainer, let me give you some insider information about that ol' lobber you're eating:

1. It isn't naturally red in color—that's what happens after it's been cooked.
2. Don't use a bib here—we'll know you're a tourist.
3. If someone from the state invites you over to their house for lobster, be aware that you're actually going over for an epic feed that usually includes not only multiple lobsters per person, but pounds and pounds of clams (steamers), corn on the cob, roasted red bliss potatoes or potato salad, sometimes coleslaw and/or baked beans, perhaps watermelon, vats of melted butter, whoopie pies and blueberry pie for dessert, and of course, some ice cold beer!

Maine—worth a visit, worth a lifetime. (Though your cholesterol may not agree!)

DID YOU KNOW?

A lobster is called a *pistol* if it has no claws; a *cull* if it has only one.

NATIONAL FUDGE DAY

"Any reviewer who expresses rage and loathing for a novel is preposterous. He or she is like a person who has put on full armor and attacked a hot fudge sundae."
—Kurt Vonnegut

One of my favorite parts about summer is the abundance of things to do outside, especially all the annual fairs and festivals that seem to stretch right through to autumn. Beyond the staple and traditional midway attractions at most fairs, there is the plethora of community-related booths and exhibition halls showcasing some of the finest handcrafted goods in the area. And among the local vendors—in my experience—there are usually some serious fudge makers selling flavors as basic as chocolate, maple, and pumpkin to more unique options like peanut butter goat's milk, mudslide, and strawberry cheesecake. For me, it's a treat each year to get a piece, and because of its density, one small block seems to last me days—which is usually when it's time to attend another fair!

The history of fudge here in the States is hazy. Food folklore suggests it could have resulted from a "fudged up" batch of caramels, which thus resulted in the sweet's name (better the PG version of the word than the mother of all swears, right?). It's also thought that the first fudge recipe may have been popularized by a female student at Vassar College, who acquired it from a schoolmate's cousin in Baltimore sometime in the late nineteenth century.

What flavor will you celebrate today with?

NATIONAL EAT YOUR VEGGIES DAY

"We are indeed much more than what we eat, but what we eat can nevertheless help us to be much more than what we are." —Adelle Davis

Have you noticed? June is a month that's positively filled with dessert. We've already had multiple cake- and chocolate-themed days thus far, and of the thirteen remaining days this month, *most* of them are sweet, not savory. I don't know about you, but as the weather gets hotter (and I grow more realistic about this year's failed attempt at having the perfect beach bod because I chose to eat the year instead), I grow less and less interested in heavy, sugary things.

What I do crave is colorful, locally grown produce. I couldn't be more thrilled that today is National Eat Your Veggies Day; it not only breaks up all these dessert days from each other, but it also falls smack-dab in the middle of National Fresh Fruit and Vegetables Month!

Everybody knows that a diet rich in fruits and vegetables is healthier for you than *any* other option. Period. So today, let's focus on *where* you get your F&V. While it's easy to just pick up produce at the grocery store, try hitting up a farmers' market or a local produce stand today instead. And, if you want to do one better, many farms are open to public tours now and even offer farm shares, in which you pay a certain amount of money to a farm for a share of their crops that season. It's an excellent way to put your money back into your local economy.

Besides, I don't know about you, but I like knowing both where my food is literally coming from and who's growing it, too!

Today is also National Apple Strudel Day.

(HOW TO HAVE THE BODY OF A) GOURDESS "PASTA"

Makes 4 servings

1 small to medium-size spaghetti squash
1 cup cherry tomatoes, halved
½ (8.5-ounce) jar of sun-dried tomatoes in oil, diced
½ cup Kalamata olives, chopped
1 cup crumbled feta cheese
1 teaspoon dried basil
2 cups garlic-flavored croutons

Preheat the oven to 350°F.

Grease a baking sheet and set aside.

Cut the spaghetti squash in half, scoop out the seeds and pulp, and place cut-side down on the baking sheet. Bake the squash for 35 to 40 minutes, or until a knife easily pierces the skin.

While the squash is baking, put the tomatoes, sun-dried tomatoes, and olives in a large bowl.

When the squash is finished baking (and being mindful of how hot the squash will be), take a fork and gently scrape out the insides. It should shred apart and look like—you guessed it—spaghetti. Place the shredded squash into the bowl of tomatoes and olives. Gently mix in the cheese and basil. Toss everything together until evenly combined and coated.

Top each portion with ¼ cup of the croutons and serve with a glass of white wine.

JUNE 18 — INTERNATIONAL SUSHI DAY

"I'm not making art, I'm making sushi." —Masaharu Morimoto

The first time I ever had sushi, I was staying in a chalet with a bunch of models for Jack Daniel's during the adult spring break week in Killington, Vermont. One lunch we ordered sushi, each girl expertly asking for what they wanted in a language that sounded foreign to me. Fake it till you make it, right?

When it was my turn, I nonchalantly ordered the four things that seemed to be most popular among the other girls: a California roll (crab, avocado, and cucumber), a Philadelphia roll (smoked salmon, cream cheese, and cucumber), edamame, and miso soup. The food arrived, the girls descended. Fortunately for me, when hungry models stuff their faces, they're too busy to notice what's going on around them. This gave me the perfect opportunity to figure out (A) what the heck I was eating, and (B) how the heck to eat it all.

I have since become a serious sushi lover. That being said, I'm still by no means a pro; every time I've ever eaten it, I've dropped a roll right as it was entering my mouth. And it always lands in a bowl of soy sauce that splatters me from head to toe. But I *like* sushi! So who cares if I don't look cool when eating it? So if you've *always* wanted to try sushi but feel nervous because you don't know what you're doing, today's the day to get over it. Everybody's gotta start somewhere. And it's totally okay if you don't eat raw fish or even cooked fish. There are loads of vegetarian versions now. So grab some premade stuff from the grocery store or get a group of sushi newbies together and go out for a night of fun!

DID YOU KNOW?

The word *sushi* actually refers to any dish that's made with vinegar rice, not just fish.

Today is also International Picnic Day and National Cherry Tart Day.

NATIONAL MARTINI DAY

"One martini is alright, two is too many, three is not enough." —James Thurber

My girly drinks of choice used to be just about anything in the sour family, specifically of the amaretto, whiskey, or Midori variety. But those drinks, while visually stunning (after all, a Midori sour is the same color as green ectoplasm), didn't come in fancy, sexy cocktail glasses like martinis do.

And nothing screams "class" or "sexy dangerous double agent" more.

Traditionally made with gin and vermouth and garnished with either olives or a lemon, the original martini is one of the most popular adult beverages in the world. Like many alcoholic concoctions, where it comes from is a bit of a mystery. History shows that gin's popularity rose during Prohibition because it was easy to manufacture illegally (and you thought bathtub alcohol was that of food folklore!). And once Prohibition was over, there was plenty of the pine-flavored stuff to go around, thus solidifying it as a staple drink in our country, regardless of where the martini originated.

Today, celebrate with a traditional martini, one made from vodka, or feel free to stray off the beaten path and try a flavored version, like a watermelon or an espresso martini. Even though they're not technically considered a *real* martini, they're still *really* delicious!

DID YOU KNOW?

James Bond's martini (a Vesper) is three measures of Gordon's (gin), one of vodka, half a measure of Kina Lillet (a French aperitif wine), shaken well until ice cold, and then finished with a large, thin slice of lemon peel.

NATIONAL VANILLA MILKSHAKE DAY

"Accept what people offer. Drink their milkshakes. Take their love." —Wally Lamb,
She's Come Undone

Vanilla milkshakes just scream all things nostalgia, don't they? They conjure the image of a simpler time, like when courting involved one milkshake and two straws. Or of friends all meeting up at Arnold's drive-in from *Happy Days* or at The Max from *Saved by the Bell* to talk about age-old problems of high school and relationships.

They're a drink that has not only become part of the Americana legacy, but also embodies a certain frame of mind; even in this day and age there are diners all over the world that try to recreate that milkshake shoppe feel.

Today was certainly a trip down memory lane for me. While I was making my milkshake, I couldn't help but think about my Barbies. When I was really young, I had a pretty impressive collection of them. (This was before Legos took over my life.) And one year, Santa got me the Barbie Soda Shoppe, which not only had a jukebox, condiments, cutlery, scoops of ice cream, and the individual components to build hamburgers, but also had a *working* soda fountain, and the stools Barbie and friends sat on doubled as drinking glasses! I put all manner of weird things in the fountain to see what would come out of the spigot—including milkshakes.

Which are better going into the belly than they are coming out of miniature plastic tubes!

Today is also National Ice Cream Soda Day.

JUNE 21
NATIONAL PEACHES AND CREAM DAY

"One does a whole painting for one peach and people think just the opposite—that particular peach is but a detail." —Pablo Picasso

Not to be outdone by its cousin strawberries and cream, which we celebrated exactly a month ago (page 167), today is National Peaches and Cream Day! And it couldn't fall during a more perfect time of year, as today is usually when the summer solstice happens. For many people nothing truly invokes the spirit of summer like that of a ripe peach. Its sweet, juicy flesh is refreshing in the hot, humid weather; its golden color symbolic of long, sunny days.

There are lots of ways to celebrate today and ring in the season of pool parties, BBQs, and tans—how will you? A peaches and cream–flavored martini or daiquiri with some friends sounds nice. You could indulge with a giant bowl of ice cream (although, do note: July 17 is actually National Peach Ice Cream Day, page 230), or with peach slices topped with Greek yogurt and granola. There are peaches and cream–flavored lollipops, fudge, popsicles, pies, shortcakes, crêpes, and tarts, too!

Why not just throw a peaches and cream party and try grilling the fruit glazed in a little honey? Top it with some fresh whipped cream, and you've got the makings of a perfect summer get-together.

DID YOU KNOW?

Peaches were once known as Persian apples.

NATIONAL ONION RING DAY

"Onion rings in the car cushions do not improve with time." —Erma Bombeck

Onion rings are the superior side dish to burgers, chicken fingers, and just about every other bar food you can think of. There, I said it. Now I know there are french fry enthusiasts who are shaking their heads in disagreement right now, but let's agree to disagree today. (After all it *is* National Onion Ring Day; french fries will have their moment in the spotlight on July 13.)

When you think about it, if you decided to eat your way across this great country of ours, you might not ever run into the same type of onion ring twice since it seems everybody does a little something different to their batter. Sometimes it's so thin it's like the little fried onions you get in the can; sometimes the batter is so thick it's like

fried dough surrounding the onion. They can be crunchy like a potato chip or melt-in-your-mouth like a chocolate truffle.

For me, nothing tops the onion rings that achieve both of those textures in one bite. Especially the ones made from local mom-and-pop shops on the coast—the way they just dump their onion rings in a big brown paper bag, pour some salt into it, and shake the whole thing up. Drowned in ketchup, grease seeping through the bag, and the salt air mixing with the salt on the onion rings.

It's a profound experience.

Today is also National Chocolate Éclair Day.

204 / EAT THE YEAR

JUNE 23 — NATIONAL PECAN SANDY DAY

"Having in my life been bitten by the jaws of both victory and defeat, I must rush to add that success is to failure as butter pecan ice cream is to death." —Rupert Holmes

If you like that sweet-and-salty flavor combo, that melt-in-your-mouth and crunchy textural combo, then today's food holiday is for you! The pecan sandy is a perfectly balanced cookie that can be an excellent alternative for people who don't like—or can't process—chocolate.

Pecan sandies—similar to the *sablé*, which is a French version of shortbread and means "sand"—are crumbly cookies (sometimes they're a little more soft like a sugar cookie than a shortbread; both kinds are totally acceptable today!) that are made with the addition of buttery-flavored pecans.

It's funny, isn't it? If someone we love really likes a particular food, we end up also feeling a strong attachment to it—even if we don't personally like it. Despite not being my favorite thing, I still feel quite warmly toward pecan sandies. They were my mom's favorite cookie at one point (she suggests eating them frozen), and for the rest of my life now they'll *always* make me think of her. And so I appreciate today's food holiday simply because of that.

DID YOU KNOW?

The pecan tree is the official state tree of Texas.

NATIONAL PRALINES DAY

"There is only one difference between a long life and a good dinner: that, in the dinner, the sweets come last." —Robert Louis Stevenson

Pralines, depending on where you're located, can represent a variety of different things. Belgian-style pralines are chocolates filled with soft fillings. (As bizarre as this sounds, the butcher near my house as a kid had some of the best—I remember them being shaped like sea shells!) French-style pralines are caramelized sugar-coated nuts that are ground up and used as an ingredient in other sweets; and American-style pralines are a confectionary similar to fudge or brittle made from sugar syrup, sometimes cream and nuts. They're the kind I decided to *try* and make today.

I'm not going to sugarcoat it: My celebration of National Pralines Day was nothing short of dramatic. While the candy and nut mixture was coming to a boil on my stovetop, an entire bag of coffee fell out of my freezer and grounds spilled absolutely everywhere. Despite my best efforts to multitask—cooking, wiping down grounds from every inch of my refrigerator, trying to prevent the pet rabbit from both eating and rolling around in the grounds like a dog—the pralines ended up burning.

But you know what? I wouldn't change a thing about that moment! Because that's the *fun* thing about celebrating these food holidays—even if they don't go according to plan, you'll always remember *how* you celebrated the day. (The grounds frozen to the inside of my freezer help remind me, too!)

JUNE

25

NATIONAL CATFISH DAY

"Fresh-caught fried fish without hush-puppies are as man without woman, a beautiful woman without kindness, law without policemen." —Marjorie Kinnan Rawlings, Cross Creek Cookery

While we call all of these fun food and drink celebrations "national" holidays, most of them don't actually have any official governmental backing. But today does! In 1987, President Ronald Reagan authorized an official proclamation observing June 25th as National Catfish Day in recognition of the "value of farm-raised catfish" in America.

Part of President Reagan's proclamation acknowledged that the catfish industry in the U.S. was a thriving one and was imperative to our economy. He also recognized that catfish was a nutritious and delicious, inexpensive protein.

Fried, blackened, Cajun baked, in an amandine sauce, a hash, tacos, or a po'boy—know it's your civic duty to "observe this day with appropriate ceremonies and activities." So—get to eatin'!

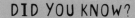

DID YOU KNOW?

The catfish has up to 100,000 taste buds.

Today is also National Strawberry Parfait Day.

NATIONAL CHOCOLATE PUDDING DAY

"If you're an ant, and you're walking along across the top of a cup of pudding, you probably have no idea that the only thing between you and disaster is the strength of that pudding skin." —*Jack Handy,* Deep Thoughts

Every food lover has a list of dishes that make them go weak in the knees time and time again, for whatever reason. For some, it might be beef Wellington—a dish perhaps they could make themselves, but choose not to when someone else has, in their eyes, already perfected it. For others, it might be *gofres y crema*—a sugary dessert waffle topped with a thick creamy icing that they associate with a particularly blissful holiday in Spain. And then there are those of us who are mesmerized by simpler foods crafted for us out of love; for me,

that's my mom's chocolate pudding. And regardless of how full I am, I always have room for some!

It doesn't matter how old I get or how many other versions I try, only hers will do. It's cold, creamy, and forms a thick, chewy "skin" on top that makes my mouth water at the very thought of it. In a pie shell, in a bowl, topped with whipped cream or not—it's absolutely one of my favorite things in the world to eat and the only way I'd want to celebrate today's food holiday.

NATIONAL ORANGE BLOSSOM DAY

"A man ought to carry himself in the world as an orange tree would if it could walk up and down in the garden, swinging perfume from every little censer it holds up to the air." —Henry Ward Beecher

Perhaps the idea of eating flowers doesn't appeal to you, especially ones that are as fragrant as the orange blossom. This white flower—with five long, separated petals in the shape of a star—is used in perfumes, soaps, and incense because of its sweet, citrusy smell. It can also be found in tea, honey, baked goods, and in chocolate sauces.

Still not doing it for you?

What if I told you that the Orange Blossom is also the name of a classic cocktail probably stemming from the Prohibition era? Sounds a little more tolerable, doesn't it? The basis of the drink is orange juice and gin; some versions also call for the addition of a sugar or sweet vermouth, grenadine, or Cointreau. Garnish with either a slice of orange or an orange peel, and you've got yourself a sweet and citrusy, flower-free Orange Blossom!

DID YOU KNOW?

The orange blossom became the state flower of Florida in 1909.

Today is also National Indian Pudding Day.

NATIONAL CEVICHE DAY

"And it is discipline in the equality of men, for all men are equal before fish."
—Herbert Hoover

What is America but a melting pot of other cultures? Our diversity is something we've always been proud of. And our different traditions are reflected in our music, our art, and our food. Today isn't necessarily a food holiday that originated in the U.S., but it's one we've begun to adopt.

Today is *Día Nacional del Cebiche* —or National Ceviche Day—in Peru (and now elsewhere in the world, too). Ceviche is raw fish that's marinated in citrus juices and spices. After a few hours, the acid from the citrus kind of "cooks" the fish (scientifically speaking it's a chemical process called *denaturation*—it alters the texture of the fish without losing that raw taste). It's a staple dish in Peru, so much so that it was declared part of their cultural heritage in 2004. Four years later the Ministry of Production in Peru took it one step further and declared June 28 as National Ceviche Day.

So join in with the rest of the world today and celebrate a beautifully crafted dish!

Today is also National Tapioca Day.

NATIONAL ALMOND BUTTERCRUNCH DAY

"God gives almonds to those who have no teeth." —Spanish proverb

Today almost got the best of me. For some strange reason, I was convinced that I didn't know what this mysterious "almond buttercrunch" food was. At one point, I was pretty set on just buying a Butterfinger candy bar and some almonds, chopping them both up, throwing them onto some ice cream, and calling it a day.

And wouldn't you know, if I had, I wouldn't have been too far off the mark!

Almond buttercrunch was made famous by confectionary geniuses Harry L. Brown and J.C. Haley (of Brown & Haley), who developed a log-shaped toffee, chocolate, and almond candy in 1923. They called it Almond Roca, *roca* being Spanish for "rock" (given the candy's hard texture

this seemed fitting). A few years later in 1927, they began packaging it in tin containers that helped extend the product's shelf life. This made it easier to ship to troops stationed all over the globe during World War II. To this day, the candy is still being made in the same factory where it all began 'lo those many decades ago.

Makes sense to me why it has its own food holiday!

DID YOU KNOW?

Almonds are part of the Prunus family, which includes peaches, apricots, nectarines, plums, and cherries.

JUNE 30

NATIONAL ICE CREAM SODA DAY

"Not to like ice cream is to show oneself uninterested in food." —Joseph Epstein

Of the many food legends about the creation of the ice cream soda, one of the most common is that it was invented in Philadelphia, Pennsylvania, in the late nineteenth century by a man named Robert McCay Green when he ran out of cream—or was it ice? History has a way of making things as fuzzy as today's sweet drink is! For his flavored sodas, he decided to improvise by substituting it with some vanilla ice cream. Whether that's true or not, Green still instructed that his tombstone be engraved with "Originator of the Ice Cream Soda" (which it was!).

Who knew ice cream was such serious business?

By the way, the date of today's food holiday is hotly contested. Some people claim National Ice Cream Soda Day is June 20th, and others claim June 30th. You know what I think? There's nothing wrong with celebrating it on *both* days!

DID YOU KNOW?

"Brain freeze" is a type of headache someone gets after eating or drinking something cold that touches the roof of their mouth. The body's nerves tell their brain that they need to warm up, and so it responds by rapid constriction and swelling of blood vessels.

Today is also National Mai Tai Day.

JULY IS...

JULY IS ALSO...

National Baked Bean Month
National Berry Month
National Bison Month
National Blueberry Month
National Culinary Arts Month
National Grilling Month
National Horseradish Month
National Hot Dog Month
National Ice Cream Month
National Lasagna Awareness Month
National Picnic Month
National Pickle Month
National Watermelon Month

. . .

3rd Sunday—National Ice Cream Day
Last Thursday—National Chili Dog Day

NATIONAL GINGERSNAP DAY

"And if someone pays you such a kindness as to make up a tale so you'll enjoy a gingersnap, you go along with that story and enjoy every last bite." —Clare *Vanderpool,* Moon Over Manifest

Whether you appreciate them or not, you can't deny the fact that gingersnap cookies have one of the most distinct flavors in the baked-goods kingdom, which is probably why there's such a divide between folks who appreciate their unique, robust flavor and those who would rather stay far, far away from them!

Have you ever noticed that ginger—a rhizome, not a root!—tastes very pungent and has a spicy kick that tingles your sinuses similar to the way horseradish does? Regardless of that sensation (which, like the flavor, some people can't stand and others weirdly like—I'm one of those people!), ginger has some really awesome health benefits, including, among other things, migraine, indigestion, nausea, and menstrual cramp relief.

So even though these may not be your favorite treat in the world, you should probably eat one today anyway. When else is eating cookies actually good for your body?!

Today is also National Creative Ice Cream Flavor Day.

STOKER'S SOFT GINGER COOKIES

Makes at least 2 dozen cookies

Note: This cookie dough needs to be refrigerated overnight.

- ½ cup (1 stick) unsalted butter, at room temperature
- ¾ cup brown sugar, firmly packed
- 2 large eggs, well beaten
- 3 tablespoons ground ginger powder
- ¼ cup dark molasses
- ¾ cup boiling water
- ¾ teaspoon baking soda
- 3 cups all-purpose flour, divided
- 2 teaspoons baking powder
- ¾ teaspoon salt
- ½ teaspoon cinnamon

The day before:
In a large bowl, cream together the butter, brown sugar, and eggs. Stir in the ginger, molasses, water, baking soda, 2½ cups of flour, baking powder, salt, and cinnamon. If the dough seems too wet, stir in the other ½ cup flour. When everything is combined, wrap the dough in plastic wrap and refrigerate overnight.

The day you bake the cookies:
Preheat the oven to 400°F.
    Grease a baking sheet and set aside.

Remove the dough from the refrigerator. Using an ice cream or cookie scoop (or just eyeball it), make golf ball–size balls of dough. Roll the balls in your hand before placing them on the baking sheet. Bake the cookies for 10 minutes. These cookies should not spread, so expect them to stay in the same little ball shapes you rolled them into.

Tip! This recipe can also be used to make cupcakes or loaves, but you should know the dough can be incredibly difficult to work with. Be prepared to use extra flour to stop it from sticking to everything.

JULY
02

NATIONAL ANISETTE DAY

"Alcohol is the anesthesia by which we endure the operation of life."
—George Bernard Shaw

It's okay if you've never heard of anisette before. That's one of the beautiful things about celebrating food and drink holidays—you get to explore parts of the culinary world you may have never had a reason to venture into before!

Anisette is a colorless anise-flavored liqueur that tastes similar to black licorice, and it's a sweeter-tasting cousin to The Green Fairy (absinthe), pastis, ouzo, and sambuca. Anisette has a very potent, bitter flavor when consumed straight, so it's usually mixed with something else (like water).

My little corner of the world didn't carry anisette, but they did carry sambuca. So to celebrate today's holiday, I made a drink called Liquid Asphalt—one part sambuca, one part Jägermeister—and drank it while sitting outside on the street (which is covered in what? That's right—asphalt!). It seemed clever at the time . . . and much more so after a couple drinks!

DID YOU KNOW?

Anisette is made from anise seed, which is part of the parsley family.

JULY 03 — NATIONAL EAT BEANS DAY

"Better beans and bacon in peace than cakes and ale in fear." —Aesop

Black, navy, kidney, lima, mung, pinto, green, adzuki, garbanzo, lentil, soy, pigeon pea, cannellini, black-eyed peas, fava . . .

How do you bean?

One of my favorite traditions of small-town New England living is the Saturday bean supper. It's a social time for family and community to come together and break bread. A typical meal consists of slow-cooked pea beans and salt pork in molasses, biscuits or *pain brun* (brown bread, if you are of French-Canadian heritage), coleslaw, hot dogs or slices of deli ham, piccalilli (relish eaten as a side dish, not a condiment), casseroles of all kind, potato or macaroni salads, and pie or pastries for dessert.

If you've never attended a bean supper and you want an authentic New England experience with good-hearted locals, I highly encourage you to check one out—especially during the summer, when everyone always seems to be in a genuinely happy mood. Don't worry about how to find one, either . . . we aren't shy about our love for these get-togethers and often post enormous signs on church lawns with the time and date of the next one!

Today is also National Chocolate Wafer Day.

NATIONAL BBQ SPARERIBS DAY

"I had a bag of Fritos, they were Texas Grilled Fritos. These Fritos had grill marks on them. They remind me of something, when we used to fire up the barbeque and throw down some Fritos. I can still see my dad with the apron on. Better flip that Frito, Dad, you know how I like mine." —Mitch Hedberg

I have heard that the folks in the South were locavores before it was cool. It seems every dish they make is a proud representation of whatever ingredients are freshest during that time. And however awesome you think your mom's home cooking is, Southern food is filled with a thousand times more love and soul.

The last time I visited the South, I did all manner of sinful things, including drinking, gambling, and eating my weight in BBQ food. 'Cause don't they just do it right down there?! I'm from Maine—and, we make a *lot* of good food, but BBQ isn't always one of them. I didn't know it then, but I was on the verge of becoming a vegetarian at that point in my life. It's as if I innately knew that, so my friends

and I joke that I went to Tennessee for my last "meat-eating hurrah." I drank a lot of whiskey, blew a lot of money at the casinos in Mississippi playing blackjack all night long, and ate a tremendous amount of pulled pork, smoked sausage, barbeque brisket, corn bread, coleslaw, baked beans, and sweet tea. In just the few days I was down there, I think I must've eaten BBQ nearly every meal.

Good food, kind people, and certain atmosphere of *joie de vivre*—what a fine, fine way to go out of the omnivore lifestyle.

Today is also National Caesar Salad Day, National Sidewalk Egg Frying Day, National BBQ Day, and Independence from Meat Day.

DIY SPICY BBQ SAUCE

Makes about 2 cups

1 cup ketchup
½ cup packed light brown sugar

2 tablespoons honey
2 tablespoons stone-ground mustard
1 teaspoon Sriracha or hot sauce

In a saucepan on low heat, mix together the ketchup, brown sugar, honey, mustard, and Sriracha. Stir everything until the brown sugar is no longer grainy and all the ingredients are well blended.

Remove the pan from the stovetop and let the sauce cool for 1 hour. Pour the sauce into a jar or a container with a lid and refrigerate until ready to use. This barbecue sauce tastes great on poultry, pork, and veggies.

JULY 05 · NATIONAL APPLE TURNOVER DAY

"Even if I knew that tomorrow the world would go to pieces, I would still plant my apple tree." —Martin Luther

Back on National Blueberry Popover Day (March 10, page 83)—when I foolishly thought popovers and turnovers were the same thing—we learned that a turnover is actually a folded puff pastry filled with something sweet (like lemon) or even something savory (like pork). Today is all about the apple *turn*over . . . which seems to be a little eager in its day of recognition given that fall is still more than two months away!

And, I'll be honest: Celebrating the apple turnover on July 5th was a struggle for me: It was ninety-five degrees outside with 110 percent humidity. When people think about this time of year, they think of berries—I do! Not apples. Apples are sweater-weather and foliage food, not bikini (today is also National Bikini Day, by the

way) and freckle food. It was surreal to be standing in my already-steaming-hot kitchen peeling apples with the oven on high.

It's no exaggeration when I say that I put sweat and tears into celebrating today's food holiday!

Today is also National Graham Cracker Day.

JULY 06 — NATIONAL FRIED CHICKEN DAY

"Fried chicken just tend to make you feel better about life." —Minny Jackson, **The Help**

There is something sinful about fried chicken. That crispy outside and juicy, melt-in-your-mouth inside of a perfectly prepared, golden, shimmering piece of poultry has become a staple comfort food across this great nation of ours. Not only does it seem to be an essential item at nearly every fast-food chain there is, but it also graces the menus of fine dining restaurants. It's no wonder it has its own food holiday!

And as a country we've done a pretty exceptional job of exploring all avenues of the classic dish. From Buffalo wings to popcorn chicken, chicken patties, country fried chicken, chicken and waffles, and even multiple American-Chinese food dishes like General Tso's, sesame, and mandarin chicken, we have truly mastered the art of frying chicken in ways that bring out its absolute best.

Personally, chicken nuggets (or fingers) have always been my preferred version of fried chicken. I was packed a homemade lunch every day from kindergarten to sixth grade, but not on Fridays. Friday was chicken nugget day at school. Even into my twenties, I would order them when I was at a restaurant with family, friends, or even on dates. And let me tell you: I think twentysomething boys are secretly enamored with twentysomething girls who order chicken nuggets on a first date. It shows that they aren't worried about their image and are in touch with their inner kid!

DID YOU KNOW?

There are more chickens currently living on Earth than there are people.

JULY
07

NATIONAL MACARONI DAY

"Life is too short, and I'm Italian. I'd much rather eat pasta and drink wine than be a size zero." —Sophia Bush

My mom worked second shift for a spell during my childhood. During that time, it fell to my dad to make a nutritious, filling dinner for my younger sister and me every night.

So he fed us macaroni and cheese.

Or macaroni and cheese with peas mixed in.

Or macaroni and cheese with tuna fish and peas mixed in.

Or macaroni and cheese with spam and peas mixed in.

Or macaroni and cheese with tomato soup mixed in.

And that's when my mom started making a more well-balanced dinner ahead of time for my sister and me to reheat during the nights she worked.

If you, too, were traumatized by macaroni and cheese, fear not! There are lots of other ways to celebrate today. You could go to the Macaroni Grill, or you could make macaroni jewelry, minestrone soup, pasta salad with mayo or Italian dressing and fresh veggies, deep-fried mac and cheese balls, or even use it in a casserole. (Like tuna—unless that dish haunts you, too. Trust me—I understand completely!)

Today is also National Chocolate Day and National Strawberry Sundae Day.

NATIONAL MILK CHOCOLATE WITH ALMONDS DAY

"It was inevitable: The scent of bitter almonds always reminded him of the fate of unrequited love." —Gabriel García Márquez, Love in the Time of Cholera

Despite having multiple chocolate-related food holidays, a National Almond Day (page 59), a National Chinese Almond Cookie Day (page 118), a National Almond Buttercrunch Day (page 211), a National Toasted Almond Bar Day (page 257), and a National Bittersweet Chocolate with Almonds Day (page 361), someone, somewhere still wasn't satisfied and lobbied to have today crowned as National *Milk* Chocolate with Almonds Day.

If that's not love (or obsession), I don't know what is!

Then again, when you take a look at all the big-name brands in the candy industry, it seems their preferred nut is—second to the peanut—the almond. There are almond M&Ms, Almond Joys, Hershey's Kisses and bars with almonds, and Snickers with almonds, just to name a few.

Now that I think about it, I've definitely had a love affair with each of them at some point during my life. So, yes! Milk chocolate with almonds *does* deserve its own day of recognition, because there certainly is an allure to creamy milk chocolate and the meaty crunch of an almond!

DID YOU KNOW?

Brazil considers chocolate to be one of its natural resources.

NATIONAL SUGAR COOKIE DAY

"We should look for someone to eat and drink with before looking for something to eat and drink." —Epicurus

No chocolate, no nuts, no need! If you like simple things done well, then sugar cookies hit that mark perfectly.

Not only are the buttery beauties delicious on their own, au natural, but they're also easy to doctor up for those of us who need a little extra "umph" in our lives. For example, super-soft sugar cookies with an inch-thick layer of artificially flavored, usually neon-colored, frosting topped with sprinkles? I don't care how processed those things are, they make me tingle all over. Or what about those sugar cookies shaped like little pillows, filled with raspberry jam? Few things are as delightful as they are with an iced coffee and a free afternoon.

Swoon.

Enough of this jibber-jabber! It's time to go out and enjoy one—or maybe one dozen—of these delicious little cookies. So here's wishing you and yours rivers of frosting, a small lake of jam, and a rain shower of sprinkles!

Today is also National Don't Put All Your Eggs in One Omelet Day.

NATIONAL PIÑA COLADA DAY

"My point is, life is about balance. The good and the bad. The highs and the lows. The piña and the colada." —Ellen DeGeneres, Seriously . . . I'm Kidding

Let's make each other a promise. Even though it's National Piña Colada Day and it's very tempting to sing obnoxiously and off-key, we won't do that to each other. Instead, we'll raise a glass of the sweet, smooth cocktail and toast to each other's health. Sound good?

Piña colada, which originated in Puerto Rico, means "strained pineapple" in Spanish, and it's made from pineapple juice, rum, and coconut cream. It's best served blended with ice and garnished with a wedge of pineapple and a couple maraschino cherries. Or a drizzle of chocolate syrup if you're me (seriously, try it sometime).

It was hot enough outside when I celebrated that I didn't feel like I needed to be somewhere tropical to enjoy one of my guilty pleasure drinks. I strolled down to my favorite Mexican restaurant (the same one that helped me out on National Mint Julep Day back on May 30th), and the same waitress we had on my last visit instantly asked, "What's today's food holiday?" (It was at that moment that I knew I'd be celebrating a lot more of my alcohol-themed days here!) I told her, and within minutes a pint glass full of frothy, delicious, coconutty goodness was sitting in front of me.

I think that's even better service than I might have gotten at some Caribbean resort!

DID YOU KNOW?

The piña colada became the official beverage of Puerto Rico in 1978.

NATIONAL BLUEBERRY MUFFIN DAY

"Usually, old ladies tell me to find Jesus. Look, I'm just trying to find some chai and a good vegan muffin." —Davey Havok

It's the middle of National Blueberry Month, so it only makes sense that we celebrate one of, if not *the*, most popular muffins! These delicious little cupcake-like breakfast items have been a staple at continental breakfasts and drive-thru coffee chains for ages, so of course they deserve their own day of recognition.

My college boyfriend and I would stay out all night with our friends playing video games, sneaking into the theater he worked at to watch movies before their release date, and taking long road trips to nowhere in particular. In the morning, we'd always end up at the same local mom-and-pop breakfast joint. It was small, crowded, and the walls seemed to have yellowed from years and years of fried food (and smoking before it was banned) permeating the air.

My breakfast of choice was always eggs Benedict with extra hollandaise sauce and a grilled blueberry muffin. I knew of no other place at the time that served their muffins any other way besides cold, dense, and awkwardly sticky. (Anyone else ever notice that bits of muffin always seem to get stuck to your fingers?) But to slice it in half and grill it? Sure, it didn't change the fact that it was still essentially a carb bomb, but the savory charcoal crisp that formed on the blueberry muffin elevated it in ways I had never experienced before. Try it today for a twist on your average blueberry muffin.

DID YOU KNOW?

The blueberry muffin is the official muffin of Minnesota.

Today is also National Mojito Day and National Slurpee Day.

JULY 12

NATIONAL PECAN PIE DAY

"But I would be proud to partake of your pecan pie." —Harry Burns, When Harry Met Sally . . .

While it's easy to believe that pecan pies—like turkey, canned cranberry sauce, and boxed stuffing—were part of the original Thanksgiving meal, they actually come to us via the French who settled in the South.

Call me a purist if you wish, but I don't want my pecan pie changed in any way. No maple, no caramel, no bacon, no chocolate, no sweet potatoes, no fruits of any kind (okay, maybe a little rum or bourbon would be okay!)—just give me a layer of corn-syrupy gel topped with mildly chewy, sweet pecans in a basic, nondescript piecrust, please and thank you. No whipped cream, no ice cream, no topping on the slice of any kind.

And you know what? As a matter of fact, I don't even need the piecrust, or the actual pecans for that matter. I really just want to celebrate today with a bowl of that gooey, gorgeous, brown gel.

That's my perfect pecan pie day!

Today is also National Eat Your Jell-O Day.

JULY 13

NATIONAL FRENCH FRIES DAY

"I went into a McDonald's yesterday and said, 'I'd like some fries.' The girl at the counter said, 'Would you like some fries with that?'" —Jay Leno

Oh, french fries, I promise that I didn't mean all those things I said back on June 22nd during National Onion Ring Day (page 204). I was just seduced by those sweet, fried, circular rings of infinite love. *You* are (also) the superior side dish to burgers, chicken fingers, pizza, and most all other typical bar foods. You even do a glorious job of standing alone as a meal in dishes like *poutine* (french fries topped with cheese curds and gravy), steak frites, or smothered in cheese, BBQ pulled pork, and maple sour cream.

French fries are comfort food incarnate for children and adults alike, probably because they have the ability to truly complement you as a person and your specific tastes. Doesn't matter if you're craving something fancy, exotic, uncomplicated, or even edgy, there are all kinds of toppings for fried potatoes, including ketchup, mayo, ketchup mixed with mayo, flavored ketchup (with truffle oil, jalapeño, banana, or curry), mustard, BBQ sauce, tartar sauce, ranch dressing, Sriracha, blue cheese dressing, Thousand Island dressing, flavored yogurts, cocktail sauce, hummus, tzatziki, canned chili, aïoli, horseradish, salt and malt vinegar, garlic with parsley and salt, cinnamon and sugar, kimchi, and even chutney.

When you line up all of those options next to each other, it's kind of eye-opening how beloved french fries really are generationally and universally! You could eat french fries every meal for the next month and never have the same experience twice.

Actually, if I weren't eating the year, that might be a very tempting thing to do!

Today is also National Beans and Franks Day.

PAPAS LOCAS

Makes enough for 4 people

1 (28-ounce) package frozen shoestring french fries
2 garlic gloves, minced
1 cup mayonnaise
1½ tablespoons lemon juice
1 large avocado, peeled, seeded, and cut into chunks
¼ teaspoon cumin
¼ teaspoon salt

Bake the french fries according to package directions plus 2 or 3 minutes—you want them to be as crispy as possible without burning so that they hold up under the weight of the sauce.

While the french fries are baking, put the garlic, mayonnaise, lemon juice, avocado, cumin, and salt into a blender. Blend until everything is completely creamy and without chunks.

Either place the baked french fries in a large bowl, pour the sauce over the fries, and gently combine the sauce and french fries until they are completely covered, or place the french fries out on a large platter and drizzle sauce over the top of them. Eat them with a fork or get messy and dig in with your hands!

NATIONAL GRAND MARNIER DAY

"When I read about the evils of drinking, I gave up reading." —Henny Youngman

Grand Marnier—made from Cognac using the grape varietal *ugni blanc* and bitter orange essence from the Citrus bigaradia oranges for their intense fragrance—has been around since 1880. It was first created by Louis Alexandre Marnier-Lapostolle, who named it *Curaçao Marnier*. Friend, César Ritz—founder and manager of Paris' Ritz Hotel at the time—suggested it be given a much more opulent title. And so it became Grand Marnier. Today, the company still belongs to the Marnier-Lapostolle family.

Initially I celebrated today with a Sun and Surf (which I think is supposed to be a layered shot and not just one giant beverage), made from one part Grand Marnier, one part tequila, and one part Kahlúa. Although it was heavy, it was a great drink for a balmy, sunny, bikini-wearing kind of day. But you can use Grand Marnier in more than just cocktails. It makes an excellent ingredient in dishes like crêpes, soufflés, jams, crème brûlées, cakes, breads, mousse, tiramisùs, sorbets, cheesecakes, brownies, or—probably the classiest of all—Jell-O shots!

Today is also National Macaroni Day and National Pick Blueberries Day.

MARGARITA GEL "SHOTS"

Makes 12 "shots"

- 1 (3-ounce) package lime gelatin
- 1 cup boiling water
- ¼ cup cold water
- ½ cup gold tequila
- ¼ cup Grand Marnier
- Salt, for garnish

Empty the packet of gelatin into a medium-size heat-proof bowl. Add the boiling water and whisk until the gelatin is completely dissolved. Whisk in the cold water, tequila, and the Grand Marnier. Pour immediately into 12 (2-ounce) cups, distributing evenly.

Gently place the small cups, uncovered, into an 8 x 8-inch baking dish (this will hold the cups in place). Place the baking dish in the refrigerator and chill until the "shots" are firm. Remove the shot cups from the pan, cover them, and return them to the refrigerator until ready to serve. When ready to eat, sprinkle each shot with a desired amount of salt. Bottoms up!

Tip! If you're making a double batch, use one box of lime gelatin and one box of lemon gelatin, and double all the other ingredients for a more expanded citrus flavor.

JULY 15 — NATIONAL GUMMI WORM DAY

Erin: "Gummy bears and gummy worms?" Michael: "Bears sad, worms happy. . . come on, Erin!" —The Office

When you were a kid, were you Team Red and White, or Team Green and Yellow? It seemed everybody had a very particular gummy worm preference, but it wasn't necessarily the color of the little candies that attracted kids, was it? It was the fact that they were shaped like *worms!* Bears are cute and all; fruit shapes are just boring; fish have their place; but worms scream childhood. Kids have been throwing them at each other and daring one another to eat them for generations. Thankfully, we can skip the dirt kind and go right to the gummy kind today! They're great in mud cakes; they're surprisingly awesome in ice cream; and they're super just as they are, too.

But gummy worms aren't just for eating. My sister told me she once caught a sunfish with one.

She was at our family's summer camp, fishing off the dock, when she decided to sacrifice a red-and-white gummy worm, which were, and still are, her favorite kind. (This worked out perfectly growing up since the only ones I would eat were the green-and-yellow-colored ones.) Her ten-year-old self concluded that if she loved the red-and-white ones, then the fish would probably love them, too!

She swears to this day that it was one of the easiest catches of her life.

DID YOU KNOW?

Red is the most popular color of gummy candy.

Today is also National Tapioca Pudding Day.

JULY 16 — NATIONAL CORN FRITTER DAY

"The day of fortune is like a harvest day, We must be busy when the corn is ripe."
—Torquato Tasso

As we learned back on National Corn on the Cob Day on June 11 (page 190), much of the corn grown in the U.S. ends up becoming ethanol (a fuel made from the sugars in corn that's then mixed with gasoline), feed for cattle and other animals, or high-fructose corn syrup (which appears in everything from soda to candy and ketchup to yogurt).

I think today it's best to celebrate corn in a much more unrefined state. (All sarcasm aside, corn fritters are probably more "natural" than the high-fructose corn syrup in peanut butter. By mixing it with flour, eggs, milk, and spices, and deep-frying or baking it!)

Related to the hushpuppy, corn fritters are a staple Southern comfort food. They're delicious as is or dredged through a variety of sauces, including honey mustard, sweet chili, garlic, or even marinara.

MEXICAN GRILLED CORN FRITTERS

Makes 8 or 9 fritters

3 small ears corn, husked, grilled, corn removed (about 2 cups)
1 (4.25-ounce) can diced green chilies
2 tablespoons freshly squeezed juice (from one small lime)
½ cup (soy) milk
1 tablespoon vegetable oil
¾ cup all-purpose flour
¼ cup cornmeal

1 teaspoon granulated sugar
¼ teaspoon salt
½ teaspoon cumin
3 tablespoons grated Cotija cheese (Parmesan, if you're in a bind)
Sour cream, for serving (optional)

Preheat the oven to 400°F.
Grease a baking sheet and set it aside.

In a large bowl, mix the corn with the chilies, lime juice, milk, and oil. Stir in the flour, cornmeal, sugar, salt, and cumin. Then gently stir in the cheese until everything is well combined.

Scoop the fritter batter by ¼ cups onto the baking sheet and gently pat them down. Bake the fritters for 12 minutes, flip them over, and bake them for another 8 minutes. Serve them as is or with sour cream, if desired.

JULY 17 — NATIONAL PEACH ICE CREAM DAY

"Training is everything. The peach was once a bitter almond; cauliflower is nothing but cabbage with a college education." —Mark Twain, The Tragedy of Pudd'nhead Wilson

Peach lovers, rejoice! Ice cream lovers, rejoice! Today is a day for you!

I'll be honest: I didn't even know that peach ice cream was a *thing*. After the tremendous difficulty I had finding rocky road ice cream (which I thought was a staple flavor) back on June 2nd, I wasn't expecting to find *so many* different peach-based ice creams available from *so many* different manufactures! Is peach ice cream really more beloved than rocky road? Obviously, if it has its own food day (which I think is a good testament to its popularity).

Today's food holiday also falls pretty close to National Ice Cream Day itself (some years it might even happen on the same day!), which is always the third Sunday of the month. It—along with July being National Ice Cream Month in general—was declared in 1984 by our old foodie pal President Ronald Reagan. The man definitely appreciated summertime's finest cold, creamy treat, and today—every day this month, really!—so should you.

Will you have it in a dish, a sugar cone, or a waffle cone? And remember: The more scoops you have, the harder you're celebrating!

JULY 18 — NATIONAL CAVIAR DAY

"Caviar is to dining what a sable coat is to a girl in evening dress." —Luwdig Bemelmans

It seemed that while all the other days—though sometimes random or tremendously specific—were accessible in one way or another, National Caviar Day isn't. Caviar, to me, just seems exclusive. Eating your money would make you look crazy; that's why people just eat caviar instead. Most people are never going to try this food in their entire lives, because it's excessively expensive and not something the average person craves. "Whatta ya feelin' tonight, Bob?" "Oh, y'know, a burger and some caviah." In the real world, that conversation doesn't play out that way.

Traditional caviar is made from fish eggs, specifically from sturgeon (though most edible fish eggs are referred to as caviar nowadays). And it tastes like fish and salt—really, how else would you expect it to taste? So if that isn't the most appealing thing in the world, but you still want to have a similar culinary experience, vegan caviar is available. It's made from seaweed, but it's still pretty expensive.

And hey, if you don't have the money to afford *either* luxury, celebrate nontraditionally, like I did with Texas caviar! It's a marinated salad of sorts (some folks even call it a salsa) made from black-eyed peas and veggies that taste awesome with tortilla chips.

And you won't look the least bit crazy while eating it!

"AVOIDING THE WRATH OF A THOUSAND BABY FISH" TEXAS CAVIAR

Makes 1 large bowl

Note: This dish needs to chill for 2 to 4 hours before serving.

- 2 (15-ounce) cans black-eyed peas, drained and rinsed
- 1 (14-ounce) can petite diced tomatoes, drained
- 1 (7-ounce) can diced green chilies
- 1 (11-ounce) can sweet kernel corn, drained and rinsed
- ½ medium red pepper, seeded and diced (about ½ cup)
- ½ medium green pepper, seeded and diced (about ½ cup)
- ½ medium yellow pepper, seeded and diced (about ½ cup)
- ½ medium orange pepper, seeded and diced (about ½ cup)
- ½ teaspoon crushed red pepper flakes
- ¼ cup olive oil
- 2 tablespoons red wine vinegar
- 2 tablespoons lime juice
- 1 tablespoon granulated sugar
- ¼ teaspoon garlic powder
- ½ teaspoon cumin
- ¼ teaspoon salt
- 1 or 2 (14-ounce) bags scoop-shaped tortilla chips

In a large bowl, combine the black-eyed peas, tomatoes, chilies, corn, peppers, and pepper flakes. Mix everything together.

In a smaller bowl, whisk together the olive oil, vinegar, lime juice, sugar, garlic powder, cumin, and salt. Pour the dressing over the ingredients in the large bowl and mix thoroughly. Place the bowl in the refrigerator to let flavors combine for 2 to 4 hours.

When ready, serve with scoop-shaped tortilla chips.

NATIONAL DAIQUIRI DAY

"Here's to alcohol, the rose-colored glasses of life." —F. Scott Fitzgerald, The Beautiful and Damned

If your liver's been aching just reading about all of the alcohol-related holidays that happen in July—try drinking all of them! In all seriousness, while it might seem excessive, it's true to our culinary trends and habits. People *do* tend to drink a lot more in the summer, which is associated with hot weather and vacationing. And what's a better way to enjoy lazy, carefree days or to beat the heat than with an ice cold beer?

Or a fruity daiquiri?

The image we associate with daiquiris today—blended, icy, colorful drinks perhaps with a big umbrella sticking out of the top—isn't how the cocktail started. It was originally a simple, refreshing, light drink made from sugar, lime juice, and rum poured over ice. It was created sometime around the turn of the twentieth century in Cuba.

I don't know about you, but that version sounds a lot more tempting to me than the frozen, neon-pink one does! So today, let's strip off our clothes (because it's way too hot to be in anything but swimwear) and strip away the girliness of what the daiquiri has evolved into, and let's celebrate by reclaiming the old-school version!

JULY
20

NATIONAL FORTUNE COOKIE DAY

*"You have no fortune. I didn't need a cookie to tell me that." —Carrie Bradshaw,
Sex and the City*

The fortune cookie is one of the best parts about eating Chinese food, whether you consume the little (more than likely) American-born pastry or not. And it has nothing to do with the flavor of the cookie; it's all about three things:

1. Conclusion: Your meal is over, and it's the end of some quality time with family or friends.
2. Conversation: Is your fortune hilarious or apropos to life and the complexities of your current strife?
3. Potential friendly chaffing: Especially toward the person who didn't even get a fortune in their cookie. Which, by the way, is usually me.

Sage advice, me thinks.

Here's hoping your fortune cookie today is filled. With what kind of saying? You know, it doesn't really matter—as long as it's filled with something!

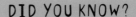

DID YOU KNOW?

Fortune cookies were also referred to as "fortune teacakes" until around World War II.

Today is also National Lollipop Day.

NATIONAL JUNK FOOD DAY

"My doctor told me to stop having intimate dinners for four unless there are three other people." —Orson Welles

The old adage "one man's trash is another man's treasure" certainly applies to today's food holiday. Not to get all philosophical here, but what exactly *is* junk food? It's usually defined as something that's "bad" for you because it has little-to-no nutritional value. But a lot of foods eaten in excess can be *bad* for you in one way or another, too. (Think about it: Eat too many carrots, and you might turn orange; not exactly the most attractive skin tone color, is it? Unless you're going for that fake tan look.)

Junk food is subjective. And, really, can food be considered *junk* when it serves a purpose of either spiritual nourishment or emotional satisfaction?

When I lived in England, every night after dinner my best mate there and I would do the same thing: Drink Jack Daniels with Diet Coke, eat a tremendous amount of chocolate, and watch really trashy TV shows. That's *my* junk food. And that's exactly how I celebrated today.

Maybe not good for the body, but definitely good for the soul!

DID YOU KNOW?

Cibophobia is the fear of food.

Today is also National Crème Brûlée Day and National Legal Drinking Age Day.

NATIONAL PENUCHE DAY

JULY 22

"I prefer to regard a dessert as I would imagine the perfect woman: subtle, a little bittersweet, not blowsy, and extrovert. Delicately made up, not highly rouged. Holding back, not exposing everything and, of course, with a flavor that lasts." —Graham Kerr

It sounds like incense, something you might call someone being an arrogant jerk, or a "trick-and-meld" game involving a forty-eight-card deck. But penuche is actually pretty similar to fudge. It's usually made with brown sugar, butter, cream, and nuts. And supposedly it's a popular candy in places like the South and New England; though as a proud New Englander, I would just like to state that I have never—in all my years—had or heard of it before today.

But that's what these food holidays are all about, right? We're broadening our gastronomical horizons! And if you live in a place where something's considered a regionally loved food and you've never had it before, don't you think you oughta?

NATIONAL HOT DOG DAY

JULY 23

"Some people wanted Champagne and caviar when they should have had beer and hot dogs." —Dwight David Eisenhower

With all the barbecues that happen between Memorial Day and Labor Day in this country, it only makes sense that National Hot Dog Day falls smack-dab in the middle of all that. I mean, what would summer be without some corn on the cob, a mound of potato salad, and a few good charcoal-grilled dogs smothered in mustard, relish, and celery salt? (Or however you prefer yours, and there are lots of different ways to do so; what a fellow tops his hot dog with says a lot about his character!

Didn't some famous author say something like that at some point in history?)

I was never a fan of hot dogs at baseball games or from street vendors, but my family has the art of hot dogs—getting them a little black and crispy-on-the-outside, and melt-in-your-mouth soft on the inside—down pat. We were never really the "steamed dog on a microwaved bun" kinda folks, though if you are, no judgment here! After all, if you're eating a hot dog (which is made from "chicken lips and feet," as my grandfather used to say) in the first place, then you're the kind of person who doesn't care what other people think of you.

So grab your veggie dog, beef franks, or red snappers and unashamedly celebrate the day!

DID YOU KNOW?

In 1957, the U.S. Chamber of Commerce officially designated July as National Hot Dog Month.

Today is also National Vanilla Ice Cream Day.

JULY 24 — NATIONAL TEQUILA DAY

"Get up and dance, get up and smile, get up and drink to the days that are gone in the shortest while." —Simon Fowler

Oh, tequila. I've seen grown women dance around the plastic sombrero that adorns some of your bottles, and I've seen grown men stumble across a completely level floor all due to your golden nectar.

Tequila—the national drink of Mexico, which is the only place in the world that can actually legally make tequila—is made from the blue agave plant. After it's matured, the sharp leaves are stripped away and the remaining *piña* is roasted, mashed, fermented, distilled, and then consumed by twenty-one-year-olds in Cancun on Spring Break every year.

For tonight's celebration I was talked into drinking something called a Paloma, which is a mix of tequila and Fresca. I'm pretty sure it was a glass of straight tequila. And I'm pretty sure if I had ordered a second one, I might have been one of those boogying-around-the-hat (whether it was real or imaginary), staggering-on-even-ground, drunky mcdrunksters.

Hey liver, you better appreciate what I spared you from tonight!

Today is also National Drive-Thru Day.

- -

JULY 25

NATIONAL HOT FUDGE SUNDAE DAY

"Always serve too much hot fudge sauce on hot fudge sundaes. It makes people overjoyed, and puts them in your debt." —Judith Olney

About a million years ago, I was standing in line at the grocery store perusing through a tabloid promoting the engagement of bat boy and iguana girl. Inside was an article about a brand-new diet that revolved around eating as much as you could at every meal. And to end the day, you could eat all the ice cream you wanted in ninety seconds at three a.m. Supposedly it helped weight loss.

Oh, how I wish that were true.

While there may be no relationship between any part-animal, part-human couples happening in reality, there *is* an incredible marriage of flavors being celebrated today: the hot fudge sundae. One of the local ice-cream stands in my home-town used to make these vertical sundaes. They were tall Styrofoam cups filled with chocolate soft serve and a core of hot fudge sauce (they even made one with hot peanut butter sauce, too!). And it was *deliriously* good. Every bite was a mix of cold, creamy chocolate ice cream and warm, rich, gooey hot fudge that made the entire thing taste a little like eating a hot cocoa!

I could definitely celebrate National Hot Fudge Sundae Day every three a.m. with one of those!

NATIONAL BAGELFEST DAY

"The battle promises to be fought with bags of bagels and bran muffins, free beer and wine, expanded legroom, baggage closets, and overhead bins."
—Ralph Blumenthal

Lender's Bagels was started in Connecticut by Harry Lender in 1927. When the company opened one of the largest bagel factories in the country in 1986 in Mattoon, Illinois—Bagel Capital of the World—Harry's son Murray hosted a free bagel breakfast. Soon, July 26 became National Bagelfest Day, a way to celebrate the bagel while encouraging more people to eat breakfast.

I could never say no to a bagel; I've even driven three hours to get one. (It was an Asiago bagel with jalapeño cream cheese; I'm sure I could've gotten it anywhere, but this particular place just made the best version.) In elementary school, one of my friends used to bring a cold bagel with plain cream cheese for lunch every day and—while it may sound unappetizing, since most people toast or at least heat up their bagels—I often traded her with whatever I had for it. It was incredibly chewy and filling and the simplicity of it made my mouth water.

Bagels are truly one of my top ten favorite foods. It's National Bagelfest Day in my world much more than once a year (more likely once a week)! One of the reasons I dig them so hard is because of how versatile they are. In this day and age there certainly is no lack of creativity with bagel or cream cheese flavor, either. So whether you prefer lox, butter and honey, cream cheese, or egg and sausage, today is the day to celebrate our holey little friends.

Today is also National Coffee Milkshake Day.

SEBAGELS

Makes 2 to 4 servings

2 bagels, any flavor, sliced in half
1 large tomato, sliced
4 slices Muenster cheese
½ cup salted cashews, finely chopped

Preheat the oven to 325°F.

Place the bagel halves on a baking sheet, sliced side up. Place a tomato slice and a cheese slice on each bagel half and then bake for 10 minutes.

Remove the baking sheet from the oven and top each bagel half with some chopped cashews. Return the baking sheet to the oven and bake the bagels for an additional 5 minutes, or until the cashews sink into the cheese. Serve.

- -

JULY 27

NATIONAL SCOTCH DAY

"Whenever someone asks me if I want water with my Scotch, I say I'm thirsty, not dirty." —Joe E. Lewis

Unlike the whiskey-related holidays previously celebrated this year, today is specifically all about Scotch—a whiskey that's been made in Scotland since the fifteenth century. And like many other alcohols, under law the drink must meet certain standards to be considered proper Scotch. Under the Scotch Whiskey Regulations of 2009, *some* of those requirements include that it must:

- be produced and distilled in Scotland from water and malted barley.
- be aged no less than three years in Scottish oak casks.
- contain no artificial or added ingredients.
- have a minimum ABV (alcohol by volume) of 40 percent (which is 80 proof).

That's serious business.

Enthusiasts will also tell you that the best way to drink your Scotch is neat, (i.e., no ice), which can dull the flavor, and *definitely* no mixers, which really muddle the entire experience. So if you were planning on celebrating tonight with any old whiskey in any old glass, maybe with a splash of some ginger ale—think again! Neat in a tulip-shaped glass is the recommended way to get the most authentic experience from today's holiday.

Today is also National Crème Brûlée Day.

JULY 28 — NATIONAL MILK CHOCOLATE DAY

"The twelve-step chocoholics program: Never be more than twelve steps away from chocolate!" —Terry Moore

Before exploring the creamy, delicious worlds of dark, white, bitter, or semi-, or unsweetened chocolate, most people start their sweet tooth adventure with the universally loved, ever reliable milk chocolate variety. And whom do we have to thank for this treat? It's generally believed that a fella named Daniel Peter developed milk chocolate with help from his pal Henri Nestlé (sound familiar?) in Switzerland during the latter half of the nineteenth century.

With so many delicious ways to celebrate chocolate, how will you choose to celebrate?

Today is also National Hamburger Day.

NATIONAL LASAGNA DAY

"The trouble with eating Italian food is that five or six days later you're hungry again." —George Miller

I don't know about you, but when I think about the height of summer—the heat, the humidity—cranking my oven up to make lasagna *totally* makes sense. All sarcasm aside, if the lasagna comes out as good as mine when I celebrated today's food holiday (I even called my dish Gasmsagana—which was overloaded with sweet nut cheese, rosemary, sun-dried tomatoes, and spicy soy sausage—because of how much of a gastronomical turn-on it was), then who cares if you have to sweat a little more than you are already to make it?

Lasagna is a hearty, traditional Italian comfort food made with layers of flat noodles and—depending on where you're from—a variety of different fillings. While many people associate a tomato-based sauce with the dish, other classical options include using a creamy béchamel sauce or even a salty, crunchy pesto. Feel free to think outside the box today, too; there are all sorts of recipes available now for deep-fried lasagna, breakfast lasagna with bacon and eggs, and even Mexican lasagna with salsa and taco shells.

Just remember to keep hydrated if you're going to be in the kitchen cooking on a hot summer's day—I suggest wine. Lots of it!

Today is also National Cheese Sacrifice Purchase Day and National Chicken Wing Day.

JULY 30 NATIONAL CHEESECAKE DAY

"Because you don't live near a bakery doesn't mean you have to go without cheesecake." —Hedy Lamarr

You're an Olympic athlete in the very first games ever played. After you compete in your sport—most likely a sprint across the stadium—you're given a large slice of . . . cheesecake. Seriously! It's widely accepted that cheesecake may have originated in Ancient Greece. Makes sense: Before or after running in extreme heat, I know the first thing I always crave is a dense slab of cheese and sugar.

Cheesecake has evolved quite a bit since then. Whether you're craving a slice of heavy, rich New York–style cheesecake; a lighter, creamier Philadelphia-style cheesecake topped with a bit of fruit; *käsekuchen*—German cheesecake—made from quark, which is a bit sour; or a sweet and creamy Italian cheesecake made from mascarpone or ricotta, there are loads of options to choose from.

Flavors are just as varied, too. What's your preference? Key lime, chocolate and peanut butter, or maybe turtle? Personally, I like a nice, thick slice of honeycomb cheesecake!

Just not immediately before or after exercising, that is.

- -

JULY 31 NATIONAL RASPBERRY CAKE DAY

"Dost thou think, because thou art virtuous, there shall be no more cakes and ale?"
—William Shakespeare, Twelfth Night

Raspberries, part of the rose family, have quite the romantic Greek mythological tale associated with them. They were believed to have been white until Ida—Zeus' nursemaid—nicked her finger on a thorn that stained the berries red forevermore. *Rubus idaeus*, the Latin name for raspberries, even translates to "bramble bush of Ida."

Raspberries scream summer to me. My uncle had big, thorny bushes of wild raspberries growing on his property. When my sister and I were younger, my mom used to bring us to his house to pick them. I remember feeling so little among the maze of (what seemed like then) tall, tall shrubs—bees buzzing past me to divebomb the sweet flesh of my screaming sister, thorns threatening to prick our tanned and freckled skin, and huge raspberries dangling ripe and juicy. For me, National Raspberry Cake Day is a perfectly placed food holiday.

Today is also National Cotton Candy Day and National Jump for Jelly Beans Day.

RASPBERRY JAM BREAKFAST CAKE

Makes one 8 x 8-inch pan (4 to 12 pieces)

10 tablespoons (1¼ sticks) unsalted butter, at room temperature

¾ cup granulated sugar

1 large egg

¾ teaspoon vanilla extract

1½ cups all-purpose flour

½ teaspoon baking powder

½ teaspoon salt

1½ teaspoons cinnamon

1 (10-ounce) jar seedless raspberry jam

Preheat the oven to 350°F.

Spray an 8 x 8-inch baking pan with nonstick cooking or baking spray.

In a large bowl, cream together the butter and sugar. Add the egg and vanilla and mix well. Slowly add the flour, baking powder, salt, and cinnamon. Mix everything together until there are no lumps—the batter will be very thick.

Spread two-thirds of the batter into the pan. Gently spread the jam across the batter. As best as you can, spread or pat the rest of the batter across the jam, making sure the jam is completely covered. Bake for 40 minutes, or until a toothpick inserted comes out clean and dry. Serve warm.

AUGUST IS...

AUGUST IS ALSO...

National Brownies at Brunch Month
National Catfish Month
National Eat Dessert First Month
National Family Meals Month
National Goat Cheese Month
National Panini Month
National Peach Month
National Sandwich Month
National Water Quality Month

. . .

1st Thursday—National IPA Day
1st Friday—International Beer Day
1st Saturday—National Mustard Day and National Mead Day
Thursday before Labor Day—National Cabernet Day
Saturday before Labor Day—International Bacon Day

NATIONAL RASPBERRY CREAM PIE DAY

"There is something in the red of a raspberry pie that looks as good to a man as the red in a sheep looks to a wolf." —Edgar Warson Howe

Back-to-back raspberry-themed food holidays? I'm okay with that; after all, 'tis the season for fresh berries! And raspberries come in all sorts of beautiful shades—red, black, purple, and even yellow/gold! But do you know how to tell the difference between a raspberry and a blackberry, which are both Alabama and Kentucky's state fruit? Unlike a blackberry, a raspberry has a hollow center when picked because its stem (called a receptacle) remains attached to the plant.

While eating the year, I lived in a big apartment next door to one of the cutest elderly couples I have ever met. Ann and Leo were French-Canadian through and through: small in stature but huge in personality and generosity. The apartment I lived in was built on land they used to own, so our backyards were adjacent. Over the years, they encouraged me to wander over whenever I wanted and help myself to their raspberry and blackberry bushes. So in the warm summer sun, I meandered across my garden into theirs and picked fistfuls of raspberries—and the first blackberries of the season—to make today's pie. Quite the luxury, let me tell you!

AUGUST 02

NATIONAL ICE CREAM SANDWICH DAY

"I am having a love affair with this ice cream sandwich." —George Bluth Sr., Arrested Development

When I think about ice cream sandwiches, two things come to mind: (1) a brick of vanilla ice cream sandwiched between two soft chocolate wafer cakes that stick to the ends of your fingertips while you're trying to eat your sweet novelty, and (2) hard chocolate chip cookies sandwiching a layer of chocolate ice cream. Me? I'll take option two, please!

In some regards, the ice cream sandwich, which probably got its humble beginning as a street cart vendor specialty, hasn't changed much. It's become a loved frozen confection worldwide. And

Stateside, you can now find them everywhere, from baseball games and ice cream trucks to all-natural food stores and gourmet restaurants. Whether you're craving a vegan version of the sweet confection or one made from mascarpone, balsamic vinegar, and ginger, ice cream sandwiches have truly blossomed into an opportunity for creative minds to show off while still embracing the inner kid in all of us.

Make your own or buy a box today—just be ready to share!

AUGUST 03 — NATIONAL WATERMELON DAY

"When one has tasted watermelon he knows what the angels eat." —Mark Twain

Juicy wedges of watermelon are another perfectly appropriate summertime food. The refreshing fruit—which is more than 90 percent water—is an ideal side dish at BBQs and picnics, as well as to good conversation and childhood memory-making moments. (Who doesn't recall having seed spitting contests with their siblings or cousins that usually got entirely out of hand?)

Watermelon is one of my mom's top five favorite foods. When I asked her why she liked them so much, she answered, "It satisfies my sweet craving without adding junk to the trunk, and when I cut one into sections, they look like big smiles so naturally that makes me smile, too." Makes complete sense to me! She's not the only person who feels so fondly toward watermelon, either. In 2007, the 110th Congress passed a resolution declaring July as National Watermelon Month.

I enjoyed big wedges of the brilliantly colored fruit while sitting outside under a maple tree in nearly 100-degree weather. I suggest you do the same. Or you could spice things up and celebrate with a watermelon margarita, salsa, soup, or even pickled rind.

Today is also National Grab Some Nuts Day.

SPICY WATERMELON SALAD

Makes enough for 2 salads as a meal,
4 to 6 as a side dish

- 1 small (6-to-8-inch-wide) red seedless watermelon, cut into cubes (about 5 cups)
- 1 cup salted pistachios
- 1 cup feta cheese, crumbled
- 1 teaspoon crushed red pepper flakes

In a large bowl, combine the watermelon, pistachios, feta cheese, and pepper flakes. Chill in the refrigerator for 1 hour. Drain before serving.

Tip! Leftovers of this are *no bueno* so eat it immediately!

NATIONAL CHOCOLATE CHIP DAY

"Chocolate is a perfect food, as wholesome as it is delicious, a beneficent restorer of exhausted power. It is the best friend of those engaged in literary pursuits."
—Baron Justus von Liebig

Of the two National Chocolate Chip Days celebrated this year, today's was my favorite. An enormous outdoor music festival was being held in my city for the first time and with it came some huge acts. I got up before dawn, walked across town to where it was being held (a giant park that overlooked the ocean), and took my place first in line for the "doors" to open hours and hours later. Midmorning, while listening to some of my favorite bands during sound check, I soaked up the warm sunshine and sat contently on the grass munching away on two dinner plate-size vegan chocolate chip cookies that tasted exactly like cookie dough. In other words: It was one of the most perfect moments I had during my journey to eat the year.

My day was possible because of a happy accident. The chocolate chip cookie was invented by Ruth Graves Wakefield at the Toll House Inn in Whitman, Massachusetts, during the 1930s. When she didn't have enough baker's chocolate to make cookies, she chopped up a bar of semisweet chocolate and tossed it into the dough instead. It didn't melt, but her guests didn't care—they loved every bite of the delicious new treat.

My hope for you today is that however big or small you celebrate today, that it is no less than epic. Then again, a *really good* chocolate chip cookie usually makes any event perfect.

NATIONAL OYSTER DAY

"All art is autobiographical. The pearl is the oyster's autobiography." —Federico Fellini

Oysters have been eaten since prehistoric days. But before *you* dive into these bivalve mollusks, let's learn a little about them, shall we? While you may enjoy oysters for their nutrients, oysters get their calories through filter feeding. Meaning they breathe in through their gills and delicious little edibles like plankton get caught in the mucus there. They have a three-chambered heart that pumps colorless blood throughout their body. But the coolest thing of all? They're protandric hermaphrodites, meaning they start off their lives as males and many eventually switch to being females. (I don't blame them, the grass is greener—or in this case, the water is bluer.)

If eating straight oysters isn't appealing, consider celebrating today with oyster mushrooms or oyster crackers! Feeling a little more daring than that? Some breweries make oyster stouts. For example, Abita uses freshly shucked Louisiana oysters in their appropriately named Imperial Louisiana Oyster Stout. And 21st Amendment Brewery makes Marooned on Hog Island, a stout that uses Hog Island Sweetwater oyster shells.

Now that's one way to celebrate today, eh?

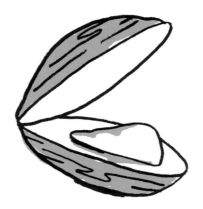

DID YOU KNOW?

Oysters are considered an aphrodisiac (and some believe that's partly because of how much they resemble the . . . um . . . female anatomy).

Today is also National Chile Pepper Day.

NATIONAL ROOT BEER FLOAT DAY

". . . the egg creams of Avenue A in New York and the root beer float . . . are among the high points of American gastronomic inventiveness." —Mark Kurlansky, Choice Cuts

The root beer float—like many food and beverages—has a foggy origin. But it's generally credited to Frank J. Wisner of Colorado. Food legend states that in the late nineteenth century he had a total revelation: He realized the snow-covered Cow Mountain looked like ice cream in soda. The next morning he put a scoop of vanilla ice cream in a glass of root beer and—voilà!—the "black cow" was created, history was made, and Steely Dan had something to sing about.

There was a 1950s-style drive-in diner near my house when I was a little kid. We went there often throughout the summer because the prices were cheap, it was easy entertainment (when you're a kid, the idea of going to a restaurant just to sit in your car and eat while girls in poodle skirts passed you food through your window was just wild— absolutely wild!), and they made some of the best root beer in the whole state. It came in oversized frosted mugs and was delicious, refreshing, and made us feel super cool and adultlike when we were drinking it.

Not gonna lie: Even now when I drink root beer out of a bottle I feel the same way.

DID YOU KNOW?

Root beer was originally made with sassafras, but it was removed in 1976 after the U.S. FDA banned it because it was carcinogenic.

AUGUST 07 NATIONAL RASPBERRIES AND CREAM DAY

"It is not well for a man to pray cream; and live skim milk." —Henry Ward Beecher, Life Thoughts

"I wondered when you'd be over," said Leo, my elderly next door neighbor. He reminded me of my own late grandfather, kindness radiating from every pore and quick to laugh right from the depths of his soul. I walked across his yard to where he was sitting comfortably in a lawn chair playing with his kitten, Minou. "It's National Raspberries and Cream Day! So can I please have some berries?" I asked, pretending to beg.

"Of course! They're all yours! Do you know where they are? Of course you know where they are. Let me show you where they are," he pushed himself out of his chair and slowly, very slowly, walked me to the back edge of his property where the raspberries were flourishing. "Oh my, just look at them all. You can have as many as you want!"

I tossed one of the plentiful ripe berries into my mouth and was delighted to find that they were sweet this year, not at all tart. "You like them, hun?" he asked.

"I do. You grow some of the best." I alternated between picking and eating. "And berries are good for you—filled with antioxidants, fiber, and all sorts of healthy things. I mean, just look at you! You're the strongest fella on the block!" He put his hand to his chest and wheezed with laughter. "I don't know who you've been talking to, but I think they got it wrong!"

After just a few moments, my bowl was already full. "That's it?" he asked me playfully.

"For today," I smiled.

It's the small moments like these that make this crazy project to eat the year so sweet.

DID YOU KNOW?

Does it seem like a raspberry is broken into little segments? Well they are, and they're called drupelets.

AUGUST 08 — NATIONAL ZUCCHINI DAY

"'Do I have to explain the obvious?' I asked impatiently. 'Somebody might break in and put zucchini in our house.'" —Barbara Kingsolver, Animal, Vegetable, Miracle

I had every intention of celebrating National Frozen Custard Day today, but after visiting my farm share and seeing the bounty of beautiful zucchinis the farmer had grown, I knew that the only way to do justice on August 8th would be to celebrate with the colorful courgettes!

The prolific plant came to the U.S. most likely via Italian immigrants in the 1920s. Zucchini—which is more flavorful when it's small—is incredibly versatile. You can eat it raw, or you can grill, fry, steam, BBQ, sauté, bake, or roast it. It goes great *with* pasta or *as* a pasta replacement. (Seriously—slice it thin and use it as lasagna sometime!)

You can make stuffed zucchini boats, fritters or latkes, casseroles, bread, a classically French ratatouille, or you can use the yellow flower of the plant (*flor de calabaza*) in an authentic Mexican soup or quesadilla. My preferred way? On pizza! One of my favorite pizza joints in Maine makes a zucchini, summer squash, and spinach pie, and it's absolutely gorgeous-tasting.

And exactly how I plan on celebrating again today!

Today is also National Frozen Custard Day.

ZUKE CHIPS

Makes 1 or 2 servings

- 1 medium zucchini
- 1 cup sour cream
- 2 tablespoons taco seasoning
- 2 cups panko crumbs
- ¼ cup grated Parmesan cheese

Preheat the oven to 450°F.

Lightly grease a baking sheet and set it aside.

Slice the zucchini into ¼-inch slices and set them aside.

In one bowl, mix together the sour cream and the taco seasoning.

In a second bowl, mix together the panko crumbs and cheese.

Take a zucchini slice and dip it in the wet mixture so that it has a thin layer covering it completely. Place the wet zucchini slice in the dry mixture, covering the slice completely on both sides (pat the crumbs firmly onto the zucchini slice), and gently lay it onto the baking sheet. Repeat this process with the remaining zucchini slices. Bake for 30 minutes, or until the zucchini chips turn dark brown but are not burned. Use the leftover sour cream/taco seasoning mix as a dip, if so desired.

AUGUST 09 — NATIONAL RICE PUDDING DAY

"When they didn't give him boiled mutton, they gave him rice pudding, pretending it was a treat. And saved the butcher." —Charles Dickens, The Schoolboy's Story

Remember way back on March 2nd (page 76) when we discovered that banana cream pie was the favorite dessert among U.S. Armed Forces in a 1951 survey? Well, their *least* favorite dessert at the time was rice pudding. And I can understand why; generally, I'm averse to savory dishes that try to be desserts. Until today, the thought of rice pudding always made me cringe.

I like rice (especially when it's the bed to a curry duvet). I like pudding (homemade chocolate with a thick skin is what dreams are made of). But the two together just never made sense to me, probably because I never had a quality version before. A good rice pudding should be smooth and creamy like pudding (duh), but also have the chewy consistency of properly cooked rice. Crunchiness, stickiness, or soupiness are probably the reasons for my previous dislike!

And if you're still not feeling rice pudding, think of it this way: It's a dish that's long been associated with religion. It's believed that Buddha's final meal before enlightenment was a bowl of the stuff; and, in certain folklore, specifically Dutch and Flemish, rice pudding or porridge is given to people who go to heaven (and it's eaten with a golden spoon).

Kind of makes you look at the stuff in a whole new light, no?

NATIONAL S'MORES DAY

Buzz Lightyear: "Don't worry, Woody. In just a few hours you'll be sitting around a campfire with Andy making delicious hot Schmoes." Woody: "They're called s'mores, Buzz." —Toy Story

You can always tell what season it is based on how the shelves are stocked at a grocery store. Everything becomes quite pink, with an abundance of flowers and Champagne on sale, as we approach Valentine's Day; with the Super Bowl, trays and trays of party food like finger sandwiches, chips with dip, and football-shaped snacks appear throughout the store; and, with summer—much to the delight of most kids everywhere, because it signifies the end of school year and the beginning of staying up late—comes rows and rows of graham crackers, chocolates, and marshmallows.

Not having a campfire is no excuse not to celebrate this season's perfect dessert, either. You can still participate in this delightfully ooey, gooey sandwich by using a microwave (just be careful your marshmallow doesn't explode) or even an open candle (though a scented one might make your s'more slightly bizarre-tasting).

However you celebrate today—out in the woods or curled up on the couch—I hope it's one filled with wonderful childhood memories.

DID YOU KNOW?

The first mention of a s'more is in the 1927 publication of *Tramping and Trailing with the Girl Scouts.*

NATIONAL RASPBERRY BOMBE DAY

"Fruits each in its season, are the cheapest, most elegant and wholesome dessert you can offer your family or friends, at luncheon or tea. Pastry and plum pudding should be prohibited by law, from the beginning of June until the end of September." —Marion Harland, The Century

Have you had enough of our friend the raspberry, which we've now celebrated four times in the past twelve days? Well, don't despair, because this is the last we'll see of our bramble friend for some time. Besides, how could a day where you get to blow up your food not excite you?

Oh, there're no explosions happening today. A traditional bombe, or *bombe glacée*, is actually a layered, frozen dessert shaped in a spherical or dome-shaped mold. Typically it combines sherbet, ice cream, heavy cream, chopped nuts, candied fruit, and sometimes even a little alcohol (like rum or kirsch). Once it's all been layered and frozen, you're left with a beautiful, colorful dessert even the most burned-out-on-raspberries food lover would appreciate.

A little less exciting than some pyrotechnics, but it is what it is.

Hey, at least August is National Eat Dessert First Month! So use today as the perfect excuse for eating ice cream before (or as) every meal!

DID YOU KNOW?

Batology is the study of fruits in the bramble family, like raspberries.

Today is also National Raspberry Tart Day.

NATIONAL JULIENNE FRIES DAY

"You don't have to cook fancy or complicated masterpieces—just good food from fresh ingredients." —Julia Child

I think today just further proves the United States' love for junk food. Having a National French Fry Day about a month ago on July 13 just wasn't enough, so today we celebrate National *Julienne* Fries Day. Besides, what a joke of a cut regular, crinkle, curly, waffle, steak, home, or wedge fries are, right? They don't show supreme knife skills like julienning does, which is clearly the more sophisticated way to prepare small strips of potato you're going to then deep-fry and smother in ketchup, gravy and cheese, or salt and vinegar.

Who knows why today needed its own food holiday. Could it be because the world-famous golden-arched fast-food joint has made the cut fry iconic? Maybe it's to secretly celebrate those machines that chop, slice, and dice in one swift movement sold on three a.m. infomercials? Most likely we celebrate today because of just how delightfully easy it is to pick up these long, fun, crispy fries!

DID YOU KNOW?

Lachanophobia is the fear of vegetables.

Today is also National Toasted Almond Bar Day.

NATIONAL FILET MIGNON DAY

"If you're going to get a steak, make it a sirloin or filet mignon. They're the real cut above the rest." —Jayne Hurley

If someone lovingly calls you *ma petite mignon*, they're probably not referring to you being the cut of meat we're celebrating today. In the French culture, *mignon* actually means "cute/cutie" or even "dainty." I'm sure if filet mignon could talk, it would disagree with being called such a mushy term of endearment, as it's considered to be the King of Steaks. The meat, which comes from the tenderloin of beef (the length of area that runs parallel to both sides of the spine), is thought to be the most tender and expensive cut available.

So if you crave "melt-in-your-mouth" meat, this is the way to go.

For a serious flavor explosion, try topping your filet with a sauce like béarnaise, Cognac and cream, mustard, or even with blue cheese butter or Parmesan-garlic butter. Good side dishes include wild mushroom risotto, rice pilaf, butternut squash, steamed asparagus, baked potato with all the fixings, or a wedge salad.

After celebrating today, I'm not sure you'll be feeling so dainty afterward!

NATIONAL CREAMSICLE DAY

"Cream doesn't rise to the top, it works its way up." —Dutch proverb

When burly men approve of a girly drink, you know it's gonna be delicious. One summer at the liquor store, I came across some whipped cream–flavored vodka. The moment my fingers curled around the neck of the bottle, a pretty rugged-looking fellow appeared out of nowhere and said in crazed addict speed, "Doyouputorangesodainyours?" I blinked at him. "What?" He motioned to the vodka, "Orange soda. Do you put orange soda in yours? It makes it taste like a creamsicle." I am sure this is *not* one of the manliest things he's ever said.

Inspired by his vote of confidence, I decided to buy it. Another muscular, flannel shirt-wearing, bearded man got in line behind me. He tapped me on the shoulder and said, "I drink mine with orange soda. It's awesome." "So I've heard," I responded in amusement. After paying for my alcohol, I walked out to my car only to be harassed one more time by another grizzled, unassuming local guy who yelled across the parking lot, "Looks like you forgot the orange soda!"

So I bought some orange soda. I mixed it with the whipped cream vodka. And—wouldn't you know—it tasted just . . . like . . . a creamsicle!!!

Those men were right.

What they forgot to tell me is how smoothly the drink goes down. A little too smoothly. Like I-can't-feel-my-legs-anymore-because-of-how-many-of-these-drinks-I-gone-done-drank smoothly. So today I pay homage to the strange men who materialized out of nowhere to talk me into what they probably consider a very, very guilty pleasure drink.

DID YOU KNOW?

The 50/50 Ice Cream Bar is an alternative name for a Creamsicle.

AUGUST 15 — NATIONAL LEMON MERINGUE PIE DAY

"Our store is called The Pie Hole. As in shut your. Or in this case "open your" because it's real good." —Olive Snook, Pushing Daisies

When I was in my teens, I was fascinated with sweet yet tangy, creamy lemon meringue pie, mostly I think because of its height. (And as a vertically challenged youth, I was enamored with just about anything tall . . . still am, really!) It just seemed like when I ordered a piece I was actually getting twice as much pie than I would with other flavors. After the traditional layer of crust and filling (lemon curd in this instance), there was also an enormous tier of fluffy egg whites, too. Which led me to believe that if I wanted more bang for my buck, lemon meringue pie was definitely the way to go.

August 15th is also National Relaxation Day! So today is the perfect opportunity to take a break from everything that stresses us out and float away on a sweet, heavenly cloud of meringue-topped lemon pie!

DID YOU KNOW?

Elizabeth Coane Goodfellow is credited for introducing lemon meringue pie to America.

AUGUST 16 — NATIONAL RUM DAY

"There's naught, no doubt, so much the spirit calms as rum and true religion." —Lord Byron

Avast! It's time to let your inner pirate out: It's National Rum Day. (Too bad National Talk Like a Pirate Day isn't until September 19, eh?)

Rum is made from distilled sugarcane by-products (like molasses). And unlike many other types of liquor, there's no one universally defined set of regulated standards for its production (like we learned there is on National Tequila Day, July 24, and National Scotch Day, July 27). Different countries have different rules for it.

Since we've already celebrated the spirit a couple different ways this year, take the opportunity to enjoy it today in a way that perhaps isn't represented on the food and drink calendar (yet). You could make Bananas Foster, rum balls, rum raisin ice cream, or use it in a marinade. If you're dead-set on drinking, try a Bahama Mama, Dark and Stormy (drink an extra one for me, please!), Mojito, Hurricane, Zombie, or my personal favorite beachside drink: coconut-flavored rum in diet cola with as many maraschino cherries as the bartender will let me have!

So yo, ho, ho and a bottle of grog to you today, mateys!

Today is also National Bratwurst Day.

RUMBERRIES AND ICE CREAM

Makes 4 servings

Note: Part of this recipe needs to be refrigerated for 30 minutes.

   1 pint red raspberries
   ¼ cup dark spiced rum
   1 tablespoon honey
   1 pint chocolate ice cream

Place the berries in a bowl with an airtight cover and set them aside.

In a small bowl, whisk together the rum and honey until they are combined. Pour the rum mixture over the berries, cover the bowl, and put the bowl in the refrigerator for 30 minutes. After 30 minutes, gently flip the bowl of berries upside down and then right side up again to coat them completely with the rum mixture. Return the berries to the refrigerator to chill for an additional 30 minutes.

Scoop the ice cream into four serving dishes. Remove the berries from the refrigerator, drain them (saving the liquor for drinks, if you want), and spoon them onto the ice cream. Serve immediately.

NATIONAL VANILLA CUSTARD DAY

"The belly rules the mind." —Spanish proverb

Custard, the thicker cousin to pudding (and not the Civil War general), has been around since Medieval days when it was used in pies and tarts. When you think about how it's used today, you'll notice that tried-and-true concept hasn't changed much—it's found in crème brûlée, trifles, flan, éclairs, or the classiest (and my favorite) way of all: inside doughnuts.

Did you know that vanilla is one of the most expensive spices there is? That's because it's so labor intensive to cultivate. (Seriously, have you ever purchased vanilla beans? When I made today's food holiday, just two of them cost me twelve dollars! As a diehard chocoholic that certainly made me view vanilla in an entirely new, respect-filled light!)

If it's exceptionally hot out and you didn't get the chance to celebrate National Frozen Custard Day back on August 8 (page 253), why not combine the two today? There are very few things in life that taste quite as exquisite as dense, velvety, *rich* (as just learned) frozen custard in any flavor!

DID YOU KNOW?

The Aztecs called vanilla *tlilxóchitl*, which meant "black flower."

NATIONAL ICE CREAM PIE DAY

"Everyone likes pie. But people like pie à la mode even better. In the pie of life, arts is the ice cream." —Peter Krause

I was under some bizarre impression that ice cream pie was ridiculously difficult to construct. In my mind, it was a time-consuming process with lots of layers and ingredients and melting and stickiness and frustration (much like I imagine making a baked Alaska or bombe glacée from scratch is like).

And then I realized it didn't have to be so complicated—ice cream, after all, never should be. I could just toss some (ginger and caramel-flavored) ice cream into a premade (graham cracker) pie shell and call it good. So that's what I did. And y'know what? Not only was it a less messy way to eat ice cream, but it also came out *awesome*.

I'm glad simplicity still tastes so darn good this deep into eating the year.

With so many different ice cream and piecrust options available now, what will your flavor combination be?

DID YOU KNOW?

One of the major ingredients in ice cream is actually air.

Today is also National Soft Serve Day.

NATIONAL HOT AND SPICY FOOD DAY

"My favorite time of day is to get up and eat leftovers from dinner, especially spicy food." —David Byrne

Today you shouldn't be saying anything but "My mouth is on fire," or "Please, pass the milk," or *"Why did I do this to myself?!"* It's all about hot and spicy foods, whether that's salsa, hot wings, kimchi, jerk chicken, or vindaloo.

In my opinion, life is a lot like food: It's better when it's spicier, not saltier. After all, capsaicin (the chemical compound that makes peppers hot as we learned on January 16, International Hot and Spicy Food Day, page 24) can improve digestion and also lower blood pressure. Too much salt, on the other hand, can make you retain fluid—which keeps in the very stuff you should be expelling from your body to stay healthy and balanced.

I don't know about you, but I'd rather live a life that's clean of crap; one where I can breathe deeply and deal with everything thrown at me calmly.

Spice. Not salt.

Here's to a happy National Hot and Spicy Food Day every day of the year!

Today is also National Potato Day.

THE SECRET SWEET POTATO RECIPE

Makes 6 to 8 side servings

2 (20- to 24-ounce) cans sweet potatoes, drained

½ cup light brown sugar, packed

½ teaspoon nutmeg

½ cup (1 stick) unsalted butter, cut into chunks

1 teaspoon vanilla extract

Place the sweet potatoes in a large microwave-safe bowl. Sprinkle the brown sugar and nutmeg on top of the potatoes. Place the butter on top of the brown sugar. Place the bowl (uncovered) in the microwave and cook for 5 minutes. Remove the bowl, gently run a knife through the sweet potatoes to make the pieces smaller, stir everything, and cook for another 5 minutes.

Remove the bowl from the microwave, add the vanilla, and mash the sweet potatoes to a consistency of your liking.

NATIONAL LEMONADE DAY

"I believe that if life gives you lemons, you should make lemonade. And try to find someone whose life gives them vodka, and have a party." —Ron White, Blue Collar Comedy Tour Rides Again

Every summer, kids all over the United States learn entreprenural skills by continuing the deep-rooted custom of starting lemonade stands in their neighborhoods.

Let me rephrase that: *Some* kids in *some* parts of the country will start a lemonade stand while others will get an early dose of what governmental red tape feels like, because it's actually now illegal in certain parts of the U.S. to start a lemonade stand. Unless, that is, you *pay* for a permit to do so and/or register with the city clerk's office for an employer identification number. Even then, you may *still* need to receive permission from your local Department of Health and Human Services. And, for some states, taking a certified food protection course is required, too.

Since I wasn't able to break the law and buy some of that street-grade lemonade (let's make it sound as thuggish as some local governments make it out to be), I asked some friends what they do when they want to get a fix. The resounding answer was: Sweeten your lemonade with maple syrup.

My advice to you is the same (if you, too, are being prevented by The Man from a refreshing-drink-for-twenty-five-cents-style transaction on someone's front lawn). You will not be disappointed by the flavors. It's mellow and tastes both sweet and tart in the most natural way possible.

Today is also National Chocolate Pecan Pie Day.

PINK LEMONADE OF LOVE

Makes 2 to 4 drinks

1 cup lemon juice
$^2/_3$ cup organic pure maple syrup
2 teaspoons grenadine

In a pitcher, combine the lemon juice and 3 cups of water. Pour in the maple syrup and whisk vigorously until completely blended, then whisk in the grenadine. Refrigerate the lemonade until cold and serve it over ice.

Tip! Juice from the little plastic lemon-shaped bottles works just as well as the fresh stuff!

- -

AUGUST 21 — NATIONAL SPUMONI DAY

"Seize the moment. Remember all those women on the Titanic who waved off the dessert cart." —Erma Bombeck

Spumoni—a molded Italian frozen dessert made (usually) from layers of chocolate, pistachio, and cherry gelato, whipped cream, nuts, and candied fruit—hails from Naples, Italy. And the U.S. isn't the only one who loves this treat, either. Canada celebrates National Spumoni Day on November 13.

Close to ten years ago, I got an ice-cream maker; I've used it only a handful of times. While it's incredibly easy to use, it can be time-consuming (and expensive) to make good ice cream from scratch. But today seemed like the absolute perfect opportunity to bring it out, dust it off, and make my very first batch of spumoni. Sweet cherry-flavored ice cream with whole chunks of creamy chocolate and salty pistachios?

I may or may not have eaten the entire thing by myself.

NATIONAL EAT A PEACH DAY

"In Hollywood, the women are all peaches. It makes one long for an apple occasionally." —William Somerset Maugham

It may seem like there are a lot of peach-related food holidays. That's because there are! This drupe (or "stone fruit," so named because of the fleshy meat encasing a hard seed) originated in China, but over centuries it has become a staple part of our own country's agriculture. So much so that in 1982 President Ronald Reagan declared—in Proclamation 4947—that July should be National Peach Month. Somehow that celebration eventually migrated into August as well. That just further proves how passionate we are about peaches!

I don't usually go out of my way to buy whole peaches; they aren't one of my favorite fruits. Truthfully, they fall somewhere in the middle of my preferred produce. However, I do think they are absolutely exceptional in savory recipes, like marinades for ribs or when grilled in salads with tangy cheeses, in chutneys that top curried chicken or—my favorite—in spicy salsa! The heat and sweet from the salsa and salt from the tortilla chip is definitely a unique mouthgasm!

Today is also National Pecan Torte Day.

HEATED PEACH SALSA

Makes about 2 cups

- 1 small yellow onion, peeled and quartered
- 1 garlic clove, peeled
- 1 jalapeño pepper, stem cut off, cut in half, seeds optional
- 1 tablespoon lemon juice
- ¼ teaspoon red pepper flakes
- 1 pint grape tomatoes, cut in halves
- 1 large peach, pitted, chopped into small pieces

Place the onion, garlic, jalapeño pepper, lemon juice, pepper flakes, and tomatoes into a food processor and pulse until the mixture is of a consistency to your liking. Empty the contents into an airtight container and fold in the peaches. Cover the container and refrigerate at least 2 hours. Serve with tortilla chips, veggies, or grilled with cheese on flour tortillas. This salsa may be kept in the refrigerator for up to 2 weeks.

NATIONAL SPONGE CAKE DAY

"Let's all go have some sponge cake and a little wine . . . " —Inspector Kemp, Young Frankenstein

Sponge cake seems simple enough; it's made from three basic ingredients: sugar, flour, and eggs. But those three items show up together in loads of different foods, so where does a sponge cake get its, well, *spongy* texture? It's all about the wrist, baby. The method of properly beating the batter needs to be just right so that it becomes aerated enough to give the cake its famous fluffy, light texture in the mouth feel. I must not have been patient enough when I was making mine, because it came out quite sticky. Still delicious (aren't most cakes delicious regardless if they come out perfectly or not?), especially slathered with orange marmalade and whipped cream!

If you, too, feel like getting your inner queen (or king) on today, celebrate with Victoria Sponge Cake. It's made with sponge cake layered with a thick spread of jam (like strawberry) and dusted with caster sugar. It was one of Queen Victoria's favorite afternoon teatime snacks. With a cuppa and some quiet time, it could quickly become yours, too!

AUGUST 24

NATIONAL WAFFLE DAY

"He sent her sweetened wine and well-spiced ale and waffles piping hot out of the fire." —Geoffrey Chaucer, The Canterbury Tales

National Waffle Day falls almost halfway between International Waffle Day each year. (Or does International Waffle Day fall almost halfway between National Waffle Day each year? Hm, something to ponder over a big stack of waffles topped with whipped cream and strawberries, maple syrup, or fried chicken, me thinks!)

Today celebrates the first U.S. waffle iron patent, received on August 24, 1869, by New York native Cornelius Swarthout. Wait . . . people actually *make* their own waffles? Get outta here! I mean, why bother when I can get them out of a box in a variety of different ways including mini, multigrain, (if that's not enough) seven-grain, blueberry, strawberry, buttermilk, chocolate chip, cinnamon—you name it!

(Okay, okay, homemade *always* tastes better; I agree. But sometimes a frozen waffle product just reminds you of your childhood, no?)

DID YOU KNOW?

The waffle cone made its world debut at the World's Fair in St. Louis in 1904.

Today is also National Peach Pie Day.

AUGUST 25

NATIONAL WHISKEY SOUR DAY

"What whiskey will not cure, there is no cure for." —Irish proverb

Whiskey sours are an excellent combination of girly-meets-manly drink. The sour mix, or lemon and simple syrup combination if you're drinking a truly authentic version (some folks even add egg whites, but that seems entirely unappealing to me), softens the sometimes painful bite of whiskey. Friends tell me this is the perfect drink for ladies to show they've got a tough side, and for fellas to show they have a sensitive side.

For me, my go-to drink as a freshly turned twenty-one-year-old was an amaretto sour. That, however, quickly led to whiskey sours, which ended up being my gateway drink to having a torrid love affair with straight-up Jack Daniel's—who, by the way, is not an easy man to love; our relationship was so tumultuous that we eventually had to part ways. Though once in a while, like on nights like tonight, we meet up and reminisce about the good old days.

As you can well imagine, tonight was one of those nights.

Walk of shame tomorrow (to my bathroom, that is)? You betcha!

Chin, chin! (To your health!)

Today is also National Banana Split Day.

AUGUST 26

NATIONAL CHERRY POPSICLE DAY

"He who likes cherries soon learns to climb." —German proverb

Around the time that I celebrated National Cherry Popsicle Day the first time, I had been put on some pretty rugged medicine that had severe dry mouth as a side effect. My doctor told me that other patients found sucking on lollipops helped them deal with it. But the only thing that seemed to satiate me was ice cubes.

But that seemed so drab and depressing that

I started calling them water popsicles! So to celebrate today, I placed halved cherries in an ice cube tray, filled each tray with some black cherry sparkling water, and froze it. Talk about mouthwatering: These cheap, simple, and refreshing cherry-flavored (water) popsicles were absolute lifesavers (and tasted mighty fine in some adult beverages, too)!

Cherries themselves are pretty impressive fruits. Among their awesome health properties, the tart version of the fruit contains naturally occurring melatonin, making them—for some people—an awesome natural sleep aid!

So whether you're trying to relax before bed, keep hydrated, or simply want to enjoy a childhood favorite icy treat, today's food holiday might be perfect for you.

DID YOU KNOW?

There are roughly 7,000 cherries on an average cherry tree.

AUGUST 27

NATIONAL BANANA LOVER'S DAY

"Intellectual property has the shelf life of a banana." —Bill Gates

"Can I have one?" a tourist wearing a cliché Hawaiian shirt asked, randomly approaching me as I sat on a bench in the park making peanut butter and banana sandwiches.

"Um . . . no. They're for me and my boyfriend," I remarked, defensively placing my hands over the sandwiches in fear that he might just help himself.

"Is your boyfriend Elvis or something?" he asked sarcastically, sneering at me before angrily storming off to rejoin his wife, who had her nose buried in a map of the city.

"What was that?" my then boyfriend asked, having just come out of the coffee shop after purchasing us a double chocolate soy latte. (What better drink to go with our sandwiches, am

I right?) I shrugged nonchalantly, "I almost got jumped for our lunch." Picking up a sandwich and taking a bite, he smiled playfully, "Just another day in the life, right?"

Actually, it was *the* most bizarre and one of the most memorable moments I had while eating the year. But I can say with absolute certainty after celebrating today: Banana lovers are serious about loving bananas. It's no wonder this food holiday exists!

Today is also National Pot de Crème Day.

SPICY 'NANAWICHES

Makes 2 sandwiches

Note: Part of this recipe needs to be refrigerated overnight.

¼ cup orange marmalade

¼ to ½ teaspoon chili powder

4 slices multigrain bread

1 large banana, peeled and sliced

½ small lemon

The day before:

In a small bowl, mix the orange marmalade with the chili powder (¼ teaspoon if you want it a little less hot, ½ teaspoon if you want it a little more). Cover the bowl tightly and refrigerate it overnight.

The day of:

Remove the marmalade from the refrigerator, stir it, and set it aside.

Toast the bread. Spread half of the marmalade on two pieces of the toast and arrange half of the banana slices on the marmalade to cover. Give the lemon a bit of a squeeze onto the bananas, and then rub the lemon onto the two plain slices of toast. Close the sandwiches (lemon-rubbed pieces of toast-side down) and serve.

NATIONAL CHERRY TURNOVER DAY

"Happiness is a bowl of cherries and a book of poetry under a shade tree."
—Terri Guillemets

If you've been eating the year from the beginning, then you know that we've become quite familiar with both turnovers and cherries—the latter of which are represented multiple times throughout the food calendar year. But in case you need a quick refresher. . . .

Turnovers are a light pastry filled with something lovely like lemon curd, apples, or even something savory like chicken and cheese. They're cousins to the empanada, the pasty, the calzone, etc. And cherries, brought to the U.S. sometime in the seventeenth century, have high levels of antioxidants (which protect our bodies from free radicals that can wreak havoc on our immune systems, and may even cause cancer or heart disease).

Whenever my family makes cherry turnovers, we usually use premade crescent roll dough that we fill with cream cheese, a sprinkle of sugar, and a handful of chopped *fresh* cherries. It's definitely *not* a unique recipe by any means (I think most people have their own variation of this type of dessert), but it *is* delicious, flaky, buttery, velvety, and sweet. Accompanied with a good cup of coffee, additional fresh fruit on the side, and time spent with someone you love? It's a moment—and a food holiday—not to be missed.

DID YOU KNOW?

Cherry trees provide food for several species of caterpillars.

NATIONAL CHOP SUEY DAY

"Chop suey, chicken chop suey, it's so hard to beat thee, smell of soy, no bok choy, I'm so happy to eat thee!" —Grandpa, Hey Arnold!

In my family growing up, we knew three different versions of chop suey, and we differentiated them by the culture they came from:

Chinese chop suey—meaning "mixed/assorted pieces" or "odds and ends" in Cantonese, it's believed to be an *American*-Chinese dish of stir-fry vegetables, meat, maybe egg, and served on rice. In my experience, it's always been a little anemic-looking and abundantly salty.

American chop suey—elbow macaroni mixed with tomato sauce and ground beef (some people add green peppers, onions, or other veggies, too), topped with cheese. It seemed parents always made it in bathtub-size vats to feed all of the kids in my neighborhood.

French-Canadian chop suey—no doubt inspired by the American-Chinese version, is a mix of vegetables and meat tossed in a slow cooker for hours and served over a slice of white bread. My great grandmother passed her recipe down to my grandmother, who passed it down to my dad, who passed it down to me only recently.

This last kind was a very prevalent food in my formative years, and to this day reminds me of generations of my heritage. I know that today's food holiday probably wasn't created with our version in mind, but I like to pretend it was!

Today is also National Lemon Juice Day, National Swiss Winegrowers Day, National Whiskey Sour Day, and National More Herbs, Less Salt Day.

AUGUST 30

NATIONAL TOASTED MARSHMALLOW DAY

"Sarcastic people tend to be marshmallows underneath the armor."
—Stephen King, 11/22/63

On National Toasted Marshmallow Day while I was in the lengthy process of getting a new phone provider, a new phone, and a new number, the sales representative asked me what I did. I told him I was a food blogger (which was far more interesting at the time than my tremendously boring office day job) eating my way through the national food holidays.

He asked what food I was celebrating that night and when I told him, he smiled really big and said, "I'm actually one of the world's best marshmallow-toasters. You know the trick? You build a fire . . . I like to do mine in a log cabin fashion. And you let it burn down real low. Then patiently . . . *very patiently* . . . you get that marshmallow golden. *Golden* is the key. It gets the very center gooey and makes the best s'mores ever."

And now you know the secret, too!

(But hey, if you like your marshmallows charred, there's nothing wrong with that, either!)

DID YOU KNOW?

Marshmallows were first used as a medicinal remedy for sore throats.

Today is also National Mai Tai Day.

NATIONAL EAT OUTSIDE DAY

"Too many of us take great pains with what we ingest through our mouths, and far less with what we partake of through our ears and eyes." —Brandon Sanderson, The Way of Kings

Wait, what? It's already the end of August? How exactly did that happen?!

While you're trying to figure out where summer went, I suggest you take the opportunity today to eat outside. Especially if you haven't done so yet this season since, for many of us, this might be the last chance to do so until next year!

And you don't necessarily have to do anything elaborate or even really go out of your way to celebrate today's "food" holiday. If it happens to fall on a weekday and you're stuck at work, why not take your lunch break outside? I've always believed that fresh air cleans out the mental cobwebs—you might find you go back to work refreshed! Or if

you haven't had a BBQ yet, you could always invite friends or family over tonight to do so.

Don't feel like cooking? Why not take advantage of the outdoor seating many restaurants have during the nicer times of the year? Few things are as pleasant as being waited on and enjoying dusk at the same time. And don't count out food trucks! Some of the best grub I have ever eaten has come out of the windows of portable restaurants. And there's nothing like grabbing a slice, a sandwich, a kebab, a cupcake, whatever, and strolling through the streets you love.

Today is also National Trail Mix Day.

MOUTH PARTY CHICKEN SALAD

Makes 2 servings

1 medium boneless, skinless chicken breast, cooked and cut into cubes

1 cup red seedless grapes, halved

¾ cup pistachios, divided

½ cup dried cranberries

¼ cup crumbled blue cheese

4 to 6 tablespoons mayonnaise

½ teaspoon celery salt

½ teaspoon black pepper

In a medium bowl, combine the chicken, grapes, ½ cup of pistachios, cranberries, and blue cheese. Gently stir in the mayonnaise—4 tablespoons for a dryer chicken salad or 6 tablespoons for a wetter salad. Stir in the celery salt and pepper, and chill in the refrigerator for 1 hour. Place the salad in two bowls, top with the remaining ¼ cup of pistachios, and serve.

Tip! Wanna make this veg-friendly? Instead of chicken, use 1 (8-ounce) package of tempeh. Sauté the tempeh in 1 tablespoon of olive oil, until golden-brown on all sides, before using it in the recipe.

SEPTEMBER IS...

01 National Cherry Popover Day / 279
02 National Blueberry Popsicle Day / 280
03 National Welsh Rarebit Day / 281
04 National Macadamia Nut Day / 282
05 National Cheese Pizza Day / 283
06 National Coffee Ice Cream Day / 285
07 National Beer Lover's Day / 286
08 National Date-Nut Bread Day / 287
09 National Wiener Schnitzel Day / 288
10 National TV Dinner Day / 289
11 National Hot Cross Bun Day / 289
12 National Chocolate Milkshake Day / 290
13 National Peanut Day / 291
14 National Cream-Filled Doughnut Day / 293
15 National Linguine Day / 294
16 National Guacamole Day / 295
17 National Apple Dumpling Day / 297
18 National Cheeseburger Day / 298
19 National Butterscotch Pudding Day / 299
20 National (Rum) Punch Day / 301
21 National Pecan Cookie Day / 302
22 National White Chocolate Day / 303
23 Great American Pot Pie Day / 304
24 National Cherries Jubilee Day / 304
25 National Food Service Employees Day / 305
26 National Pancake Day / 306
27 National Chocolate Milk Day / 308
28 National Drink Beer Day / 309
29 National Coffee Day / 310
30 National Hot Mulled Cider Day / 311

SEPTEMBER IS ALSO...

National 5-A-Day Month
National Apple Month
National All-American Breakfast Month
National Better Breakfast Month
National Biscuit Month
National Bourbon Heritage Month
National Chicken Month
National Cholesterol Education Month
National Ethnic Foods Month
National Hazelnut Month
National Honey Month
National Ice Cream Sandwich Month
National Mushroom Month
National Organic Harvest Month
National Potato Month
National Rice Month
National Whole Grains Month

. . .

Thursday before Labor Day—National Cabernet Day
Saturday before Labor Day—International Bacon Day
3rd Saturday—International Eat an Apple Day
Last Wednesday—World School Milk Day

NATIONAL CHERRY POPOVER DAY

"One must ask children and birds how cherries and strawberries taste."
—Johann Wolfgang von Goethe

If you're eating the year, you know that our country is particularly fond of the cherry. And why wouldn't we appreciate the little fruit as much as we do? After all, thanks to George Washington, cherry trees stand as a representation of how much more important the truth is over material goods.

Cherries—a stone fruit similar to peaches, plums, and even almonds—are not only delicious, but also have some pretty great health benefits. Not only do they help our immune systems because of their high levels of antioxidants, but they also contain melatonin; so the next time you're hoping for some restful sleep, trying drinking a glass of tart cherry juice!

If you want to spice things up a little, instead of celebrating with cherries the fruit—why not celebrate with cherry *tomatoes* instead? A rosemary, Gruyère, and cherry tomato popover could be an amazing and unique way to commemorate today's food holiday. Sweet or savory—make sure you pop a popover into your mouth today!

DID YOU KNOW?

In 1912, Japan sent the U.S. 3,020 cherry trees—or *sakura*—as a gesture of goodwill and friendship.

NATIONAL BLUEBERRY POPSICLE DAY

"The sharper is the berry, the sweeter is the wine." —Proverb

Today's (in my opinion) appropriately placed food holiday is bittersweet; it's one of the last summery treats we celebrate before we transition into autumn. And what better way to do so than with one of the season's favorite fruits and refreshers? Besides, the blueberry popsicle is often so outshined by cherry, grape, orange, lime, and even root beer–flavored ones, that it's nice that the brilliantly blue-colored version gets an entire day dedicated to it!

Popsicles (the actual brand, not just the term most people use for all ice pops) were accidentally created in 1905 by Frank Epperson, an eleven-year-old boy who left a stick in his drink overnight. When he discovered it the next morning, the drink was frozen, but he was able to use the stick to pull it out, hold it, and lick it! He called his ingenious invention Epsicles. In the early 1920s, Epperson patented the idea, changed the named to Popsicle, and sold the rights to the Joe Lowe Company based in New York.

I have no doubt that Epperson would have celebrated today; and I'm sure he would have been delighted that we celebrate his novelty three separate times during the year!

DID YOU KNOW?

Maine is the largest producer of wild blueberries in the world.

SEPTEMBER 03

NATIONAL WELSH RAREBIT DAY

"Many's the long night I've dreamed of cheese—toasted, mostly." —Robert Louis Stevenson, Treasure Island

Welsh rarebit, or Welsh rabbit, has nothing to do with bunnies (mine was breathing a sigh of relief today). Actually, it's toast topped with a savory, thick cheese sauce. In this day and age, it's usually made from Cheddar mixed with beer or wine and other ingredients like spices, mustard, or Worcestershire sauce. Food folklore suggests the ironic name is actually an insult that originated in the seventeenth or eighteenth century: While rabbit was poor man's food in England, cheese was the poorer man's option in Wales because they couldn't afford *any* meat.

Even now, the third Monday of January in the U.K. (and elsewhere in the world) is considered Blue Monday; it's seen as the most depressing day of the year (crap weather + lack of daylight hours + debt from Christmas = utter gloominess). Collier's Powerful Welsh Cheddar declared that Blue Monday should also be the U.K.'s National Welsh Rarebit Day, because it's seen as such a satisfying comfort food. (Which, we know, is the perfect thing to eat when you're feeling particularly gloomy!)

You can celebrate Welsh Rarebit Day a variety of ways. Buck Rarebit has a poached egg either on top of or beneath the cheese; blending the cheese sauce with tomato soup makes the dish a Blushing Bunny; and a Hot Brown (even less traditional than the other two options) adds turkey and bacon to the recipe.

NATIONAL MACADAMIA NUT DAY

"Worldly riches are like nuts; many a tooth is broke in cracking them, but never is the stomach filled with eating them." —Rabbi Nachman of Breslov

We all have a food we splurge on once in a while, whether it's because of its high-calorie content or high price. For me, macadamia nuts are hands-down one of my favorite foods. I love the way they're so creamy that they practically melt in your mouth while not having that same grainy texture other nuts do. Unfortunately, because of how ridiculously expensive they are, I only get to indulge on them a couple times a year. Make that a *few* times a year now that I know about National Macadamia Nut Day.

Indigenous to Australia, macadamia trees can produce nuts for over one hundred years! While the Aborigines had been eating the nuts for centuries, they were first classified in the late 1800s by botanist Ferdinand von Mueller. He named them after his friend and colleague Dr. John Macadam.

Celebrate today by creaming your macadamia nuts into a vegan nut cheese, grinding them up to use as a crust on fish or a pork tenderloin, using them in a stuffing or a butter, or tossing them into your baked goods for a little extra pizzazz.

Today is also National Eat an Extra Dessert Day and World Chocolate Day.

MACLLDAMIA CAKE (MACADAMIA + APPLE!)

Makes 8 to 12 servings

- ½ cup applesauce
- 1 cup brown sugar, packed
- 2 large eggs
- 1 teaspoon vanilla extract
- 1½ cups all-purpose flour
- 1 teaspoon apple pie spice
- ½ teaspoon baking powder
- ½ teaspoon baking soda
- 1 medium green apple, cored, peeled, chopped (about 1 cup)
- 1 cup macadamia nuts, chopped
- Goat's milk caramel sauce, for topping (optional)

Preheat the oven to 350°F.

Spray an 8 x 8-inch baking pan with nonstick cooking or baking spray. Set it aside.

In a large bowl, cream together the applesauce, brown sugar, eggs, and vanilla.

In a small bowl, combine the flour, apple pie spice, baking powder, and baking soda.

Add the dry ingredients gradually to the wet ingredients, and then stir in the apples and macadamia nuts. Mix well. Spread the batter into the pan and bake for 50 minutes, or until a toothpick inserted comes out clean and dry.

Allow the cake to cool completely in the pan. Cut into eight or twelve pieces and serve topped with goat's milk caramel sauce or even caramel sea salt ice cream.

SEPTEMBER 05 · NATIONAL CHEESE PIZZA DAY

"The perfect lover is one who turns into a pizza at four a.m." —Charles Pierce

Growing up, my birthday parties were always held at a local pizza parlor. You've never met a kid who loved cheese pizza as much as I did. But then I became a know-it-all, hormonally charged, gastronomically rebellious teenager and decided that I *loathed* pizza. I refused to touch the stuff for over six years, and it drove my parents, my friends, and my friends' parents all crazy. Seriously, what kid doesn't eat pizza?

I'm thrilled that I can say it was just a phase; a stupid, nonsensical phase that lasted far too long, and I'm doing everything I can now to make up for it. My relationship with cheese pizza is healthier than ever. Sometimes I wonder if maybe we don't love each other too much. But you know what they say: If you love something, set it free. And if it comes back to you, then it's yours.

This love? This girl-on-pizza love? It was *always* meant to be.

HOMEMADE CHEESE 'ZA

Makes 1 pizza, 4 servings

Note: This dough takes 1½ hours to prepare before baking.

Crust:

- 1 envelope dry yeast
- 1 teaspoon granulated sugar
- 3 cups all-purpose flour
- 1 teaspoon salt
- 2 tablespoons unsalted butter, at room temperature

Sauce:

- 1 (12-ounce) can tomato sauce
- 1 teaspoon dried oregano
- 1 teaspoon dried parsley
- ½ teaspoon garlic powder
- 1 (8-ounce) bag shredded mozzarella cheese (about 2 cups)

After baking:

- ½ cup Thousand Island dressing
- 2 tablespoons grated Parmesan cheese
- 1 teaspoon crushed red pepper flakes

Preheat the oven to 350°F.

Grease a baking sheet and set it aside.

With a fork, gently mix together 1½ cups of warm water, the yeast, and sugar in a small bowl. Set the bowl aside for 15 minutes.

In a large bowl, mix the flour, salt, and butter together—this will be crumbly. Gradually stir in the yeast mixture until a ball of dough forms. Let the dough sit in the bowl, covered with a dry kitchen towel, for 1 hour and 10 minutes. Remove the dough from the bowl and put it in the middle of the baking sheet. Using your fingers, spread the dough out from the center to the edges until the dough has been stretched out over the entire baking sheet without springing back toward the middle.

When the dough is stretched and in place, cover it with the tomato sauce, oregano, parsley, and garlic powder. Top the pizza with the cheese and bake for 30 to 40 minutes, checking the bottom to make sure the crust doesn't burn. When the pizza's finished baking, slather it evenly with the Thousand Island dressing, and then top it with the Parmesan cheese and red pepper flakes. Cut and serve.

SEPTEMBER 06 — NATIONAL COFFEE ICE CREAM DAY

"I had always thought that once you grew up you could do anything you wanted—stay up all night or eat ice cream straight out of the container." —Bill Bryson

I can be a huge coffee snob; my friends have even been known to call me a high-maintenance customer because of my sometimes extraordinarily long and complicated coffee orders. But while I love a good cup of coffee, I'm not always a huge coffee ice cream fan. Unless there's giant chunks of ooey, gooey chocolate brownie in it, then I guess it's okay. Or caramel swirls. Or alcohol. Those all improve the flavor of just about anything.

Now that I think about it, coffee ice cream is also pretty awesome as an afternoon pick-me-up. When I celebrated today's food holiday, I was fortunate enough to walk out of my office at noon, arrive at the closest ice cream place at 12:04 p.m., and eat a scoop of coffee ice cream with Oreo cookie chunks in the park by 12:07 p.m. And it was sunny and muggy, making for the perfect end-of-summer and midday treat!

DID YOU KNOW?

Coffee is the second most traded commodity in the world after oil.

NATIONAL BEER LOVER'S DAY

"Give beer to those who are perishing, wine to those who are in anguish; let them drink and forget their poverty and remember their misery no more." —Proverbs, 31:6-7

I took up running the same year I decided to eat the national food holidays (which was one of my smarter ideas looking back, given all the calories I was consuming). I'm (still) awful at running, but I love doing it. One night, after going on a four-mile loop around the cove in my city, a friend and I stopped at a bar. Some guy she knew was there, and he offered to buy me a drink. Believe it or not, this never happens to me so I jumped at the opportunity to take him up on it. However, he was completely hammered when he asked, so I thought the polite move would be to order what the rest of his party seemed to be drinking—Allagash White (a locally crafted beer).

And it was more than just a mouthgasm—it was a *lifegasm*. I had never really been a beer fan until that moment. Never had I tasted such a beautiful, refreshing, flavorful, bubbly drink before! Dear drunk boy in the bar who couldn't figure out my name (probably because every time he asked me, I told him a different one): You changed my life that night.

So today, I toast you, good sir: Cheers! You made celebrating (and genuinely *wanting* to celebrate) today possible! You . . . made me . . . a beer lover!

DID YOU KNOW?

The phrase *rule of thumb* may have originated from brewers who used to use their thumbs to test the maturity of their beers.

Today is also National Acorn Squash Day, National Salami Day, and National Napoleon Day.

SEPTEMBER 08

NATIONAL DATE-NUT BREAD DAY

"If bread is the first necessity of life, recreation is a close second." —Edward Bellamy, Looking Backward

Did you know National Date-Nut Bread Day is actually celebrated twice in the year? It's true: It's celebrated today and on December 22 (page 411). You would think with *all* the other food options our melting pot of a country has to offer, we could've been a little more creative and not repeat any food holidays. But this particular bread is just so wildly popular and loved that it absolutely had to be celebrated twice!

Dates grow on palm trees, and the word comes from the Greek *dáktulos*, meaning "finger," which refers to the shape of the fruit. Because they've been part of our diets for so long, it's difficult to pinpoint their exact origin, though it's believed to have been in the Persian Gulf.

After celebrating yesterday's National Beer Lover's Day a little too excessively, I took the easy way out today and bought a quick bread mix from my local grocer, tossed some cinnamon-coated walnuts I had in with it, and *voilà!* National Date-Nut Bread Day part one complete!

DATE, NUT, AND FRIENDS BREAD

Makes one 9 x 9-inch loaf

3 cups all-purpose flour

3 tablespoons granulated sugar

4 teaspoons baking powder

½ teaspoon salt

½ cup macadamia nuts, coarsely chopped

2 ounces dark chocolate chips (about ½ cup)

½ cup dried dates, roughly chopped

1 (12-ounce) bottle Belgian-style wheat ale

½ cup candied orange peel (page 357-358)

Preheat the oven to 350°F.

Grease a 9 x 9-inch loaf pan and set it aside.

Mix together the flour, sugar, baking powder, salt, nuts, chocolate chips, and dates. Stir in the beer, one-third of the bottle at a time, until everything is incorporated and the dough is sticky. *Gently* fold in the orange peel so the sugar coating doesn't come off the peels.

Place the dough in the pan and bake the bread for roughly 50 minutes, or until a toothpick inserted in the middle comes out clean.

SEPTEMBER 09 — NATIONAL WIENER SCHNITZEL DAY

"There is no more sincere love than the love of food." —George Bernard Shaw

Whether you're celebrating today because you genuinely love the schnitz' or just love saying the words *wiener schnitzel* because they make you giggle, today is definitely a food holiday for carnivores. *Wiener schntizel* means "Viennese cutlet" in German. It's an Austrian comfort food that's traditionally made from a boneless veal cutlet that's pounded thin, breaded, deep-fried, and then served with potato salad or french fries and a lemon wedge.

Stateside, wiener schnitzel is often associated with hot dogs because of the fast-food chain of the same name (though it started in 1961 as *Der Wienerschnitzel*). They sell chili cheese dogs, bacon-wrapped dogs, corn dogs, cheeseburgers, pastrami sandwiches, chicken fingers, french fries, and even jalapeño poppers.

However, if you were hoping to celebrate National Wiener Schnitzel Day squared (y'know, eating schnitzel at the chain itself), note that the restaurant doesn't actually sell the stuff!

Today is also National I Love Food Day and National Steak au Poivre Day.

NATIONAL TV DINNER DAY

"Who bothers to cook TV dinners? I suck them frozen." —Woody Allen

There's been such a negative stigma about TV dinners in the past. Stereotypically, the media has portrayed them as food you eat when you're too busy to eat real food, *or*—worse than that—you eat them because you're alone and have become entirely defeated by life; the only energy you can muster to feed yourself is to throw a prepackaged frozen block of undistinguishable food into the microwave and eat it disinterestedly in front of your TV or computer screen while mentally running through the events of your life, wondering what could have prevented the moment you're in.

How depressing.

In reality, TV dinners have evolved quite a bit since they were originally created. Actually, they've become quite fashionable and a sign of a smart person on-the-go. Because, for an extremely reasonable price, you can now have *any* kind of meal you want whether that's vegetarian, vegan, organic, soy-free, lactose-free, GMO-free, carb-conscious, low-sodium, or low-calorie within mere minutes!

So grab a TV dinner, turn on your favorite show, and hunker down on the couch! Celebrating a food holiday doesn't get much easier, does it?

NATIONAL HOT CROSS BUN DAY

"We have no right to luxuries while the poor want bread." —Thomas Day

Hot cross buns are sweet rolls made with spices and raisins or currants. They're marked with a cross on the top, usually in white icing, which is thought to represent the crucifixion of Jesus. Served toasted with a little butter, jam, or honey, they're traditionally eaten on Good Friday.

But that was six months ago.

(It makes no sense, I know. Then again, by now

I'm sure you've noticed that the timing of many food holidays doesn't make much sense. So just go with it!)

Apparently, the hot cross bun has a tremendous number of superstitions surrounding it too, including:

- Buns baked on Good Friday won't go bad during the next year.
- Buns can be used for medicinal purposes; they help a sick person get better.
- If you carry a hot cross bun on a boat, it'll protect you against a shipwreck.
- If you hang one in your kitchen, it will protect your home against fire.
- And if you share a bun with another person and chant "Half for you and half for me, between us two shall goodwill be" you'll have enduring friendship . . . or at least until the next Good Friday (or National Hot Cross Bun Day)!

SEPTEMBER 12 — NATIONAL CHOCOLATE MILKSHAKE DAY

"The only emperor is the emperor of ice-cream." —Wallace Stevens, "The Emperor of Ice-Cream"

Aren't we lucky that we're not celebrating today's food holiday back in the 1800s when a milkshake was an eggnog-like drink made from whiskey and eggs—anybody else make an "eww gross" face at the thought of that combination? Thankfully, in the early twentieth century it evolved into the drink we know it as today.

Though if you want to celebrate today in the seriously old-fashioned way and try to recreate that eggy alcoholic beverage, then kudos to you! That's taking your food holidays very seriously indeed!

For some strange reason, despite the simplicity of a milkshake, it's an art form I just can't seem to master. They always come out either too runny or like cement. After the subpar vanilla milkshake I made back in June, I knew that today I wanted to take myself out on a date for one. (Which is sort of like the modern, independent woman's version of the classic image of a single milkshake with two straws for couples going steady back in the 1950s.) A local artisanal gelato shop in my town makes these deliriously good pazzo shakes, and today I had one with dark chocolate *sorbetto* and soy milk. It was thick and creamy, and I was thankful I didn't have to share any with a letter jacket–wearing stud!

SEPTEMBER 13

NATIONAL PEANUT DAY

"If you can't control your peanut butter, you can't expect to control your life."
—Bill Watterson, The Authoritative Calvin and Hobbes

Peanuts, specifically peanut butter, have been around longer than you might think. It's believed that the Aztecs actually mashed peanuts into a thick paste. I'm not sure what they were doing with it or eating it with, but I'm guessing it wasn't one of the following ways: peanut butter and jelly sandwiches; peanut butter and banana sandwiches; peanut butter, bacon, and honey sandwiches; peanut butter and chocolate anything; peanut butter and apples; peanut butter and pretzels; peanut butter and tuna fish sandwiches; peanut butter and cheese; and peanut butter in celery topped with raisins.

Been there, done that on all of these combinations. And let me just say, despite what you might think: mega noms.

Peanuts are also excellent for your heart. They're jacked full of monounsaturated fats that can lower the risk of heart disease and reduce cholesterol. Unless, that is, you're eating them salted at one of those restaurants that let you throw the shells on the floor. (I know I'm supposed to do this at places like that, but—c'mon now—my momma raised me better than that.)

So many options to celebrate this super food today . . . how will you?

Today is also International Chocolates Day, National Fortune Cookie Day, National Snack a Pickle Day, and National Cachaça Day (Brazil).

SPICY THAI PASTA SALAD

Makes 4 dinner servings or 8 side servings

Note: This dish needs to be refrigerated for at least 2 hours (or overnight) before serving.

- 1 (16-ounce) box tricolored rotini
- 1 small to medium zucchini, washed and cut into small chunks (1½ to 2 cups)
- 1 small to medium summer squash, washed and cut into small chunks (1½ to 2 cups)
- 1 (8-ounce) bar Colby Jack cheese, cubed
- 1 (12-ounce) jar or bottle of Thai spicy peanut sauce, divided

Boil the pasta according to package directions.

While the pasta is cooking, place the zucchini, summer squash, and cheese in a large bowl.

When the pasta has cooked to your preferred tenderness, drain it well and add it to the bowl of vegetables. Add half the peanut sauce and toss to coat. Refrigerate for a couple of hours or overnight.

Prior to serving, mix in the remaining sauce for additional heat and spice.

Tip! This dish works both as a hot potluck-style dish or a cold salad for an end-of-summer picnic!

SEPTEMBER 14 — NATIONAL CREAM-FILLED DOUGHNUT DAY

"Mr. Scorpio says productivity is up 2 percent, and it's all because of my motivational techniques, like doughnuts and the possibility of more doughnuts to come."
—Homer, The Simpsons

One of the foods I've been enjoying nearly my entire life is the cream-filled doughnut. While jelly-filled doughnuts definitely have their place in the food kingdom, in my opinion nothing beats fried dough filled with cold, silky cream. According to my mom, when I was in my "doh-doh" (that's kid lingo for *doughnuts*) phase, she would take me to the local bakery to get one chocolate cream-filled doughnut and one regular cream-filled doughnut. She'd cut them in half so we could each enjoy a side. I, however, would squish the two halves together to make one perfect doughnut.

"You did a helluva job, but it was so messy that after a few times you decided to just get a Boston cream because to you it tasted exactly the same. Just with less mess," my mom explained. "Personally, I don't think cream-filled doughnuts and Boston cream doughnuts taste anything alike, but try telling that to a determined three-year-old!"

How could I not celebrate with a Boston cream doughnut today? And to be honest, I didn't even know the aforementioned story until *after* I had purchased one!

DID YOU KNOW?

Per capita, Canadians consume the most doughnuts.

Today is also National Eat a Hoagie Day.

NATIONAL LINGUINE DAY

"Tomatoes and oregano make it Italian; wine and tarragon make it French. Sour cream makes it Russian; lemon and cinnamon make it Greek. Soy sauce makes it Chinese; garlic makes it good." —Alice May Brock

One of the negatives about attempting to eat the entire year through is that you won't frequently have the option to eat whatever it is *you* want every day. Your gastronomical life will be dictated by whatever the calendar says. Every now and then, though, a food holiday *will* come around that genuinely excites you. For me, National Linguine Day was one of those moments. It also helped that my sister was home for the first time since National Blueberry Pie Day back in late April!

She and I made an enormous bowl of linguine with a creamy, spicy pesto topped with chewy, tangy sun-dried tomatoes—flavors that beautifully complement each other. Much like my sister and I do with each other. (I'm the pesto; she's definitely the tomatoes!)

Linguine is a flat pasta that means "little tongues" in Italian. It originated in the coastal region of Liguria, Italy, which is known for its beautiful beaches and picturesque views of the Alps. This area of the country is known for its olive oil, seafood, pesto, and white wine.

Which, if you ask me, sounds like a recipe for a perfect way to celebrate today!

Today is also National Crème de Menthe Day and National Double Cheeseburger Day.

GREEN PESTO FOR A GODDESS

Makes about 1 cup

- 2 cups packed arugula, rinsed and dried
- ½ cup pistachios
- 3 garlic cloves
- 1 tablespoon plus 2 teaspoons lime juice
- ¼ cup olive oil
- ⅛ teaspoon salt
- 1 (8.5-ounce) jar sun-dried tomatoes in oil, drained (oil reserved)

Place the arugula, pistachios, and garlic cloves in a blender and pulse a few times until everything has broken down. Blend in the lime juice and olive oil. At this stage the pesto will be very thick. Add the salt and oil from the sun-dried tomatoes.

Tip! If you're going to use this pesto with linguine, dice up the sun-dried tomatoes you didn't use and mix them in with the sauce-covered cooked pasta. Also tastes great on pizza or as a straight-up dip!

SEPTEMBER 16 — NATIONAL GUACAMOLE DAY

"You know what I need? I need a tortilla chip that can support the weight of guacamole!" —Ellen DeGeneres

Avocados are one of my top five favorite foods ever. *Ever.* They're sexy and versatile. They're awesome as is, in brownies (seriously), as a textural replacement for cheese, but most of all, they're amazing when they grow up to become guacamole!

Today is *El Grito de la Independencia* (which is Spanish for "The Cry of Independence"); it's the day Mexico celebrates its independence from Spain. I'm not entirely sure if that's why National Guacamole Day is on September 16, but it makes sense. Apparently guac was first concocted by the Aztecs. The name—*āhuacamolli*—is derived from the Nahuatl dialect; it translates to "avocado sauce" (*āhuacatl* = avocado; *molli* = sauce). Interestingly enough, *āhuacatl* also translates to "testicles" (because the Aztecs believed avos and testes were shaped alike . . . which they are).

Sometimes premade food stuffs are acceptable. And on past food holidays I've even said that there's no shame in using them. But when it comes to guacamole, it should *always* be made fresh from scratch. Besides, how people make their guac says a lot about them! For example, the addition of Greek yogurt might imply that they like things smooth and controlled. Mangoes and roasted garlic in guac could signify that they're both playful and filled with surprises. And if they add a lot of chile, well, it's safe to assume they like to keep things spicy!

See? I told you avocados were sexy.

Today is also National Cinnamon-Raisin Bread Day.

EASY BEGINNER'S GUAC

Makes 1 medium-size bowl

3 medium ripe avocados

1 medium tomato, diced (about ¾ cup)

1 medium jalapeño, seeded and diced (about 2 tablespoons)

3 garlic cloves, minced

2 tablespoons freshly squeezed juice (from one small lime)

½ teaspoon cumin

¼ teaspoon salt

⅛ teaspoon crushed red pepper flakes

¼ cup Greek yogurt (optional but highly recommended)

Seed the avocadoes and spoon the flesh into a medium bowl. Add the tomato, jalapeño, garlic, lime juice, cumin, salt, pepper flakes, and yogurt. Using a fork, mix everything together, and then use the back of the fork to smash some—not all—of the large avocado chunks. The guacamole should have chunks in it. When the guacamole is a consistency to your liking, chill it in the refrigerator for 1 hour before serving.

NATIONAL APPLE DUMPLING DAY

"Comfort me with apples: for I am sick of love." —The Song of Solomon, *2:5*

One of my favorite things is autumn in New England: the way the leaves change, the way people slow down as if taking a breather between the summer and holiday rush, and all things apple related. Over the years people have come to know me for my obsession with apple trees, apple picking, apple cider, and apple dumplings.

When I got my first car, it was September and I was seventeen. Unsure of where to go with my newfound freedom, I took a trip to the orchard in town, a place where I had found peace, stillness, and restoration throughout my entire life. The winding road there is lined with long-armed trees that reach overhead. And in fall, the leaves erupt with colors of gold, red, and orange, creating a stained-glass effect when the sun shines its brightest. Even in rain, the sound of the drops hitting the leaves brings with it a sense of calm unlike anything else I've experienced.

When I arrived, I bought an apple dumpling smothered in warm vanilla sauce and ate it while meandering through the rows and rows of trees that were heavy with fruit. In that moment I felt as if autumn were both in me and all around me; a very spiritual moment all thanks to a McIntosh encased in pastry dough! Anyway, it became a weekly ritual for me from Labor Day to Thanksgiving (when the orchard closed). And as the years ticked by, it became an annual one, too.

Without knowing it, this is the food holiday I have probably celebrated the most in my life.

NATIONAL CHEESEBURGER DAY

"You can find your way across this country using burger joints the way a navigator uses stars." —Charles Kuralt

I always hated it when whoever was running the grill at a BBQ would ask, "Do you want cheese on your burger?" Really?! That's like asking someone if they would rather sunbathe in the rain or the sunshine. I think the answer will almost always be sunshine, or in this case *cheese*. Equally frustrating was when cheeseburgers weren't even an option. This told me my host was either (A) the most unthoughtful human being on the planet (because who doesn't buy cheese for a BBQ?!), or (B) blatantly lying to me and didn't want to share what was in the refrigerator. This is America! Land of life, liberty, and cheese on everything! And I demand cheese on my burgers!

The origin of the cheeseburger is a little questionable. It happened sometime in the 1920s or 1930s, but loads of different people and places take credit for the obviously ingenious creation. (I know I would!)

Do yourself, and your guests, a favor: Buy extra cheese today (and *every* day you invite people over for a cook-out)!

DID YOU KNOW?

Mayor McCheese was the cartoon cheeseburger mayor of McDonaldland from 1971 to 1985.

Today is also National Rice Krispies Treat Day.

SEPTEMBER 19

NATIONAL BUTTERSCOTCH PUDDING DAY

"Invention, my dear friends, is 93 percent perspiration, 6 percent electricity, 4 percent evaporation, and 2 percent butterscotch ripple." —Willy Wonka, Willy Wonka and the Chocolate Factory

Move over, vanilla. Hold your horses, chocolate. Today is all about butterscotch!

Butterscotch, a sticky, sweet substance similar to toffee, is usually made from brown sugar and butter (sometimes cream, corn syrup, or vanilla are added, too). It was invented sometime in the 1800s. My first taste of it came via my grandmother's Hopscotches—a family-favorite dessert made from butterscotch chips, peanut butter, mini marshmallows, and a can of crunchy Chinese (chow mein) noodles that were formed into little clusters.

Once a year—usually for my sister's birthday—my mom makes something she calls Mush in a Bucket, and I've known since the beginning of eating the year that it was how I wanted to celebrate today's food holiday. It's a delicious layered blend of textures—spongy, creamy, whipped—and flavors including spice, butterscotch, and vanilla. And it's a fun dessert because it was meant to be messy! Or, in this case, mushy!

However, mine didn't come out as good as hers usually does. I'm convinced that she's withholding information from me when it comes to her recipes. I made this Mush in a Bucket *exactly* like she explained, and yet it still came out mediocre compared to when she makes it. I really think that the additional ingredient of Vitamin L (that's *love*) when making something for someone enhances a dish much more than when you just make it because that's what the calendar says!

MUSH IN A BUCKET

Makes 8 servings

Note: If possible, use a very large bowl to make this dessert. A glass bowl shows off the layers best but any large bowl will work. Also note that part of this recipe needs to be refrigerated for an hour.

- 1 (16-ounce) package spice cake mix
- 2 (3.4-ounce) boxes instant butterscotch pudding
- 1 (8-ounce) container whipped topping

Bake the spice cake in a 9 x 13-inch pan according to package directions and set it aside to cool.

Make the pudding according to package directions, leaving it in the bowl you made it in. Refrigerate the pudding to allow it to settle.

When the cake has cooled, cut it in half. Using your hands or a spoon, scrape and crumble half of the cake from the pan into the bowl, layering it evenly across the bottom. Using half of the pudding, layer it by *small* spoonfuls evenly onto the top of the crumbled cake. Don't try to *spread* the pudding—the crumbled cake will stick to the spoon. Remember: This is a layered dessert.

Take the second half of the cake and crumble it onto the top of the pudding. With your hands or the back of a spoon, gently press the cake onto the pudding. Gently—as before—layer the rest of the pudding onto the crumbled cake. By now the bowl should be almost full. Cover the cake with plastic wrap and refrigerate for 1 hour.

Remove the bowl from the fridge and the plastic wrap, and layer the top evenly with the whipped topping. Serve it by digging a large spoon directly down into the center of the "mush" to get all the layers. Refrain from going back for thirds!

NATIONAL (RUM) PUNCH DAY

"There's naught, no doubt, so much the spirit calms as rum and true religion."
—Lord Byron

Whether you're celebrating innocently or more R-rated, today's holiday is flexible because it's all about interpretation!

Punch made its way to us via British sailors who had been to India sometime in the sixteenth or seventeenth century. The beverage originates from the Hindi word *panch*, which means "five." It's in reference to the five ingredients used in the original drink: water or tea, alcohol, sugar, lemon, and spices (which sounds to me exactly like the components of a hot toddy).

I was on a date at a concert when I celebrated today the first time. We went up to the bar to order drinks, and I asked if they made rum punches. "Like . . . the pink, fruity drinks?" the bartender asked with a raised eyebrow. Feeling judged and realizing my reputation was on the line, I quickly said, "Um, yeah. But it's totally for him, though." I nodded toward my date. "He's too ashamed to ask himself. I don't want one. I want . . . a manly beer drink." And I pounded my fist on the bar and grunted. I'm pretty sure both the bartender and my date just rolled their eyes.

Guess who ended up drinking most of that rum punch (*and* ordered a second one)? I'll give you a hint: It wasn't me!

DID YOU KNOW?

Located and produced in Barbados, Mount Gay Rum is the oldest brand of rum in the world.

NATIONAL PECAN COOKIE DAY

"Cookies are made of butter and love." —Norwegian proverb

We sure do love the pecan, don't we? And why wouldn't we? It's the only nut tree actually native to our country. Plus—among other health benefits—it's packed full of protein, unsaturated fats, and antioxidants. So go ahead, my fellow citizens—feel patriotic about the pecan!

Since we've already celebrated the ultimate pecan cookie, the pecan sandy, back on June 23rd (page 205), why not do something creative with your food holiday today? I attempted to make pecan cookies with black pepper and cranberries. If you're not feeling as daring (and I don't blame you!), why not combine seasonal flavors with the nut and make either pumpkin-pecan cookies with a caramel drizzle or sandwiches using apple cookies and butter pecan ice cream?

If you do, save me a couple. (I'm guessing you've already figured out that the black pepper thing didn't work out so well for me.)

NATIONAL WHITE CHOCOLATE DAY

"White Chocolate. Intense, sweet. But not deep. Okay for prom dates or flings, but not to get serious. Milk chocolates are guys you could date for like a few months, and dark chocolates are for love." —E. Lockhart

White chocolate has always bothered me. I don't know what it is, but that glossy sheen and ivory, old-glue color never seemed appetizing. It all just seemed . . . *fake*. But my family is filled with white chocolate lovers, so every Easter as a kid I received multiple hollow, white-chocolate bunnies named Sunny or Honey; and at Christmas there were pretzels dipped in white chocolate coated in candy cane bits. (All right, I confess: Those *are* actually delicious-tasting.)

I was onto something as a youth, I just didn't know what. It wasn't until my college baking course that I came to learn that white chocolate isn't even chocolate. It's a chocolate derivative containing cocoa butter, milk, and sugar, but no actual cocoa solids. What an imposter!

White chocolate thrives off confusion, though: There's a healthy debate among food bloggers as to whether National White Chocolate Day is actually on September 22nd or September 23rd. Which means (if you're playing it safe) white chocolate has weaseled its way into being celebrated on back-to-back days!

How sneaky.

DID YOU KNOW?

Milton Hershey was scheduled to ride the Titanic, but at the last minute changed his plans and caught an earlier boat out.

Today is also National Ice Cream Cone Day.

SEPTEMBER 23 — GREAT AMERICAN POT PIE DAY

"I want there to be no peasant in my kingdom so poor that he cannot have a chicken in his pot every Sunday." —Henry IV

In 2002, Marie Callender's declared the first ever Great American Pot Pie Day on the first day of fall, which happened to be September 23rd that year. (The physical date stuck, and people have historically always celebrated it today rather than the actual first day of autumn.) They believed that with cold weather, people craved heartier dishes—like pot pies—and wanted GAPP Day to be the kickoff to pot pie season. To celebrate that first year, Marie Callender's donated a portion of the proceeds of their pot pies sold on September 23 to the ConAgra Foods Feeding Children Better Foundation.

While the Great American Pot Pie Day might not be as common a food holiday as others, it still deserves its place. If you're not feeling like a traditional version, why not make a taco pot pie or a seafood pot pie? Want more ideas? Okay! How about a pot pie with a chicken Alfredo or Sloppy Joe center? All you gotta do is take what you love, put it between two piecrusts, and bake it up.

SEPTEMBER 24 — NATIONAL CHERRIES JUBILEE DAY

"You can't serve up hearts like cherries jubilee." —Leonard Bailey

French chef Auguste Escoffier definitely knew that a way to a woman's heart was through her stomach. Not only is he credited with creating Peach Melba (which is celebrated January 13, page 21) for Australian opera singer Dame Nellie Melba and pears Hélène (celebrated on March 15, page 88) in honor of the operetta *Le belle Hélène*, but he is also credited with today's food.

Escoffier created this classic *flambéed* (which is French for "flamed/flaming") dessert made with cherries and liqueur (usually brandy or kirsch), in theory, for one of Queen Victoria's jubilee celebrations because cherries were one of her favorite foods. It was either for her Golden Jubilee in 1887 (fiftieth anniversary of ruling) or her Diamond Jubilee in 1897 (sixtieth year), but it's uncertain which one.

If the idea of intentionally lighting alcohol on fire makes you nervous, fear not! There are other ways to celebrate while still keeping in tradition with the flavors of today's food holiday. If you'd like to avoid alcohol altogether, you could make cherries jubilee–flavored cheesecake, pudding, cupcakes, or trifle. Or, if you'd like to drink your holiday (and there's nothing wrong with that), try a cherries jubilee martini or a Champagne cocktail.

SEPTEMBER 25 — NATIONAL FOOD SERVICE EMPLOYEES DAY

"Businesses often forget about the culture, and ultimately, they suffer for it because you can't deliver good service from unhappy employees." —Tony Hsieh

Jobs within the food service industry may be some of the most underappreciated there are. Today is all about taking the time out to genuinely thank those people who make feeding us possible. From waitstaff to bar backs, cooks to delivery drivers, grocery cashiers to in-store food demo promoters—show some love today (and every day).

I asked some friends—a bar back, a bartender, a server, and a chef—what things customers do that food service employees appreciate. If you aren't already, try implementing them as you celebrate National Food Service Employees Day today and every day you go out. To be an exceptional customer:

- Make eye contact and have *real* conversations with the people serving you. Don't ignore them, talk over them, or talk *at* them when they're trying to serve you. Sure, they're paid to engage with you, but many genuinely do want to create a positive rapport with you during the time you're with them.
- Tip well if they've provided fast or polite service, or when you see your server has clearly gone out of his or her way for you.
- Don't be on your cell phone when ordering or checking out.
- Don't treat a restaurant or bar like a dumpster.

- The food industry can be very competitive and difficult to succeed in. Don't belittle anyone's job (many famous chefs started as dishwashers). After all, you've worked hard just to have extra money to go out; the people serving you are working just as hard to obtain a better life, too. So show some compassion.

DID YOU KNOW?

Mageirocophobia is the fear of cooking.

Today is also National Crab Meat Newburg Day.

SEPTEMBER 26

NATIONAL PANCAKE DAY

"Drama is very important in life: You have to come on with a bang. You never want to go out with a whimper. Everything can have drama if it's done right. Even a pancake." —Julia Child

While pancakes aren't terribly difficult to make, they can be time-consuming—especially if you're like me and burn the first two (or twelve) before finding your pancake-making groove! But I'm absolutely fascinated with them, because they seem to be one of the most universal foods there is. Lots of different cultures throughout the world have a variation on the batter-in-a-hot-greased-pan food. And just as varied are the items people top their pancakes with. Are you a whipped cream and fruit kind of person? What about butter, jam, honey, flavored maple syrup, chocolate sauce, powdered sugar, apple compote, or a dairy product like sour cream, yogurt, or cottage cheese?

Personally, one of my favorite indulgences *in the world* is a stack of three pancakes. In between the first two layers, I like to spread peanut butter; between the second and third layer, I put a thick schmear of cream cheese; and then I drown the whole thing in maple syrup. Every time school was canceled because of snow, my mom would make this for my sister and me. She learned it from her time working at a fishing camp in Maine. The hearty breakfast was filling enough to sustain both fishermen and camp staff during long, hard days working in the cold. If you've never tried that combination of flavors before, you are missing out, my friend!

SNOW DAY PANCAKES

Makes 6 pancakes (or 2 stacks of three)

2 tablespoons vegetable oil
1 cup all-purpose flour
1 tablespoon granulated sugar
1½ teaspoons baking powder
½ teaspoon baking soda
¼ teaspoon salt
2 teaspoons vanilla extract
1 cup milk
¼ cup creamy peanut butter
2 ounces plain cream cheese
¼ to ½ cup maple syrup

Coat the bottom of a large frying pan with the oil and set it to medium-high heat.

While the pan heats, mix the flour, sugar, baking powder, baking soda, and salt together. Add the vanilla and milk to the dry ingredients, and mix together well (it's totally okay if it's still lumpy).

Pour the batter, ¼ cup at a time, onto the heated pan and cook until there are either bubbles across the top of the pancake or the edges of the pancake look cooked. Flip the pancake over and cook for another 2 to 4 minutes, or until the pancake is cooked through. Continue making the rest of the pancakes (for a total of six).

To serve, spread 2 tablespoons of peanut butter on one pancake. Top with a second pancake, spread 2 tablespoons of cream cheese on top, finish with a third pancake, and cover the stack with ¼ cup of the maple syrup. Repeat this process with the other three pancakes to make a second stack. Find a friend, dig in, and feel full!

NATIONAL CHOCOLATE MILK DAY

"There's no use crying over spilled milk, unless your tears are chocolate syrup."
—Patrick Cassels

If you're ever looking for a good conversation starter, why not ask someone about their chocolate milk preference? It seems weird, but you're sure to get a variety of answers. (And probably a flood of childhood memories associated with the drink, too!) Some people like premade stuff. But is it best out of cardboard, glass bottles, or cans? And those who would rather make it from home usually have pretty strong feelings about the quality of milk they use, and whether or not powder or liquid chocolate is best. My house was Team Liquid, and my sister and I always debated about whether the syrup went in before the milk or after. (The answer, by the way, is *always* before.)

Bet you never stopped to think that chocolate milk was such serious business before, have you?

Today's not just for lactose lovers, either! One of the best chocolate milks I've ever had *in my life* is Earth Balance's chocolate soymilk. It is creamy, rich, and pairs really well with a *grilled* peanut butter and banana sandwich!

DID YOU KNOW?

The cocoa press was invented in 1828 by the Van Houten company in Amsterdam.

Today is also National Corned Beef Hash Day.

NATIONAL DRINK BEER DAY

"Give me a woman who loves beer and I will conquer the world." —Kaiser Wilhelm

After eating the year, people asked me what my favorite food holiday was. There were so many wonderful moments, unexpected finds, and delicious meals consumed that it was difficult for me to narrow it down to one. But National Drink Beer Day certainly stands out.

It fell on my city's monthly "art walk," something that I *love* attending. The galleries are so full that artists spill out onto the streets to sell their crafts; there are vendors selling everything from vegan cookies to authentic ethnic food; there are also buskers, dancers, flame-throwers, jugglers, etc., everywhere.

A friend and I decided to start the night at a local café with pints of my favorite brew (which I discovered only weeks before on National Beer Lover's Day). They went down a little too easy, so we got a second round. And then a third round. And then, well, the rest of the night is a bit hazy. I know I drank red wine at every art gallery we stopped at, was politely escorted away from the snack table of one gallery for eating all of their spinach-artichoke dip, danced to someone playing the accordion, had a passionate conversation with some animal activists about how much I love bunnies, spent too much time allowing a magician to do card tricks for me (there's a video of that somewhere, too), and ended the night eating a burrito from my favorite food truck sitting in a park under the stars.

Good food, good company, laughter, loving, and living.

Could you ask for a better night?

DID YOU KNOW?

Prohibition lasted thirteen years, ten months, nineteen days, seventeen hours, and thirty-two and a half minutes. Afterward, President Franklin Roosevelt said, "What America needs now is a drink."

Today is also National Strawberry Cream Pie Day.

NATIONAL COFFEE DAY

"Coffee should be black as hell, strong as death, and as sweet as love."
—Turkish proverb

After oil, coffee is the second most valuable traded commodity in the world.

And yet many coffee producers are forced to work in poor conditions where there's a lack of health and safety requirements. They're kept in poverty and debt and paid far less than the actual costs of production because of the desire for cheap labor to help keep consumer (that's us) prices low.

Over the years, industrial coffee bean production has also become a terribly un-ecological thing. While it was originally developed as a shade-grown crop, a new technique called sun cultivation, which increases the amount of coffee beans grown, promotes the destruction of forests, monocropping (when the *same* crop is grown on the *same* land year after year without any rotation), and chemical fertilizers/pesticides. These three things can lead to massive environmental problems like pollution, degradation of soil and water sources, deforestation, and even animal extinction.

So how do you go out and enjoy National Coffee Day now?

I'm sure you've heard it before, but fair trade is the way to go, not only for coffee, but also for tea, herbs, spices, sugar, flowers, grain, etc. But what is fair trade? Basically, it's a market-based social movement that aims to help producers in developing countries by advocating the payment of higher prices. It also helps to alleviate exploitation and promote sustainability.

Today is also National Goose Day and National Mocha Day.

NATIONAL HOT MULLED CIDER DAY

"Never praise your cider, horse, or bedfellow." —Benjamin Franklin

The last part of the year is my favorite time to be alive. The summer weather gracefully bows out, allowing autumn to colorfully explode before it, too, steps aside to let the holidays—the culmination of each passing year—take center stage. For me, it's difficult not to be anything but blissfully happy during these last few months, especially when I've got a mug of hot apple cider, which has always been one of my favorite drinks.

Mulled refers to both a heated and spiced beverage. In this case, apple cider (which is the superior option over apple juice in my opinion) is slowly warmed with the addition of spices like cinnamon, nutmeg, cloves, or ginger, and slices or peels from citrus fruit. Mulled cider is a cousin of wassail, which comes from the Middle English phrase *waes haeil*, meaning "be in good health." (Remember Mulled Wine Day on March 3rd?)

Appropriately enough, I celebrated today after having gone to the Johnny Appleseed Festival in Leominster, Massachusetts, where Jonathan Chapman (Mr. "Appleseed" himself) was born on September 26, 1774. Johnny Appleseed—an incredible man of faith—was a nurseryman who used his land to plant apple seeds before transplanting those seedlings to give to the settlers who, by law, needed to plant fifty apple trees their first year after establishing a homestead.

Seems like today is the perfect day to toast such a thoughtful man!

Today is also National Chewing Gum Day.

"MULL IT OVER" CIDER

½ gallon apple cider

1 teaspoon apple pie spice

1 tablespoon maple syrup

1 orange, peeled and sliced into ¼-inch-thick slices

4 cinnamon sticks

1 vanilla pod, sliced open

Spiced rum (optional)

Pour the apple cider in a 2-quart pot. Whisk in the apple pie spice and maple syrup until incorporated. Add the orange slices, cinnamon sticks, and vanilla pod. Mix gently to stir everything together.

Place the pot (uncovered) on the stove on medium-low heat and bring it to a simmer. Simmer the cider for 25 to 30 minutes before serving.

For an extra kick, add an ounce of spiced rum to your mug or glass before serving.

OCTOBER IS...

OCTOBER IS ALSO...

National American Cheese Month
National Apple Month
National Applejack Month
National Caramel Month
National Chili Month
National Cookbook Month
National Cookie Month
National Country Ham Month
National Cranberry Month
National Dessert Month
National Eat Better, Eat Together Month
National Fair Trade Month
National Harvest Month
National Pasta Month
National Pickled Peppers Month
National Pizza Month
National Popcorn Poppin' Month
National Pork Month
National Pretzel Month
National Seafood Month
National Spinach Lover's Month
National Sun-Dried Tomatoes Month
National Tomato Month
Vegetarian Awareness Month

. . .

1st Wednesday—National Kale Day
2nd Friday—World Egg Day
3rd Saturday—National Sweetest Day

WORLD VEGETARIAN DAY

"Until he extends the circle of his compassion to all living things, man will not himself find peace." —Albert Schweitzer, Kulturphilosophie

In 1977, the North American Vegetarian Society started World Vegetarian Day on October 1 as a way to promote the benefits of a plant-based diet, which includes, but is not limited to, better health and wellness, sustainability, and compassion.

Vegetarians do not eat animals. Not animals on land, or air, or sea. So do yourself a favor and never again ask a veggie if he or she eats seafood (if they did, they'd be called pescetarians).

There are many, many reasons why going vegetarian can be a good idea. For example, it:

- reduces the risk of obesity, heart disease, high blood pressure, high cholesterol, stroke, arthritis, cancer, and diabetes.
- not only helps you poo with regularity, but it also increases both energy and endurance. (Which is why they say vegetarians have a better sex life than omnivores do!)

- reduces exposure of animal-to-human disease transmissions *and* food-borne pathogens.
- encourages a more efficient use of grains, land, and fresh water.
- prevents a sentient being from suffering. Paul McCartney wasn't kidding when he said, "If slaughterhouses had glass walls, everyone would be vegetarian."

Today (and every day in October as it's Vegetarian Awareness Month) is meant to encourage open conversations about the vegetarian diet and lifestyle. So go ahead: Ask questions, be informed, and skip the meat today!

For more information check out *WorldVegetarianDay.org*.

Today is also National Homemade Cookie Day.

PINEAPPLEY FRIED RICE

Makes 4 servings

Note: Part of this recipe needs to be refrigerated for 3 hours.

- 1 cup uncooked white rice
- 4 tablespoons olive oil, divided
- 2 large eggs
- ⅓ cup soy sauce or Bragg's Liquid Aminos
- 1 (20-ounce) can pineapple chunks, drained
- 1 small bundle scallions, ends discarded, white and greens chopped (about ¼ cup)
- ½ (16-ounce) bag frozen broccoli florets

Cook the rice according to package directions (usually that's 1 cup white rice boiled in 2 cups water), spread out on a greased baking sheet, and put in the fridge to cool for 3 hours.

After 3 hours, drizzle 2 tablespoons of olive oil in a frying pan. Scramble the eggs to about 75 percent finished—not too cooked, not too watery. Transfer the eggs to their own bowl. Add the rest of the olive oil to the pan, turn the pan to medium-high (nice and sizzly!), and add the rice. While stirring constantly and slowly, add in the soy sauce. Add the egg and continue to stir. Stir in the pineapple, green onions, and broccoli. Fry until the broccoli is cooked through, then serve in a bowl and chow down!

Tip! Don't want to use eggs? Make a quick tofu scramble on the side instead. Just take one block of extra firm tofu and mash it with a fork until it breaks down into little pieces. Mix in 1 teaspoon of turmeric, 1 teaspoon of dehydrated onion flakes, and a pinch each of garlic powder, salt, and pepper. Pour 2 tablespoons of olive oil in a pot on medium-high heat. Add the tofu and cook until it becomes firm and begins to brown (this should take from 15 to 20 minutes). Add to the recipe above in place of the scrambled egg!

WORLD FARM ANIMALS DAY

"The greatness of a nation and its moral progress can be judged by the way in which its animals are treated." —Mahatma Gandhi

World Farm Animal Day was founded in 1983 as a way to educate people on animal cruelty and advocate against animals being *used* as a food commodity. They chose October 2nd because it was Mahatma Gandhi's birthday. An active and outspoken vegetarian, he promoted love, nonviolence, and justice toward sentient beings. Gandhi said, "I hold that the more helpless a creature, the more entitled it is to protection by man from the cruelty of man."

I was particularly fond of today because when I celebrated I had a "farm animal" as a pet—a mini rex rabbit named Boone. I had never entertained the idea of getting an animal friend while living the glorious bachelorette life because I didn't want to be tied down to anything, but the moment I laid eyes on him I fell in love. His stubby little arms and perky ears were both humorous and adorable, and I was amazed at how much personality Boone had—he was funny, outgoing, loving (on his terms), and pretty relaxed. (Unless he was hungry; that was when his real T. Rex side came out!)

Every day—not just on World Farm Animals Day—I'm thankful for the impact he's had on my life. Boone was (and still is) my personal reminder of the compassionate diet I abide by. As it's the second day of Vegetarian Awareness Month, I encourage you to try and eat a plant-based diet today—eat like a bunny!

DID YOU KNOW?

Geese mate for life. They faithfully love their significant other and even mourn for them when they die.

Today is also National Fried Scallops Day.

NATIONAL CARAMEL CUSTARD DAY

"Though we eat little flesh and drink no wine, Yet let's be merry; we'll have tea and toast; Custards for supper, and an endless host, Of syllabubs and jellies and mince-pies, And other such ladylike luxuries. . . ." —Percy Bysshe Shelley, "Letter to _____"

Caramel custard, flan, or *crème caramel*, is a creamy, rich custard that's covered in soft, gooey caramel (crème brûlée, on the other hand, has a hard, crunchy top because the sugar's been caramelized under a torch or broiler).

The best version of caramel custard I've ever had was flan from Santa Cruz de Tenerife in the Canary Islands. While living there, the man I taught English to and I once spent an afternoon in a park—it was completely enclosed by a fence and *full* of vegetation from floor to ceiling. Taking a break from walking around in the intense heat, we bought flan from a local bakery and settled on a bench in the park.

As we ate and people-watched, we discussed (he spoke in English; I responded in really bad Spanish) the person who had just been crowned the world's fastest texter. Is there anything particularly remarkable about this moment? No, but it stands out to me—especially today—because I never thought I'd find myself eating caramel custard in a region of the world I hadn't heard of before until I was living there.

It doesn't matter if you've never been to Spain. Authentic flan can easily be made at home or bought at a restaurant. And that's one of the best parts about many of these food holidays—it gives you the opportunity to explore different cultures!

NATIONAL TACO DAY

"You know how I feel about tacos. It's the only food shaped like a smile. A beef smile." —Earl Hickey, My Name is Earl

Are you Team Hard Taco or Team Soft Taco?

Soft shell tacos are definitely the cleaner and more authentic option, but the hard shell taco is more modern and trendy. People stuff *everything* into these crunchy, yellow U-boats of love, including scrambled eggs and bacon for breakfast tacos or chocolate and ice cream for dessert tacos.

I was traumatized by tacos in my youth. When the first express taco stand opened in my town, my parents used to go there often because tacos were only a dollar a piece. They would buy ten soft shell tacos and ten hard shell tacos, dump them in the middle of the kitchen table with packets of sauce varying in degrees of spiciness, and we would have a dinner free-for-all. It wasn't long before all that remained were crumbled up wrappers and queasy stomachs.

Those were the good ole days (when I had an iron stomach)!

Today is also Kanelbullens Dag (Cinnamon Rolls Day in Sweden) and National Vodka Day.

NORMA'S CHA CHA GIRL TACOS

Makes 8 to 10 tacos

1 teaspoon cumin

½ teaspoon garlic salt

3 tablespoons olive oil, divided

1 small to medium summer squash, washed and cut into bite-size pieces (about 2 cups)

1 small to medium zucchini, washed and cut into bite-size pieces (about 2 cups)

8 to 10 jumbo shrimp, deveined and halved or 1 (8-ounce) package tempeh

1 avocado, skinned and seeded

1 tablespoon plus ¼ teaspoon ranch dressing

8 to 10 corn tortillas

1 cup pico de gallo or salsa

¼ cup cilantro, for topping (optional)

4 medium radishes, thinly sliced, for topping (about ½ cup) (optional)

In a small bowl, combine the cumin and garlic salt. Set aside.

Sauté the summer squash and zucchini in two tablespoons of olive oil in a pan on medium heat for 8 to 10 minutes, or until the squash starts to look translucent and begins to brown. Set the pan aside.

While the vegetables are sautéing, if you're using shrimp, rub them with the cumin and garlic salt mixture. If you're using tempeh, cut it into ¼- to ½-inch strips and rub with the cumin and garlic salt mixture.

Pour the remaining olive oil into a skillet and sauté the shrimp (or tempeh) on each side until cooked, about 2 minutes per side. Set aside.

With a fork, smash the avocado with the ranch dressing until well combined.

To build the tacos: Place two shrimp halves or a few pieces of tempeh into each tortilla and some of the squash-zucchini mixture. Top each taco with some avocado ranch dressing, some pico de gallo or salsa, and sprinkle of cilantro, and some radish slices, if desired.

- -

NATIONAL APPLE BETTY DAY

"And when you crush an apple with your teeth, say to it in your heart: 'Your seeds shall live in my body, And the buds of your tomorrow shall blossom in my heart, And your fragrance shall be my breath, And together we shall rejoice through all the seasons.'" —Kahlil Gibran, The Prophet

Every autumn my mom makes a pan of her famous apple crisp using locally grown apples. The cinnamon and nutmeg spiced tart apples, topped with a crumbly mixture of melt-in-your-mouth oats, brown sugar, and butter, and a dollop of whipped cream is absolutely divine. It's something I look forward to all year long!

Little did I know that in many states across the nation apple crisp is synonymous with both apple crumble and Apple (Brown) Betty. The original Apple Betty, which showed up in the mid-nineteenth century, was made from apples and stale bread toasted into breadcrumbs before being sweetened. If you're used to apple crisp or crumble, today would be a great day to try that authentic Apple Betty recipe.

Some of the better apples to bake with, in my experience, include Winesap, Rome, Granny Smith, Braeburn, Honeycrisp, Jonagold, *Mutsu* (Crispin), Pink Lady, Cortland, and McIntosh. Feel free to experiment with different kinds today.

OCTOBER 06 NATIONAL NOODLE DAY

"You often hear about ingredients being found, whether it is corn or ancient grains, but it is not too often that you hear about something as complex as noodles."
—Greg Drescher

Noodles have been a staple food for many cultures over many (*many*) centuries. The very mention of the word *noodle* may make some people shudder (too many instant meals, no doubt); for others, though, it conjures up a variety of flavorful, distinct cuisines from around the world. Which is how I hope you celebrate today; instead of chowing down or slurping up noodles in a way that you're familiar with (or that uses a microwave to prepare), why not broaden your horizons and try something new?

Couscous, for example, is pasta made from semolina and water that's formed into small granules. It's a nuttier-tasting pasta that's popular in both North-African and Middle-Eastern countries. It's super-easy to make and tastes delicious flavored with saffron, cumin, herbs, tomatoes, or my favorite—lemon and cranberries.

Or you could try a sweet kugel, which is like a Jewish pudding that's baked like a casserole using egg noodles, cottage cheese, sour cream, butter, cinnamon, and sugar.

Don't feel like cooking? Why not take yourself out for some Pad Thai? A dish found in both Vietnam and Thailand, it's made with stir-fried rice noodles, eggs, bean sprouts, meat, or vegetables, and topped with crushed peanuts that combine spicy, sour, salty, and sweet flavors.

SWEET WHITE HOT PASTA

Makes 4 to 6 servings

1 (16-ounce) box penne or rigatoni
1 (15-ounce) jar Alfredo sauce
½ teaspoon crushed red pepper flakes
1 (15-ounce) can dark red kidney beans, drained and rinsed
¾ cup golden raisins
¼ cup grated Parmesan cheese
¼ cup fine Italian bread crumbs

Preheat the oven to 350°F.

Boil the pasta according to package instructions for al dente texture.

While the pasta is cooking, pour the jar of Alfredo sauce into a 2-quart casserole dish (with a cover). Fill the empty jar with water, cover it tightly, shake it to get any leftover sauce from inside the jar, and pour the water into the casserole dish. Add the pepper flakes and whisk everything together until well combined. Gently stir in the beans.

After the pasta has cooked, drain it and fold it into the sauce. Cover the dish and bake for 30 minutes.

Remove the dish from the oven, uncover it, add the raisins, and stir everything together. Sprinkle the cheese and then the breadcrumbs across the top, keep the dish uncovered, and return it to the oven for another 15 minutes.

Remove the pasta from the oven, let it sit for 5 minutes to settle, then serve.

NATIONAL FRAPPÉ DAY

"Why does man kill? He kills for food. And not only food: Frequently there must be a beverage." —Woody Allen, Without Feathers

When you think of a frappé, what's the first thing that pops to mind? If you're anything like me, it's either a delicious, expensive frozen espresso concoction ("with soy, an extra shot, and no whipped cream, please!") or a generic term for a milkshake, especially in the New England region. And either of those is okay—frappés have certainly evolved into those kinds of beverages, but that's not how they started!

The *frappé*—which comes from the French word *frapper* or "to beat/stir"—originated in Greece at the International Trade Fair in Thessaloniki in 1957 as a chilled coffee drink using instant coffee and water. Shaken vigorously, it develops a frothy, creamy head. It can also be made with milk and sugar, too (ordering a *frappé sketos* is without sugar, *metrios* is moderately sweet, and *glykos* is sweet).

It's not that hard to make an authentic version at home—then again, it's not that difficult to stop by your local coffee shop and order one either! Whichever you choose—just make sure you celebrate!

NATIONAL FLUFFERNUTTER DAY

"Jelly beans, fluffernutter, gummy bears, ginger snaps—this is a grocery list."
—Marshall Eriksen, How I Met Your Mother

Peanut butter and jelly might be a staple lunch item for most kids throughout the States, but in New England we like to take the sticky, sweet sandwich one step further: peanut butter and fluff. (And actually, you can always tell who the former New Englanders are at the grocery store, because they load up on red snappers—hot dogs in a red-dyed casing—Moxie, and Marshmallow Fluff to take back home with them!)

The first version of Marshmallow Fluff as we know it now was created at the beginning of the twentieth century (1917 to be exact) by Archibald Query of Somerville, Massachusetts. He sold his recipe to Durkee-Mower, Inc. in Lynn, MA, a privately held company, for just $500. And now, proud Somerville (where old Archy was from) celebrates an annual "What the Fluff?" Festival every year.

In 2006, Senator Jarrett Barrios attempted to limit the amount of fluff being served in Massachusetts' public schools, because he thought the sandwich was contributing to the state's childhood obesity epidemic. His efforts were futile: An overwhelming show of public support actually got it considered (and is still being proposed) for the official state sandwich of Massachusetts instead!

Today is also National Pierogi Day.

NATiONAL SUB, GRiNDER, HOAGiE, HERO DAY

"Sonny, true love is the greatest thing in the world—except for a nice MLT—mutton, lettuce, and tomato sandwich, where the mutton is lean and the tomato is ripe." —Miracle Max, The Princess Bride

Sub. Italian. Grinder. Hero. Hoagie. Torpedo. Bomber. Dagwood. Po' Boy. Rocket. Wedge. Zep. Gatsby. Tunnel. Blimpie. Fill-in-the-blank.

Wherever you're from, whatever you call it, the concept is the same: It's a sandwich made with an oblong roll filled with meat, cheese, veggies, and a sauce or condiment of some kind. There's no official name for it, and most regions in the U.S. have their own version of it (some feature fried seafood or melted provolone, some serve 'em cold). It's a true representation of our melting pot of a country!

I've done some pretty crazy things for a good sandwich before. On a whim, two friends of mine and I once decided we wanted to experience an authentic Philly cheesesteak. What should have been an eight-hour drive from Maine to Pennsylvania turned into eleven hours because a blizzard hit us. We eventually made our way to Pat's King of Steaks, ordered a "cheesesteak wit (not *with*) onions and Cheez Whiz," jumped back into our car, and drove back home.

Was it worth it? Absolutely. If you have the freedom to do something as spontaneous as that today (or any day), I highly encourage it. The best way to see our country is to eat our country!

DID YOU KNOW?

Portland, Maine, is considered the birthplace of the Italian sandwich.

Today is also National Moldy Cheese Day.

OCTOBER 10 · NATIONAL ANGEL FOOD CAKE DAY

"He looked about as inconspicuous as a tarantula on a slice of angel food cake."
—Raymond Chandler, Farewell, My Lovely

Culinarily speaking, angel food cake is the opposite of devil's food cake; it's a light and airy type of sponge cake, whereas the latter is much more dense and rich. Personally, I like to know when I'm gastronomically ("a moment on the lips, forever on the hips") sinning. While angel food cake is lower in calories and may come off as the wide-eyed innocent dessert that has no ill intentions toward the shape of your tush, don't be fooled. Most people slather their cakes with sauces or creams that seep into the delicious layers of golden cake begging for more to be poured onto it.

I'm on to you, angel food cake!

I spent part of today wearing angel wings (it seemed appropriate) and eating a slice of pumpkin-flavored angel food cake slathered with a thick layer of locally made pumpkin butter and served with a chilled pumpkin beer (after all, 'tis the season for all things gourd). And it was heavenly, all right.

OCTOBER 11 · NATIONAL SAUSAGE PIZZA DAY

"A man taking basil from a woman will love her always." —Sir Thomas Moore

One of the best dates you can have in the early stages of a relationship is to make pizza together. It's fun, tremendously intimate, low-key, and can reveal a lot about the other person's personality. Do they take their time making pizza, savoring the process and sampling each individual component before they become one? Are they a little more at ease with themselves, playfully throwing flour at you or wiping a streak of tomato sauce down your cheek before gently wiping (or kissing) it off? Do they meticulously check the pizza when it's in the oven to make sure the cheese is brown and bubbly the way you—but maybe not they—like it? Do they take one more bite than you while eating dinner so that no matter how much you eat, they're always just a little bit more of a pig than you?

There's a tremendous amount of unsaid things happening when a couple makes pizza.

Maybe sausage is an incredibly sexy ingredient to some people—the spice, the texture, the distinct and inviting aroma. Someone obviously thought so, because it became a national food holiday. If you have a plant-based diet, don't let today be a turnoff; there are plenty of meat-free sausage and chorizo substitutes nowadays. Sausage itself may not excite you, but being able to create a masterpiece of a pizza entirely animal-free and sharing it with someone who does turn you on *should*!

SOOOOOO GOOD SAUSAGE SALAD 'ZA

Makes one 12-inch pizza

Pizza:

1 tablespoon olive oil

1 tablespoon cornmeal

1 (20-ounce) premade pizza dough (or dough from page 284)

½ cup fire-roasted tomato and garlic sauce

1 (12-ounce) sleeve chorizo, sautéed and drained

1 (15-ounce) can cannellini beans, drained and rinsed

¼ cup fresh sage, julienned

1 (8-ounce) bag shredded mozzarella (about 2 cups)

Pizza salad:

2 cups packed arugula

1 tablespoon olive oil, divided

1 tablespoon lime juice

Preheat the oven to 500°F.

Brush a baking sheet or pizza pan with the olive oil, and then sprinkle with the cornmeal (which isn't absolutely necessary but makes getting the pizza off the pan easy!). Work the pizza dough so that it stretches out onto the baking sheet or pizza pan. Cover the dough with the sauce, and then top with the chorizo, cannellini beans, and sage. Finish by topping the pizza with the cheese (so it completely covers the other toppings). Bake for 8 to 10 minutes (crust doneness is a personal preference thing, so just keep an eye on it).

While the pizza is baking, mix the arugula, olive oil, and lime juice in a bowl (use your hands to get every single leaf covered in dressing).

When the pizza is done, pull it out of the oven, let it cool slightly, and then top the 'za with the arugula salad.

Tip! Want to make this veg-friendly? Instead of chorizo, use soy chorizo (available at Trader Joe's or companies like Frieda's, El Burrito, or Melissa's).

OCTOBER 12 — NATIONAL GUMBO DAY

"Conversation is the enemy of good wine and food." —Alfred Hitchcock

As it gets colder, my body naturally craves heartier dishes (it's my internal clock telling me it's time to put the polar bear insulation back on so I can stay warm during the winter). Gumbo, I think, is an excellent food for this time of year!

But if you're not from the South, you may not be so familiar with what it is and how it differs from its culinary cousin, Jambalaya.

Gumbo is a spicy stew/souplike dish that originated in Louisiana. It's an amalgamation of different cultures—French, German, Spanish, Choctaw, and West African. Gumbo actually comes from the West African word *kimgombo* for "okra," which is considered one of the key ingredients in the dish.

It includes meat like chicken, andouille sausage, and shellfish (crab, oysters, shrimp, scallops, etc.); it's thickened with a dark roux and/or okra, and is served over a bed of rice. Jambalaya, on the other hand, is often texturally compared to paella since it's a thick rice-and-meat-seafood dish.

Now you can go into your food holiday confidently!

DID YOU KNOW?

In Cajun cooking the "Holy Trinity" is onion, celery, and bell pepper.

NATIONAL YORKSHIRE PUDDING DAY

"It's not improbable that a man may receive more solid satisfaction from pudding while he is alive than from praise after he is dead." —Proverb

One of the things I love most about traveling is sharing a meal with the locals. Food is an integral part of every household in every nook and cranny of the world. And one of the best ways to immerse yourself in someone else's culture is to experience a meal like they do—from the preparation, to pre-meal traditions, the flow in which a meal is shared and eaten, and any post-meal rituals, too.

While we celebrate National Yorkshire Pudding Day on October 13, the first Sunday of the month in February is British Yorkshire Pudding Day in England, which makes sense since it's traditional on Sundays to have a roast dinner. I have been fortunate enough to take part in a customary Sunday tea (dinner) a couple of times. The menu included roast beef, Yorkshire pudding, creamed leeks, and roasted potatoes with gravy and mustard on the side.

The Yorkshire pudding was named after a northern county in England and has been a staple in the British diet for generations. Our friends across the Pond take their Yorkshire pud very seriously, too; in 2008, the Royal Society of Chemistry decreed that a proper pudding must be at least four inches tall!

DID YOU KNOW?

The first recorded Yorkshire Pudding recipe appeared in 1737 in a book called *The Whole Duty of a Woman*. Back then it was called "A Dripping Pudding."

NATIONAL DESSERT DAY

"Work is the meat of life, pleasure the dessert." —B.C. Forbes

My parents fall on different sides of the culinary spectrum: While my dad is an appetizer guy, my mom is definitely all about dessert. I'd like to think I can be swayed either way (whenever I travel abroad, I always have a three-course meal!), but if I had to choose?

I'd be Team Dessert all the way.

My family tends to eat desserts that correspond with the season. Ice cream in the spring, strawberry shortcake in the summer, apple crisp and pumpkin pie in the fall, and brownies and cookies in the winter. To me, having that piece of chocolate or slice of cake—something, *anything* sweet—after a meal feels like perfect closure.

We're not alone in our line of thinking either—dessert comes from the French word *desservir* which means "to clear (the table)." And the concept of it has been around for centuries—the first version of desserts came to us via fruits like dates. And once sugar was manufactured and became more readily available, all classes (not just the wealthy) began enjoying a post-meal sweet. Our love with dessert has never ceased since!

October isn't just National Dessert Month, it's also National Apple, Caramel, Cookie, and Cranberry Months, too! Why not use that as inspiration as you celebrate today's food holiday?

Today is also National Chocolate-Covered Insects Day.

NATIONAL RED WINE DAY

"A man can never have too much red wine, too many books, or too much ammunition." —Rudyard Kipling

Eating the year isn't the healthiest diet in the world, so to counteract the damage you may have done to yourself in the process, I encourage you to celebrate today's holiday. After all, red wine (in moderation) can lower cholesterol, potentially reduce the chance of heart disease and stroke, and may be good for neurological health, too!

Unfortunately, I was unable to get my hands on the world's oldest bottle of wine today (found in 1867 inside a Roman sarcophagus excavated near Speyer, Germany, it dates back to A.D. 325), so my date and I settled on a cheap bottle of red from my local grocer.

We went to open it with a corkscrew. But the corkscrew broke.

We tried to open it with a Leatherman. But the Leatherman broke.

We stuck a screw inside the cork and tried to pry it out with pliers. But the screw broke.

We *very gently* chiseled away at the cork with a knife. And, finally, the neck of the bottle of wine itself broke. It was the most hard-fought glass of $3.99 wine I had ever had.

Talk about a cork tease!

*Today is also National Roast Pheasant Day,
National Chicken Cacciatore Day,
and National Mushroom Day.*

V'OLOGNESE

Makes 4 servings

2 tablespoons olive oil

1 large Vidalia onion, chopped (about 2 cups)

2 garlic cloves, minced

1 tablespoon dried basil

2 teaspoons dried parsley

2 bay leaves

¼ teaspoon crushed red pepper flakes

⅛ teaspoon salt

⅛ teaspoon black pepper

1 (14-ounce) package soy sausage, crumbled

2 cups Cabernet Sauvignon

1 (6-ounce) can tomato paste

2 tablespoons heavy whipping cream or cashew cream

1 (1-pound) box of long-strand pasta of choice

Grated Parmesan cheese, for topping (optional)

Place the olive oil into a large skillet. Sauté the onions and garlic on medium-high heat until translucent and fragrant, about 5 to 8 minutes. Add the basil, parsley, bay leaves, pepper flakes, salt, pepper, and soy sausage. Cook everything until the sausage is brown, about 8 to 10 minutes. Turn the heat down to a simmer and add the wine, tomato paste, and cream. Mix everything thoroughly and let the sauce simmer until it has thickened, about 1 hour, stirring occasionally.

Boil the pasta according to package directions, drain, and set aside.

Remove the bay leaves from the sauce and stir it through once more before serving on top of the pasta. Top with Parmesan, if desired, and serve with a smile.

WORLD FOOD DAY

"We know that a peaceful world cannot long exist, one-third rich and two-thirds hungry." —Jimmy Carter

World Food Day was created in 1979 (but first celebrated in 1981 on October 16th) by the Food and Agriculture Organization of the United Nations to heighten public awareness of and education on poverty and hunger, food safety issues, and the global food crisis. This global observance strengthens solidarity as we fight against malnutrition and attempt to eradicate hunger within our lifetime.

That being said, sometimes I think it's easier for us to choose to "feel small" against such enormous issues like this. Someone else—somewhere else—with more money, or more connections, or more time can do more than we ever could, right? Well, today I'm asking you to feel anything but small—feel empowered, feel important, feel like you—"little" you—can make a huge difference.

Take *Kiva.org*, for example: All you do is lend $25 to someone in the world. Over time, you get periodic updates about the progress of your loan, including repayments as they become available. When it has been repaid in full, you can either withdraw the money for your personal use or donate it to someone else. A few years ago I loaned $25 to a group of cattle herders in Peru. Since then I've "recycled" that same $25 (as of now) four separate times. Kiva lets you choose the borrower, and there are people in need in every sector: education, manufacturing, clothing.

So today, maybe you could sacrifice just *one dinner out* and give that money to someone in the agriculture or food sector. That's how we're going to help end world hunger—by endorsing grassroots efforts. Just think about how many lives you can touch over and over again with just $25. Loaning to Kiva was seriously one of the best things I've ever done, and I'm proud that my family and friends also participate.

Here's to a productive World Food Day that brings us one step closer to . . . being full.

Today is also National Liqueur Day.

TORTILLA DE PATATAS

Makes enough for two really piggish
people, or four normally hungry people

½ cup olive oil

3 medium russet potatoes, sliced thinly
   (about 3 overflowing cups)

1 large Vidalia onion, sliced thinly (about 2 cups)

6 large eggs, beaten

1 teaspoon dried parsley

1 teaspoon salt

½ teaspoon black pepper

Pour the oil in a large skillet on medium-high heat.
When the oil is hot, add the potatoes and onions. Cook
until the onions are translucent and the potatoes are
cooked through (easily broken when touched with a
fork), about 8 to 10 minutes. Use a slotted spoon to
transfer the potatoes and onions to a bowl and turn the
heat down to medium.

Pour the eggs into the bowl with the potatoes,
onions, parsley, salt, and pepper; mix to make sure
everything is well combined. Empty the bowl into the
skillet—the eggs will immediately start to cook (and
may pull away from the pan). Cook everything until
the bottom of the dish is brown, about 5 to 7 minutes.
Place either a large plate or a baking sheet on top of
the frying pan. Flip the pan upside down, slide the
uncooked side of the egg and potato mixture back into
the pan, and finish cooking for 2 to 3 minutes.

NATIONAL PASTA DAY

"Pasta doesn't make you fat. How much pasta you eat makes you fat."
—*Giada De Laurentiis,* Giada's Feel Good Food

Generally speaking, pasta is served in one of three ways:

1. *Pasta asciutta*—cooked pasta that's served with a sauce (like linguine in arrabbiata)
2. *Pasta in brodo*—cooked pasta that's part of a soup (like minestrone)
3. *Pasta al forno*—pasta that's used in a baked dish (like lasagna)

And since the rest of the food calendar is filled with pastas we've all heard of, why not branch out today and try a different kind, nothing too crazy, but something like:

- Cavatappi (corkscrews): goes well with chunky or thick tomato or cream-based sauces.
- Conchiglie (shells): is ideal for chunky meat/vegetable sauces with cheese, pesto, or in pasta salad.
- Farfalle (butterflies; shaped like bow ties): also works well with chunky sauces, cheese sauces, pesto, and pasta salads, as well as olive oil or seafood.
- Orecchiette ("little ears"): can be paired with meat or vegetable sauces, pesto, or in pasta salads.
- Sacchetti ("beggar's purse"): is stuffed like ravioli, but the four corners of the pasta are pulled up and meet in the center.
- Strangolapreti/strozzapreti ("priest stranglers"): is a piece of pasta rolled tightly that goes well tossed with meat or veggie sauces.
- Vermicelli ("little worms"): is used with tomato, cheese, or olive oil-based sauces, along with meat, veggies, or seafood.

Today is also Four Prunes Day.

AU PAIR PASTA

2 tablespoons olive oil

½ large sweet onion, diced

1 medium green pepper, cored, seeded, and thinly sliced

1 medium yellow pepper, cored, seeded, and thinly sliced

1 (8-ounce) can sliced white button mushrooms

2 large tomatoes, diced

1 (1-pound) box tricolor rotini (or pasta of choice)

1 cup sour cream

1¼ cups shredded sharp Cheddar cheese

1 (15-ounce) can sweet kernel corn, rinsed

Salt and pepper, to taste

Put the olive oil in a large pot and set on medium-high heat. When the oil is hot, add the onions and peppers and cook until soft, about 6 to 8 minutes. Turn the heat down to low, stir in the mushrooms and tomatoes, and cook for another 10 minutes.

Cook the rotini according to package directions, drain it, and set aside.

Fold the sour cream and cheese into the vegetable mixture. Cook for about 10 to 12 minutes, stirring occasionally, until the cheese is melted and the sauce is thick and creamy. Add the corn and pasta, stir everything together, and cook for another 2 minutes. Add salt and pepper to taste. Serve hot or cold, but I think this dish tastes way better cold!

OCTOBER 18 — NATIONAL CHOCOLATE CUPCAKE DAY

"When you look at a cupcake, you've got to smile." —Anne Byrn

At some point in recent memory, the cupcake's popularity absolutely exploded. Not only can you walk into the grocery store, buy a mix and some premade frosting for under five bucks and have "homemade" cupcakes in twenty minutes, but there are now gourmet cupcake shops that offer flavor options never before dreamed of. (I may or may not be having a love affair with Pabst Blue Ribbon cupcakes topped with Wild Turkey American Honey liqueur frosting that the local cupcake food truck sells!)

Cupcakes have become serious business.

My stress-busting activities in college included working out and baking. My parents bought me a dessert cookbook one Christmas, and I learned how to make pretty awesome peanut butter–filled chocolate cupcakes with a ganache frosting. They were *incredible*. So good, in fact, that my mom and stepdad had me make them for their wedding!

Don't feel like you need to reinvent the wheel today; sure, gourmet cupcakes with fancy ingredients may seem glamorous, but there's definitely nothing wrong with a good, old-fashioned version either!

OCTOBER 19 — NATIONAL SEAFOOD BISQUE DAY

Elaine: "Yeah. I met this lawyer, we went out to dinner, I had the lobster bisque, we went back to my place, yada yada yada, I never heard from him again." Jerry: "But you yada yada'd over the best part." Elaine: "No, I mentioned the bisque." —Seinfeld

Traditional seafood bisque is a creamy, aromatic, seasoned French soup created from the broth of crustacean—like lobster, crab, or shrimp—shells (sometimes these are even ground up to act as a thickening agent). It's unclear where the name *bisque* comes from, though. It could have stemmed from the Bay of Biscay, which borders both Spain and France, or it could have originated from *bis cuites*, a French term that means "twice cooked," which refers to the bisque-making process. What you really need to know about this dish is that it's one of *the most* luxurious comfort foods (such a combination does exist) there is: lobsters in a rich, warm cream sauce.

To some, *c'est divin* (it's divine)!

I went into today a little nervous; since I was getting so close to the end of my project, I felt like I really needed to step up my game. So I broke down the flavors of a classic seafood bisque into something I thought (especially after multiple glasses of wine) was pretty decent: a deconstructed vegan version of the bisque in sandwich form. It worked for me!

DID YOU KNOW?

Ostraconophobia is the intense fear or hatred of shellfish.

OCTOBER 20

NATIONAL BRANDIED FRUIT DAY

"Taste every fruit of every tree in the garden at least once. It is an insult to creation not to experience it fully. Temperance is wickedness." —Stephen Fry

Brandy comes from the Dutch word *brandewijn*, meaning "burnt wine." It's made from distilled grapes and (for those of you who've never had it and want a really crude comparison) is sort of similar to a whiskey in flavor, but with a much sweeter aftertaste and far less charcoal notes. (And that's exactly how I used to sell it when working as a Hennessy Girl and offering complimentary samples.)

At some point in our great culinary history, someone realized that preserving fruits in brandy for use through the wintertime was a pretty solid idea; not only could the fruit be used in desserts and what not, but the brandy itself became flavored! So today we celebrate that ingenious equation of brandy + fresh fruit + sugar = awesome.

I was a little hesitant about the concept at first. I couldn't wrap my brain around filling a mason jar full of blackberries, brandy, and sugar, giving it a good shake, and then hiding it in a dark, cool place for *x* amount of time. Unsure of the process, I only let my first batch cure for two days before feeling the neurotic impulse to check on it. Have faith and leave yours alone to age for a couple weeks (if not months) for the best flavor.

OCTOBER 21
NATIONAL PUMPKIN CHEESECAKE DAY

"Envy for a friend is like the taste of a sour pumpkin." —Peruvian proverb

Because we celebrate National White Chocolate Cheesecake Day (March 6, page 79–80), National Cherry Cheesecake Day (April 23, page 135), and National Blueberry Cheesecake Day (May 26, page 172), it's not so surprising that we would also celebrate National Pumpkin Cheesecake Day. (Because what's better than cheesecake? *Flavored* cheesecake!)

Today's food holiday makes sense given the time of year. And there's a plethora of ways it can be made: with a graham cracker or chocolate crust; with a praline swirl; topped with a sour cream or bourbon glaze; or even mixed with white chocolate or caramel flavors. This little dessert presents endless opportunities to make it uniquely your own (much like carving a face on a pumpkin itself does).

And if you're feeling a little frisky or you want something to *really* warm your soul as we continue to march closer and closer to winter, toss a little booze in your recipe to make it a drunken pumpkin cheesecake recipe. Who's stopping you?

Today is also International Day of the Nacho, National Apple Day, and National Caramel Apple Day.

OCTOBER 22 — NATIONAL NUT DAY

"Must is a hard nut to crack, but it has a sweet kernel." —Charles H. Spurgeon

Nuts, specifically peanuts, have always made me think of my grandfather.

Every day after lunch—which, to a traditional French Canadian, was his biggest meal of the day—he'd eat a handful of roasted peanuts. I was never really sure why he did this. I thought it might have been a way to cleanse the palate, but according to my mom he just really liked peanuts. "Uncomplicated man, uncomplicated tastes, uncomplicated explanation," she said. "He liked the crunch. And salted, roasted peanuts in a jar were inexpensive and his favorite nut."

He lived to be eighty-five years old. And for most of that he was a strong, healthy man. I think it was a combination of being genuinely happy with his lot in life, having a loving family, walking daily, reading frequently, and eating an abundance of fresh, homegrown produce and peanuts. After all, nuts are full of protein, vitamins and minerals, fiber, antioxidants, plant sterols, and omega fats, meaning a reduced risk of heart disease and lower cholesterol.

Personally, I trust any food that's been around for, well, *ever*. Walnuts, for example, are actually thought to be the oldest tree food known to man and date back to around 7,000 B.C.

That's food for thought!

CHEESY NUT 'N' OLIVE CUPS

Makes 15 cups, with leftover spread

- 15 frozen premade phyllo dough cups
- ½ cup walnuts
- 1 (5- or 6-ounce) jar green olives with pimientos, drained (juice reserved)
- 1 (8-ounce) package cream cheese

Bake the phyllo cups according to package directions. Remove them from the oven and let them cool.

In a food processor, pulse the walnuts until finely chopped, empty them into a small bowl, and set aside.

Put the olives in the food processor and pulse until finely chopped; empty them into another small bowl, and set aside.

Cut the cream cheese into cubes and put it in the food processor. Add the nuts, olives, and 1 tablespoon of olive juice. Pulse until everything is mixed together well, adding more olive juice if the spread is too thick.

Spoon the spread into the cooled phyllo cups. Put the leftover spread in an airtight container and refrigerate. Place the cups in a 9 x 13-inch baking dish (to keep them from sliding around), refrigerate them for 30 minutes, and then serve.

Tip! The remainder of the spread may be used on bagels, crackers, celery, or whatever you can think of.

OCTOBER 23

NATIONAL BOSTON CREAM PIE DAY

"We never make sport of religion, politics, race, or mothers. A mother never gets hit with a custard pie. Mothers-in-law, yes. But mothers, never." —Mack Sennett

Boston cream pie isn't a pie at all—it's actually a cake made from two round tiers of sponge cake, layered with a creamy custard filling, and frosted with a silky chocolate glaze or ganache. While there's nothing particularly unique about this combination of ingredients, it's one wicked awesome dessert, bub. The dessert was first created at the Parker House Hotel in Boston in 1856. Fast-forward 140 years, and this humble "pie" became the official dessert of Massachusetts.

There are so many ways to celebrate today now that the flavors of a Boston cream pie show up in everything from coffee to ice cream. To celebrate today, I went to my local grocer, bought a pie along with a pint of strawberries to go with it (a heavenly combination of flavors, by the way), went home, ate until I hurt . . . and then guilt-shared what was left with my neighbors.

Y'know, sometimes pie really is better than cake.

NATIONAL FOOD DAY

"If more of us valued food and cheer and song above hoarded gold, it would be a merrier world." —J.R.R. Tolkien, The Hobbit

National Food Day was created by the Center for Science in the Public Interest as a way to address and improve food-related issues in our country, like hunger, nutrition and diet, sustainability, animal welfare, and equality in working conditions on farms.

There are lots of ways you can celebrate today. Perhaps one of the best is by giving nonperishable food items to local food banks. In the past, I used to wonder about food and clothing drives: Do people actually get the items that other people give? The answer is *yes.*

I spent a summer working at a food bank, and I can tell you firsthand that there are so many people in our own neighborhoods who are starving. That brown bag of canned and boxed goods you put together means so much to a family in need, whether it's a humble family of refugees who made it safely out of Africa and are starting over again here in the States, or (and I saw this a lot) proud, local farmers, who are used to providing for themselves but who have lost their land/fallen on hard times for whatever reason. What you give—whatever you give (whether you donate nonperishable goods or produce from your own garden)—really does make a world of difference. If you're not sure where to give, Feeding America has a really useful food bank locator on their website at *FeedingAmerica.org.*

DID YOU KNOW?

The five basic tastes humans can detect are salty, sweet, sour, bitter, and umami (think savory).

Today is also National Bologna Day and National Good & Plenty Day.

OCTOBER 25

NATIONAL GREASY FOODS DAY

"Greasy food might not be good for your body, but it does wonders for the soul."
—*Jessica Zafra*, Chicken Pox for the Soul

Acne. Diarrhea. Acid reflux. Obesity. Diabetes. Gallstones. Sleep apnea. Asthma.

These are just some of the awesome benefits of a diet heavy in greasy foods.

But just for today, let's forget about all that. Because it's National Greasy Foods Day—an unofficial holiday devoted entirely to that glistening sinful side of the culinary world we all secretly love. Besides, greasy foods are a great hangover remedy, and they also provide relief from bad first dates, bad last dates, no dates, a broken kitchen, post-drunken karaoke nights, your wallet, your friends' wallets, etc.

So what do you crave? Crispy onion rings? A bag of potato chips? Movie theater popcorn drowned in butter? A doughnut filled with cream and covered with chocolate? Maybe a slice of pizza you need to dab your napkin on to sop up all the extra grease? Or what about deep-fried candy bars, ravioli, fritters, Coke, or anything else you can imagine?

I won't judge if you won't.

*Today is also World Pasta Day
and National Sourest Day.*

OCTOBER 26

NATIONAL PUMPKIN DAY

"We fancy men are individuals; so are pumpkins; but every pumpkin in the field goes through every point of pumpkin history." —Ralph Waldo Emerson, "Nominalist and Realist"

I have absolutely no problem with the fact that pumpkin invades *everything* I eat and drink during this time of year. Pumpkin beer, pumpkin pie, pumpkin paired with chocolate anything, pumpkin spiced lattes, doughnuts, waffles, chili, soups, and pasta like pumpkin-filled ravioli all taste like the embodiment of the latter half of autumn to me (the first part belonging to my beloved apple).

Every year since I turned eighteen, I have carved (after removing and baking the seeds, which is exactly how I encourage you to celebrate today)

the *same* face on my pumpkin: two triangle eyes— the points on the top—and a wide grin with one big tooth on the bottom of the mouth. What can I say? I like my Jack-o'-lanterns happy!

Interestingly enough, it's believed that Jack-o'-lanterns used to be made from turnips (or rutabagas, beets, potatoes, etc.), but when immigrants from the United Kingdom relocated to the States, they may have switched to pumpkins because their size and shape made them much easier to carve. I mean seriously, think about trying to carve a turnip!

Today is also National Mincemeat Day and National Pretzel Day.

WICKED-EASY PUMPKIN SEEDS

Makes 2 to 3 cups

2 large carving pumpkins

½ cup (1 stick) unsalted butter, melted

2 teaspoons salt

Preheat the oven to 350°F.

Line a baking sheet with aluminum foil and set it aside.

Cut off the tops of the pumpkins, scoop out the insides and seeds, and put everything into a colander. (Set the pumpkins aside to carve happy faces into them after you're done making the pumpkin seeds!)

Pick the seeds out of the colander, set them aside, throw away the insides, and return the seeds to the colander. Rinse the pumpkin seeds really well in warm water, lay them flat onto paper towels, and dry the seeds until they are completely free of moisture.

Spread the pumpkin seeds evenly onto the baking sheet and pour the butter over them to coat. Place the baking sheet in the oven and bake for 10 minutes. Take them out and use a spatula to flip them. Return the baking sheet to the oven and bake the seeds for another 5 minutes, and flip them again. Repeat this process until the pumpkin seeds become a deep golden-brown. Keep an eye on the seeds, as they can go from perfect golden-brown to charcoal black in just minutes.

Remove the seeds from the oven and let them dry slightly before sprinkling them generously with salt. Let the seeds dry completely before eating them. Store any leftovers in an airtight container.

NATIONAL POTATO DAY

"What I say is that, if a fellow really likes potatoes, he must be a pretty decent sort of fellow." —A.A. Milne

While the U.S. celebrates National Potato Day in October, Ireland celebrates it on August 25th. Theirs began as an initiative of the potato industry itself, and the goal was to bring attention to the vegetable's importance to the country's economy and its role in a healthy, well-balanced diet.

Doesn't matter if it's the Emerald Isle or the Land of Opportunity, I think we can all agree that the potato has been a staple food throughout our global history. Really, potatoes are the undisputed kings of starch. From Vikings to vicars, potatoes have always been the side dish of choice. Sure, rice is important, but you never hear people say, "He's a meat and rice kind of guy," do you? No! It's always "meat and potatoes."

But today it's time for the studly spud to come out from behind the shadows of whatever huge hunk of carcass it has been overshadowed by and bathe in its twenty-four hours of fame.

Today is also National American Beer Day.

POTAJE DE ERIKA

Makes 2 large bowls of soup or
4 smaller bowls

2 large potatoes, peeled and quartered
1 large onion, peeled and quartered
3 large carrots, diced
¼ cup cream or milk
¼ teaspoon crushed red pepper flakes
½ teaspoon salt
½ teaspoon black pepper

Boil the potatoes, onion, and carrots until soft; drain. Place the vegetables in a food processor or blender and liquefy. Add the cream, pepper flakes, salt, and pepper. Eat immediately.

NATIONAL WILD FOODS DAY

"And John himself was clothed in camel's hair, with a leather belt around his waist; and his food was locusts and wild honey." —Matthew, 3:4

My sister is my favorite foodie. When we were little, I used to blindfold her, go into the kitchen, mix a bunch of random ingredients together, and force her to eat them. And she always guessed what they were correctly: "Um . . . ranch-flavored tortilla chips, orange juice, leftover ham salad, capers, and mint jelly?"

She has the palate of a champion and an iron stomach to boot. And she is one of the only people I know who'll seriously try anything once (which has led her to eat a whole different kind of wild food!). I appreciate her for this. Growing up, she loved prepackaged foods, so when I asked what her thoughts were on National Wild Foods Day I was surprised when she answered, "With wild foods you know where you stand, because you know what's in it. I

mean, seriously, some of the processed foods are made with eight-syllable, man-manufactured, preservative chemicals—while they might taste absolutely delicious, sometimes they make me wonder what's being done to my insides. You can't deny the pure flavor of food grown outside."

And that's what today is all about—eating foods found growing naturally in the wild. (But as I've reminded you before, this doesn't mean you should run outside and eat the first mushroom you find!) Educate yourself or take a trained professional with you and enjoy some of the hidden delicacies nature has to offer.

Today is also National Chocolate Day and Global Champagne Day.

NATIONAL OATMEAL DAY

"It is a hard matter, my fellow citizens, to argue with the belly, since it has no ears."
—Marcus Porcius Cato

Because I got chicken pox at such an old age (I was almost fifteen; it was traumatic), I have really bad memories of oatmeal baths and lotions. As a result, I went quite a few years before eating the stuff again. When I started considering a career as an Olympic athlete (seriously: I even tried out for the United States Bobsled and Skeleton Federation once), oatmeal became one of the staple foods in my diet. I would go snowboarding from nine a.m. to nine p.m., and both oatmeal and peanut butter sandwiches were what sustained me. (Probably because oatmeal is loaded with complex carbs, water-soluble fiber, and B vitamins, which translates to slower digestion, stabilized sugar levels, and a boost in energy.)

I don't eat much oatmeal anymore, as I've given up my dreams of competitive sports for now (although competitive eating has always intrigued me). I do keep oatmeal in the house at all times, though; it's one of my favorite foods to eat when it's snowing outside. And since I choose to live in Maine, it could snow at *any* given moment.

And one must always be prepared for a freak July blizzard!

AMY'S OATY BALLS

Makes 13 if you're using the veg recipe;
16 if you're using the meat recipe

1 pound ground turkey
1 spicy Italian sausage link, casing removed
½ cup grated Parmesan cheese
½ cup quick oats
1 small bundle fresh parsley, chopped (about ¼ cup)

Preheat the oven to 350°F.

Grease a baking sheet and set it aside.

In a large bowl, use your hands to mix the turkey, sausage, cheese, oatmeal, and parsley together. Form the mixture into 2-inch balls and place them on the baking sheet.

Bake the meatballs for 20 minutes, flip them over, and bake for another 10 minutes. Check the meatballs to make sure the centers are fully cooked—you may need to cook them for another 5 minutes.

Remove the meatballs from the oven, drain off the fat, and serve them as is, in sauce, over pasta, or in sandwiches.

Tip! Wanna make these veg-friendly? Use 1 (14-ounce) sleeve of Lightlife's Gimme Lean Sausage instead of ground turkey and 1 (12-ounce) sleeve of soy chorizo (I prefer the Trader Joe's kind) instead of a spicy Italian sausage link. Bake the meatballs for just 30 minutes, flipping once halfway through. Remove from the oven (there will be no fat to drain off—yay!) and use however you like!

OCTOBER 30
NATIONAL CANDY CORN DAY

"All the candy corn that was ever made was made in 1911." —Lewis Black

Love 'em or leave 'em, candy corn has become synonymous with Halloween. I don't particularly like candy corn, but every year around this time I feel obligated to eat some. It just doesn't feel like the end of autumn until I do!

George Renninger of the Wunderle Candy Company is usually credited with the invention of candy corn (which once went by the name of Chicken Feed) sometime in the 1880s. It was supposed to resemble a kernel of corn. People ended up really fancying the candy, too, because it was one of the first to feature three different colors! And in

almost one and a half centuries since their creation, candy corn hasn't changed in taste, look, or design.

Talk about staying true to who you are!

So whether you like the actual candy corn or the little pumpkins that sometimes come with it (I know people who think the pumpkins taste better, even though they're made with the same ingredients!), make sure you pop at least one piece of candy corn in your mouth today.

Today is also National Buy a Doughnut Day.

NATIONAL CANDY/CARAMEL APPLE DAY

"Lemme just talk to you for a second about something that I think is good for America: caramel apples. . . . I had one last night. Delicious. Not talking about candy apples. I think candy apples are a danger! You crack 'em, they're very sharp. You candy apple crowd need to wake up!" —Stephen Colbert

How are you celebrating tonight? Are you trick-or-treating? I did until I was twenty-five years old, by the way; I made a bet with my mom for $50 that I could do it until I was thirty because of how young I look. At twenty-five, she handed me $25 and asked me to stop. I think she was embarrassed for me.

Hitting the town all dressed up "just because," or having a quiet night in? However you choose to celebrate today, a caramel apple seems like the quintessential end-of-October treat to enjoy before going into the official holiday season.

There's some debate as to whether today is National *Caramel* Apple Day or National *Candy* Apple Day. You know what I think? There's no wrong answer (especially since caramel *is* a kind of confectionary)! It's all a matter of preference since most places sell both options now. So if you like that sticky, crunchy, sweet red-candy shell, go with that. If you like the softer, gooier, melt-in-your-mouth texture of caramel, well that's all right, too.

Me? I'm Team Caramel. How could I not be? In this day and age, creative culinary minds have added everything from chocolate, peanut butter, sea salt, candies, and dried fruits to the already-delicious treat!

Just make sure that whichever one you go with, you have a toothpick or toothbrush on hand.

NOVEMBER IS...

NOVEMBER IS ALSO...

National Apple Month
National Fun with Fondue Month
National Georgia Pecan Month
National Good Nutrition Month
National Peanut Butter Lover's Month
National Pepper Month
National Peppercorn Month
National Pomegranate Month
National Raisin Bread Month
National Roasting Month
Vegan Awareness Month

. . .

1st Wednesday—National Eating Healthy Day
1st Thursday—Men Make Dinner Day
3rd Thursday—Beaujolais Nouveau Day
4th Thursday—National Turkey Day
4th Thursday—Stuffing Day
4th Friday (or day after Thanksgiving)—National Leftovers Day

WORLD VEGAN DAY

"Flesh-eating by humans is unnecessary, irrational, anatomically unsound, unhealthy, unhygienic, uneconomic, unaesthetic, unkind, and unethical. May I elaborate?" —Helen Nearing, Simple Food for the Good Life

Not only is it World Vegan Day, it's the start of Vegan Awareness Month! Today is an annual celebration that brings to light the benefits of an entirely plant-based diet and lifestyle. It was established in 1994 by Louise Wallis, who was the president and chair of The Vegan Society in the U.K. at the time.

Vegans not only avoid eating sentient beings, but they also avoid animal by-products like eggs, dairy, honey, wool, leather, down, or silk, as well as any products that *contain* animal (some cosmetics have snail slime in them, for example) or were tested *on* animals. Sugar is also questionable, as some of it is processed through bone char, which gives it that impeccable white color.

There are lots of reasons why people choose to go vegan. For some, they feel like it's a more sustainable lifestyle, helping to preserve the environment. Others find it's a far healthier and more natural diet. Some do it for ethical, spiritual, and compassionate reasons, as they don't want to endorse or contribute to the unnecessary violence and exploitation of animals. And, still others do it for cultural reasons: The first vegan boy I ever dated didn't relate to a "steak and women masculinity" and felt veganism was a very positive assertion of his belief in the type of man and individual he was and wanted to be.

Whatever your reason . . . go vegan today! And once you realize it's not as difficult as you might think, try participating weekly in Meatless Mondays.

Today is also National French Fried Clams Day and National Vinegar Day.

THAI FOR TWO-ISH

Makes 2 to 4 servings

½ cup coconut milk

½ cup hoisin sauce

2 tablespoons Bragg's Liquid Aminos or soy sauce

2 teaspoons zest and 2 tablespoons freshly squeezed juice (from one medium lime)

1½ tablespoons packed brown sugar

1 teaspoon grated fresh ginger

2 tablespoons olive oil, divided

1 (8-ounce) package tempeh, cut into cubes

1 (8-ounce) can sliced water chestnuts, drained and rinsed

1 (14-ounce) can baby corn, drained and rinsed

2 cups frozen broccoli florets, thawed

1 cup cooked jasmine rice (optional)

Thai Lime & Chili Cashews from Trader Joe's (optional)

In a medium bowl, whisk together the coconut milk, hoisin sauce, Bragg's, lime zest and juice, brown sugar, and ginger until everything is well combined. Set the sauce aside.

Drizzle 1 tablespoon of the olive oil into a large skillet and sauté the tempeh on medium-high heat until all sides are golden-brown, about 8 to 10 minutes. Add the water chestnuts, corn, broccoli, and remaining olive oil. Continue sautéing until the broccoli is cooked through, about 4 to 6 minutes.

Turn the heat down to low, add the sauce, and stir until everything is well combined. When the sauce has thickened slightly, turn the heat off. Serve as is or, if desired, over jasmine rice and topped with Thai Lime and Chili Cashews.

Tip! Double-check that the hoisin sauce you get doesn't contain (or isn't manufactured on the same equipment) as fish.

NATIONAL DEVILED EGG DAY

"If I wanted to bring a large number of deviled eggs, but I didn't want to share them with anyone else, can you guarantee fridge space?" —Ron Swanson, Parks and Rec

What's the common thread at New Year's Eve parties, Easter, Memorial Day BBQs, Fourth of July, Labor Day BBQs, Thanksgiving, and Christmas? If your guess is deviled eggs, you're right on! This popular little hors d'oeuvre shows up at just about every get-together there is. Why? Could be because they're easy to pop into your mouth, making them the quintessential finger food, or maybe because generation after generation has always made them for family gatherings (and tradition can be hard to break).

My sister and I used to love deviled eggs. Sadly, so did all our cousins. If we didn't get to Thanksgiving (for example) early enough—despite the fact that our aunts always made *multiple* platters of them—the deviled eggs would all be eaten. I think our parents always thought we were eager to spend time with our family, when in reality we wanted to be the first at every get-together to stake our claim on the eggs. If this sounds like you, don't be embarrassed by your love. Instead of being tardy or showing up embarrassingly early to your next party, take control and make the deviled eggs yourself . . . that way you can make an extra batch just for yourself!

DEVILISHLY GREEN EGGS (WITH A BACON SURPRISE)

Makes 24 halves

Note: This dish takes 1 hour to prepare and 1 hour to chill.

12 large eggs

8 slices bacon or tempeh bacon

1 avocado, skinned, seeded, and chopped

½ cup mayonnaise

1 teaspoon Sriracha or hot sauce

¼ teaspoon salt

1 or 2 jalapeños, seeded and diced

¾ teaspoon lime juice

Gently place the eggs in a large pot, fill the pot with cold water to cover the eggs completely, bring them to a boil, and boil them for 5 minutes. Leaving the pan on the burner, turn off the heat, place a lid on the pan, and let the eggs sit (covered) for 45 minutes to finish cooking.

While the eggs are sitting, cook the bacon in a skillet until it's crispy. Place the bacon on 2 or 3 paper towels to dry. Cut six slices of bacon into four pieces each (twenty-four—one for each egg half) and set them aside. Crumble the other two slices of bacon and set the crumbles aside.

After the eggs have cooked, drain the pan and run cold water over the eggs until the shells feel cool to the touch, about 2 to 3 minutes. Gently peel the eggs, discard the shells, and cut each egg in half lengthwise. Gently remove the yolk from each egg half and put the yolks in a medium bowl. Place the whites on a serving tray, plate, or the bottom of a flat container.

Add the avocado, mayonnaise, hot sauce, salt, jalapeños, and the lime juice to the yolks in the bowl. Mash everything (a fork works great for this) until it is smooth.

Spoon the yolk filling equally into the twenty-four egg white holes. Place one of the twenty-four pieces of bacon onto each of the deviled green eggs, then sprinkle the bacon crumb over the top. Cover with plastic wrap and chill for 1 hour before serving.

NOVEMBER 03 NATIONAL SANDWICH DAY

"Too few people understand a really good sandwich." —James Beard

Popular food lore says that John Montagu (the fourth Earl of Sandwich) loved to gamble so much that he refused to stop to eat. One night he asked his servants or the cook to bring him lunch meat tucked between two slices of bread so he could eat with one hand and keep gambling with the other.

The ultimate in convenience, no?

Anyway, the moral of the story is to not let food snobs turn their nose up at you when you proudly proclaim that sandwiches are among your favorite foods. If it was good enough for an earl, it's good enough for you!

It might be difficult choosing exactly how you want to celebrate today—there are just so many sandwich options! Finding the right one really depends on your mood, the season, and your frame of mind. If you're feeling autumnal and nostalgic, maybe a turkey, cranberry, and stuffing sandwich on a sub roll sounds good. Seems appropriate for this time of year, doesn't it?

Or maybe you might want something with more levity and energy like a hummus, cucumber, and sprouts sandwich on multigrain bread. I know I could certainly polish off one or two of those and still feel good about myself. What about something sexy yet substantial like Dubliner cheese and avocado slices on sourdough bread? If I were a sandwich, I think that's what I'd want to be. Maybe with a couple slices of apple, too!

NATIONAL CANDY DAY

"There's nothing as cozy as a piece of candy and a book." —Betty MacDonald,
Mrs. Piggle-Wiggle's Magic

I think it's safe to assume that simply saying the word *candy* invokes all sorts of delightful memories for most of us. For my sister, it was when our parents let us walk to the convenience store alone—the ultimate feeling of responsibility when we were younger—to buy candy cigarettes and buttons, wax bottles filled with "juice," Sixlets, Warheads, Ouch! Bubble Gum, Tongue Splashers, and Swedish Fish.

Whether you prefer chocolate, taffy, jawbreakers, jelly beans, gummies, lollipops, licorice, or even gum, you can't deny it: Candy is universal. It's a language we all speak; offer someone, regardless of age or nationality, a piece of candy, and he or she becomes an instant friend. It's how I won favor with the Spanish boy I au paired for in Ireland. He and I would walk to the shopping center, and we would both fill a bag at the candy kiosk. His was always filled with brightly colored crunchy things, and mine was a collection of cola-flavored gummies and chocolate-covered honeycomb.

Delightful, indeed!

DID YOU KNOW?

Candy was once advertised as a health food.

CANDIED ORANGE PEELS MY WAY

Makes about 2 cups

Note: This dish should be made the day before serving.

- 4 medium oranges
- 3 cups granulated sugar, divided
- 4 ounces dark chocolate chips (about 1 cup) (optional)

Line a baking sheet with waxed paper and set it aside.

With a sharp knife, peel the skins from the oranges. If the pith is thick, gently slice off as much as you can (it's okay if you don't get it all). Cut the peels into ¼- to ½-inch wide strips and set them aside.

Place 2½ cups of water into a 2-quart saucepan with 2 cups of the sugar. On medium-high heat, allow the sugar to dissolve completely before adding the peels. (Do *not* stir unless the sugar is not melting evenly. Then one quick stir should be okay.) Allow the mixture to come to a boil before turning the heat down to low. Simmer for 35 minutes, giving the pan a shake every 5 or 6 minutes to redistribute everything.

Drain the sugar water from the peels, making sure to shake off any excess water. Set the peels in a colander on a towel to allow all of the water to drain.

Spread the remaining cup of sugar on the baking sheet with waxed paper. Shake the peels in the colander one last time, and then place them evenly on the sugar.

Gently roll the peels around in the sugar so that they are evenly coated. Place the sugar-coated peels on a wire rack to dry. (I usually find a window with a cool breeze and place my oranges there.) After 4 to 5 hours, they should be quite dry and beginning to harden.

If using chocolate, melt it in a double boiler or in the microwave. Dip half of each candied peel into the melted chocolate, place the peels onto the waxed paper-lined baking sheet, and refrigerate for 1 hour to harden before eating.

Tip! It's best *not* to make these when it's humid out!

NOVEMBER 05 NATIONAL DOUGHNUT APPRECIATION DAY

"An actor without a playwright is like a hole without a doughnut."
—George Jean Nathan

I am a foodie who can appreciate a good doughnut; the sweet treat and I have had a serious love affair since I was born. One day, when I was quite young, I was carrying a box of doughnut holes up my aunt's very steep driveway. However, the bottom of the box unfolded, opened, and doughnuts started rolling down the hill. I screamed, "Oh no—doh-doh's are falling!" I sat down as fast as I could, slamming the box onto my lap to prevent any more from falling out. Pretty ingenious for a three-year-old—I must have saved at least half the box. Oh, the things we do for love!

A fella named Adolph Levitt helped the doughnut industry explode. He was a Russian-born immigrant and is credited with creating the first automated doughnut machine. It was featured at the World's Fair in Chicago in 1934. The doughnuts being mass-produced by the impressive, futuristic machine were called "the hit food of the Century of Progress."

Today is just one of many doughnut holidays celebrated this year. So help keep the industry alive and well by splurging at one of your favorite bakeries today!

NOVEMBER 06 — NATIONAL NACHOS DAY

"Why is it so hard to find an exercise bike with a nice little basket where I can put my nachos?" —Ron Alderson

I wish every day could be National Nachos Day. They're one of my favorite foods to eat and make at home. I'm so embarrassingly messy and gluttonous when I eat them that it's best if I'm where no one can see me and/or get in my way and potentially lose a hand as I plow through a mountain of them.

I don't mess around when it comes to nachos.

Food legend says that nachos were created by Ignacio "Nacho" Anaya in Piedras Negras, Mexico, in 1943. Wives of U.S. soldiers stationed at a nearby fort went to eat at a place called the Victory Club after it had already closed for the night. Not wanting to disappoint his customers, maitre d' Ignacio whipped together a dish for them (he must have known how dangerous a hungry woman can be) and called it *Nachos Especiales*; it consisted of fried corn tortillas, melted Cheddar cheese, and sliced jalapeño peppers. Word spread through Texas and Mexico about his new snack, and it became so popular that Ignacio eventually opened his own nacho-based restaurant.

No matter how you like your nachos—with guacamole, pico de gallo, olive tapenade, sweet potato chili, crabmeat, or pulled pork—my one suggestion is to go big or go home!

(Although if you're "going big" with your nacho toppings, you might want to stay home to enjoy them!)

THE TROPICAL MOUNTAIN

Makes 4 to 6 servings

1 (13-ounce) bag tortilla chips
1 (15-ounce) can vegetarian refried beans
½ cup coconut milk
½ cup sweetened shredded coconut, divided
1 (8-ounce) bag shredded pepper jack cheese
    (about 2 cups)
1 cup chipotle salsa
1 ripe mango, peeled, seeded, and cubed
1 ripe avocado, peeled, seeded, and cubed
1 lime, cut into wedges, for garnish

Turn the broiler on.

Line a baking sheet with aluminum foil and place the chips on it, spreading them out to a single layer.

In a bowl, mix the refried beans together with the coconut milk and ¼ cup of the shredded coconut. Scoop this mixture into a large plastic baggy, snip off one corner of the baggie, and squeeze the contents evenly onto the chips. Sprinkle the remaining coconut and all of the cheese evenly across the top of the nachos.

Broil the nachos until the cheese is melty, bubbly, and beginning to brown, about 7 minutes.

Take the nachos out of the oven and top them evenly with the salsa, mango, and avocado. Serve with wedges of lime and cold beer, if desired.

NATIONAL BITTERSWEET CHOCOLATE WITH ALMONDS DAY

"Happiness. Simple as a glass of chocolate or tortuous as the heart. Bitter. Sweet. Alive." —Joanne Harris, Chocolat

We've had both a National Bittersweet Chocolate Day (January 10, page 18) and a National Almond Day (February 16, page 59), but what haven't we had yet? A National Bittersweet Chocolate with Almonds Day!

So here we are.

What's awesome about bittersweet chocolate? Not only is it a good source of natural antioxidants, which can reduce the risk of cardiovascular disease, stroke, and high blood pressure, but chocolate is also known to release neurotransmitters like serotonin and dopamine, which make us feel happy.

And, as if that isn't enough, almonds have been known to stabilize sugar levels (which helps prevent diabetes), lower cholesterol, and improve the health of hair and skin.

Put them together and it's kind of like you have some superhuman food, right? No wonder today has its own food holiday!

DID YOU KNOW?

Eating almonds increases sperm count.

INTERNATIONAL STOUT DAY

"May your glass be ever full. May the roof over your head be always strong. And may you be in heaven half an hour before the devil knows you're dead." —An Irish toast

Working as a Guinness Girl, I was always so shocked when women in particular were turned off by the drink. "It's so heavy, and you know I'm trying to watch my weight," was my favorite excuse. Amusing to me (and I told them as much) was that the malt beverage they clutched in their hand contained an average of 280 calories. A pint of Guinness was roughly around 170.

My very first pint was at The Quay's Bar in the Temple Bar of Dublin, Ireland, on St. Patrick's Day. It really doesn't get much more genuine than that, does it? I was twenty, living in Ireland, and working as an au pair for a Spanish woman. We lived with a German woman, her son, and her Slovakian au pair. The household decided to go out and celebrate St. Patrick's Day together with our friends from Mexico, Poland, and Northern Ireland—it's

one of those unique moments in time you could never imagine yourself in and when you do, you don't forget a single detail! Our eclectic crew entered Quay's Bar, ate a hearty, traditional meal (bangers and mash for me), and toasted with pints of Guinness and tumblers of Bailey's.

Cliché? Maybe. Authentic? Entirely!

DID YOU KNOW?

In 1759, Arthur Guinness signed a 9,000-year lease on the abandoned St. James Gate Brewery in Dublin.

Today is also National Cappuccino Day, National Harvey Wallbanger Day, and Cook Something Bold and Pungent Day.

NOVEMBER 09 | NATIONAL SCRAPPLE DAY

"Pull into the truck stop and get yourself some scrapple made out of sexy."
—Disco DJ, Starsky and Hutch

Scrapple is a mixture of ground pork scraps (think the leftover bits like brains, fat, organs, skin, etc.), broth, cornmeal, and seasonings like thyme, sage, and cayenne that are formed into a loaf, refrigerated to cool and set/congeal, before being sliced and fried. It was introduced Stateside as *pon haus* by the Pennsylvania Dutch. Similar foods to scrapple include livermush (made from pig liver and head), which is served in the South, and white pudding (made from pork fat and meat), which is popular in parts of the U.K.

Scrapple tastes a bit like a crispy, grainy, gamey meatloaf or sausage. It can be eaten for breakfast with eggs and home fries, or in sandwiches, and is often topped with ketchup, maple syrup, honey, molasses, mustard, horseradish, or even applesauce.

It may not sound appetizing, but don't scrap today . . . step out of your comfort zone and give this dish a chance to show you why it's so beloved.

NOVEMBER 10 | NATIONAL VANILLA CUPCAKE DAY

"A lot of movies are about life, mine are like a slice of cake." —Alfred Hitchcock

Does life get any sweeter?

The first printed reference to one of these deliciously small cakes-for-one can be traced to an 1828 book called *Seventy-five Receipts for Pastry, Cakes, and Sweetmeats* by Eliza Leslie.

But where exactly does the word "cupcake" originate? There are two possibilities:

1. Miniature cakes were often made in individual cups (this was before the muffin tins, obviously).

2. "Cup cakes" were cakes that were made with ingredients measured out by the cupful. They were even referred to as "1234 cakes," because they were made with four easy-to-remember ingredients: one cup of butter, two cups of sugar, three cups of flour, and four eggs.

Vanilla cupcakes are delicious as is, but if you're looking for a little extra oomph, why not jazz them up with lavender, chopped nuts, a drizzle of caramel, or even some white chocolate (which no one would see coming given the similar appearance?).

DID YOU KNOW?

Hostess Cupcakes were first sold in 1919.

NOVEMBER 11 · NATIONAL SUNDAE DAY

"You know, all that really matters is that the people you love are happy and healthy. Everything else is just sprinkles on the sundae." —Paul Walker

Regardless of how full I am after eating a big meal, I always have room for ice cream. My (irrational) reasoning is that, because it melts, it doesn't actually fill you up anymore—it just sort of dissolves into the cracks of the food already sitting in your stomach and digesting. However silly it may sound, it usually works on whomever I'm trying to persuade to eat dessert with me.

That being said, could you handle one of the world's most expensive sundaes? Called "The Golden Opulence" and served at Serendipity 3 in New York, it was introduced in 2004 to celebrate the restaurant's fiftieth anniversary.

For $1,000 you get:

- five scoops of rich Tahitian vanilla bean ice cream that's infused with Madagascar vanilla and covered in a 23K edible gold leaf.
- a drizzle of the world's most expensive chocolate (Amedei Porceleana) and chunks of rare Chuao chocolate (made from cocoa beans harvested near the Caribbean Sea on the coast of Venezuela).

- toppings like exotic candied fruits from Paris, gold dragets, truffles, and marzipan cherries.
- a glass bowl of Grand Passion Caviar, a dessert caviar made from salt-free American Golden caviar (known for its sparkling golden color) that is placed on top of the sundae.
- the sundae served in a Harcourt crystal goblet with an 18K gold spoon.

The whole thing is sweetened and infused with fresh passion fruit, orange, and Armagnac.

So . . . you in?

DID YOU KNOW?

Sugar is actually the only taste humans are born craving.

NOVEMBER 12 · NATIONAL PIZZA WITH EVERYTHING (EXCEPT ANCHOVIES) DAY

"A tavola non si invecchia." (At the table with good friends and family, you do not become old.) —Italian proverb

Today is not for the faint of heart because it's all about celebrating pizza with absolutely any- and everything you can think of. (Except anchovies—who wants fishiness overpowering all the other awesome flavors of a pizza, anyway?)

So what will you put on top of your pie today?

Maybe a "BLT"-style 'za with ranch dressing, sliced tomatoes, mozzarella cheese, and prosciutto, topped with fresh, shredded lettuce before being served? Or how about a Philly cheesesteak pizza? One that has gooey provolone, green peppers, onions, mushrooms, and steak shreds? That could be good. I make a pretty mean vegan pizza with potatoes, leeks, tempeh bacon, and a cashew cream sauce. Perhaps I'll whip that up again!

For me, today is all about being creative and not eating "just cheese" or "pepperoni." So I splurged and went with smoked tomatoes, Taleggio cheese, and leeks with fresh arugula dressed in olive oil on top—with no anchovies, of course.

Take the flavors you like, toss them on some pizza dough, and have a very happy National Pizza with Everything (Except Anchovies) Day.

Today is also National Chicken Soup for the Soul Day.

NOVEMBER 13 — NATIONAL INDIAN PUDDING DAY

"If you do your fair day's work, you are certain to get your fair day's wage— in praise or pudding, whichever happens to suit your tastes." —Alexander Smith

Indian pudding is a popular dessert here in the Northeast, but there are still plenty of locals who've never heard of it before. It's a rich, spiced pudding-meets-custard-meets-porridge type of dessert that originated in colonial times, and it calls for cornmeal instead of flour. The main ingredient? Molasses—something our region definitely has an abundance of!

With Thanksgiving so soon, this seems like an appropriately placed food holiday in our calendar of eats. Indian pudding, when done well (it has to be dense, not runny), is both comforting and delicious. If you've never had it, today's the perfect time to try it. A friend of mine suggests that, regardless of which recipe you use, it's much easier to make Indian pudding (his favorite food) by sight, smell, and soul.

Which I'd say is true for any time you cook!

NOVEMBER 14 NATIONAL PICKLE DAY

"Hunger is the best pickle." —Ben Franklin

I have a cousin who *loved* pickles. So much so that one summer he announced that he'd be perfectly content if all he got for Christmas was a jar of them. My family, perennial jokesters that they are, decided to make that a reality. Christmas day came, and there were dozens and dozens of jars individually wrapped under the tree waiting for him. Joke was on the rest of us, though—my cousin was genuinely delighted that we had listened to him and got him exactly what he wanted.

I like pickles, too (not as much as my cousin did—not sure I've ever actually met anyone else as besotted with them as he was), and I'm thrilled that they have their own food holiday. The consummate condiment, pickles are *more* than just something you tuck away into a hamburger for a bit of a sour crunch. After all, pickles are to cucumbers what french fries are to potatoes . . . a simple veg that can be dressed up and made into a star!

There are loads of different types of pickles—which comes from the Dutch word *pekel* for "brine"—to choose from today, including kosher dill, sour, half-sour, sugar-free, reduced-sodium, sodium-free, garlic, garlic dill, zesty dill, bread and butter, spicy bread and butter, and gherkin. Or you could chow down on *pickled* things like beets, watermelon, ginger, jalapeños, or green beans. Still not enough of a crunch for you? Why not try pickle-flavored potato chips or popcorn?

Just don't admit you love pickles too much . . . you never know who's listening!

DID YOU KNOW?

Acerophobia is the fear of sour foods.

Today is also National Spicy Guacamole Day.

NATIONAL CLEAN OUT YOUR REFRIGERATOR DAY

"One of the very nicest things about life is the way we must regularly stop whatever it is we are doing and devote our attention to eating." —Luciano Pavarotti, Pavarotti, My Own Story

Maybe I'm interpreting it wrong, but "cleaning out your fridge" sounds less like an unpleasant task of throwing away mysterious food items and more like an opportunity to eat delicious things you totally forgot were there! Think of today as a treasure hunt of sorts.

Although I do feel obligated to repeat the old adage: "When in doubt, throw it out." We've come this far into eating the year, and while we've chowed down on some pretty crazy stuff, I just can't handle the idea of you risking your health on some salsa you're unsure is green from tomatillos or green from mold!

Today is the perfect opportunity to practice the "out with the old and in with the new" concept too, as you bin everything that's unnecessary to create space for all those holiday goodies that will be coming in and out over the next month and change. You'll appreciate this in a week or so when you aren't trying to either (A) delicately pull something out of the Jenga-like situation happening in your fridge, or (B) cram something into your overly crowded refrigerator and thus perpetuating the Jenga-like situation.

See, if ever there were a "food" holiday we needed—today is it!

DID YOU KNOW?

Before the invention of the refrigerator, icehouses were used to provide cool storage for most of the year.

Today is also National Bundt Cake Day, National Spicy Hermit Cookie Day, and National Raisin Bran Day.

SHEPHERDESS PIE

Makes 2 to 4 servings

- 1 tablespoon olive oil
- 14 ounces ground pork or soy sausage
- 1 medium sweet potato, peeled and cubed (about 2½ cups)
- ½ large cauliflower, cut into florets (about 2½ cups)
- 2 tablespoons salted butter
- ½ teaspoon salt
- ¼ teaspoon black pepper
- 1 (15-ounce) can creamed corn
- 1 (15-ounce) can sweet peas
- 1 teaspoon paprika

Preheat the oven to 350°F.

Pour the olive oil into a skillet. On medium heat, brown the ground pork or soy sausage in the oil until cooked through, drain, and set aside.

Fill a medium saucepan with water and bring it to a boil. Add the sweet potatoes and cook for 10 minutes. Add the cauliflower and cook for another 10 to 15 minutes, or until the potatoes and the cauliflower are tender.

Empty the vegetables into a colander, shake out any excess water, and return them to the saucepan. Add the butter, salt, and pepper, and mash until everything is creamy.

Place the cooked sausage evenly across the bottom of a 9 x 9-inch casserole dish. Top the sausage with the corn and top the corn with peas. Spread the pan of mashed vegetables evenly over everything, sprinkle with paprika, and bake for 45 minutes.

Tip! Want to make this veg-friendly? Use Lightlife Gimme Lean Sausage instead. To make it vegan, use Earth Balance spread instead of butter.

NATIONAL FAST FOOD DAY

"Prepared and fast foods have given us the time and freedom to see cooking as an art form—a form of creative expression." —Jeff Smith, The Frugal Gormet Keeps the Feast

The term "fast food" was put in the *Merriam-Webster Dictionary* in 1951 as a result of all the burger and fried chicken stands popping up throughout the United States. But the concept of fast food definitely doesn't belong to us. It originated in Ancient Rome where they had street vendors with bread, olives, and wine (that's like my *perfect* fast food situation).

I can just hear the herbivores and health-conscious eaters out there crying out about what an awful food holiday today represents. But "fast food" doesn't strictly mean rolling up at a drive-thru of some evil corporate establishment that represents The Man and having them hand you back a paper sack filled with processed, high-fat, low-quality, underwhelming crap.

Fast food can simply mean edible sustenance that was prepared and served quickly. And sometimes—as a person eating a plant-based diet—*that's* what I really miss: ease and convenience. I spend so much time in the kitchen cooking that sometimes all I want is a break. And if there are companies out there that are creating delicious, healthy, and compassionate meals that I don't have to personally make from scratch? That's fast food to me.

So let's celebrate that, yeah?

DID YOU KNOW?

White Castle opened the first hamburger chain in 1921.

NOVEMBER 17 — NATIONAL BAKLAVA DAY

"Everything is a miracle. It is a miracle that one does not dissolve in one's bath like a lump of sugar." —Pablo Picasso

Crispy, paper-thin layers of phyllo dough, chopped pistachio nuts, and a rich syrup made of honey, vanilla, cinnamon, and lemon.

Baklava may be one of the stickiest, *sexiest* desserts out there.

So whom do we have to thank for this sweet, messy treat? (Seriously, every time I eat baklava I somehow get flakes of it stuck in my hair.) Unfortunately, it's hard to recognize greatness at the moment of occurrence, so there isn't exactly a clear answer. Whoever created the first baklava had no idea what delicious, cuisine-altering dessert they were making. So, whoever created it—the Assyrians, the Chinese, or the Greek guy from the pizza shop who first introduced me to it (and to cheese calzones with no sauce inside but *cold* sauce served on the side when I was eighteen)—thanks!

Today is also National Homemade Bread Day.

NOVEMBER 18 — NATIONAL APPLE CIDER DAY

"When eating fruit, remember who planted the tree; when drinking water, remember who dug the well." —Vietnamese proverb

Apple cider is a raw beverage made from apples. Unlike apple juice, it's unfiltered, unsweetened, and likely unpasteurized if you're getting it right from an orchard—which is the best way to drink apple cider in my opinion, because you won't get it fresher anywhere else!

Growing apples was easy and cheap during colonial times, so it didn't take very long for hard cider to become one of the early states' favorite adult beverages; and, since water quality was questionable back then, it made for the perfect excuse to *only* drink ciders and other libations. ("What's that, Martha? The water looks a little brown today? Pints for breakfast it is!")

Whether you're celebrating today with the hard stuff, with a flavored hot doughnut, or with a mug of your favorite orchard's fresh cider, hot or cold, I hope today you can take a moment to slow down, take a deep breath before the rush of the holiday madness, and revel in the view of wherever you are in your life right now.

Today is also National Vichyssoise Day.

CROCK-POT APPLESAUCE

Makes 6 to 8 servings

Note: This dish needs to cook for 4 hours before serving. This applesauce also freezes easily.

- ½ cup apple cider
- 1 teaspoon vanilla extract
- 8 large apples (a combination of McIntosh and Cortland work best) peeled, quartered, and cored
- ¼ cup packed light brown sugar
- 2 tablespoons ground cinnamon
- ½ teaspoon ground nutmeg

Pour the apple cider and vanilla into a Crock-Pot. (You might think that this is not enough liquid but the apples are filled with water and will reduce to liquid.) Add the apples, brown sugar, cinnamon, and nutmeg. Stir to completely coat the apples. Cover the Crock-Pot and set it on low for 4 hours.

Turn off the Crock-Pot and mash the contents to a consistency of your liking. Serve hot or cold.

Tip! The biggest thing to remember with this recipe? Peel those apples! It really will make a huge difference.

NATIONAL CARBONATED BEVERAGE WITH CAFFEINE DAY

"It's all I have left in my life, caffeine and a poodle." —Brad Garrett

Soda. Pop. Soft drink. Whatever you call it, one thing's for sure: We can't get enough of these sugar-sweetened, bubbly, caffeinated drinks that come in a variety of options, including cola, root beer, ginger ale, cream, citrus, orange, and grape. We've even gone so far as to create Thanksgiving dinner flavors like green bean casserole, green pea, sweet potato, Brussels sprouts, turkey with gravy, dinner roll, mashed potato and butter soda, wild stuffing, cranberry, pumpkin pie, fruit cake, and antacid. (No, seriously—and kudos to Jones Soda for trying out such unique flavors, and for raising money for both St. Jude Children's Research Hospital and Toys for Tots in the process.)

Try not to drink too many sodas (or energy drinks, even if you feel like you might need one as you keep up with either eating the year *or* all the holiday craziness). After all, you don't want to fill up too much before Turkey Day!

DID YOU KNOW?

In 1767, Dr. Joseph Priestley created the first artificially (and drinkable) carbonated glass of water.

NOVEMBER 20 NATIONAL PEANUT BUTTER FUDGE DAY

"Nothing takes the taste out of peanut butter quite like unrequited love."
—Charles M. Schultz

"I fudged up" is the nicer way of saying the R-rated version of "I messed up," right? I know it's National Absurdity Day and all, but it *really* is actually a correct use of the word! One food legend on the history of the candy we're celebrating today states that supposedly a chef botched up a batch of caramels one day and accidentally created what we now know as fudge.

If that's the case, then some mistakes really are epic triumphs!

With my pitiful attempts at making fudge when I celebrated my first year (it always turned out more like a goopy ice-cream topping), I probably should have just gone to the candy store and bought some. But I had been craving a certain flavor profile, and I really needed to conquer my fear of—to put it delicately—fudging up fudge.

So I crafted a peanut butter, bacon, and maple glazed version of the candy that was a little too delicious. Just remember: Sharing is caring. So don't eat it all yourself!

SWEET MEAT FUDGE

Makes one 8 x 8-inch pan

Note: Part of this recipe needs to sit for at least an hour before serving.

½ cup (1 stick) unsalted butter

¾ cup chunky all-natural peanut butter

½ teaspoon vanilla extract

1 teaspoon salt

3 cups confectioners' sugar, divided

¼ cup maple syrup

6 strips bacon, cooked crispy, dried on paper
   towels, crumbled

Grease an 8 x 8-inch pan. Set it aside.

In a medium saucepan, heat the butter, peanut butter, vanilla, and salt together on medium heat until melted. When the mixture comes to a boil, quickly stir in 2 cups of the confectioners' sugar, a little bit at a time, until the mixture thickens. Spread the fudge in the pan.

Quickly whisk together the remaining cup of confectioners' sugar with the maple syrup to make a glaze. Pour the glaze over the top of the fudge to completely cover. Top the fudge with the bacon, pressing them gently into the glaze. Cover tightly with plastic wrap and set aside for at least an hour. You can refrigerate it, but please note: You'll need to let it come back to room temperature before cutting it into pieces and serving.

Tip! Wanna make this veg-friendly? Use vegan butter and your preferred f'acon. (Mine's Turtle Island Smoky Maple Bacon Marinated Tempeh.)

NATIONAL GINGERBREAD DAY

"Everybody needs beauty as well as bread, places to play in and pray in, where nature may heal and give strength to body and soul." —John Muir, **The Yosemite**

Well, hello, National Gingerbread Day—we meet again! It's been such a long time since we first ran into you back on June 5. How was your summer? Are you ready to shine during the season most people associate you with?

The tradition of gingerbread during the holidays comes to us most likely from Germany. They've been making a gingerbread-like sweet called *lebkuchen* since the thirteenth or fourteenth century.

Sure, you could celebrate today with a gingerbread person (many bakeries sell both genders now, so I'm being politically correct!). But it is my strong belief that whenever it's deemed socially acceptable to play with your food, you should always jump at the opportunity to do it. So today I suggest celebrating with a gingerbread house–making kit, which can be loads of fun regardless if you have kids or are just a kid at heart. Though I strongly advise against making one with someone in either the construction or architectural industries; I did once, and lemme tell you: They take things way too seriously!

DID YOU KNOW?

Nuremberg, Germany, is the gingerbread capital of the world.

NATIONAL CASHEW DAY

"Two handfuls of cashews give you the therapeutic equivalent of a prescription dose of Prozac." —Dr. Andrew Saul, Food Matters

I was raised by a family who believed that mom-and-pop stores were a vital part of any community. Whenever we had the opportunity to gas up, buy our groceries, or support in any way, shape, or form our local economy, then that's what we did. Not only is it a more personal experience, but you know exactly where and to whom your money is going.

It was sad to grow up and watch several of those locally owned stores either close their doors or be bought out by major corporations because of the drastic change in our economy.

There was this place in my hometown called Mary's Candies, and they were one of the longest-surviving stores. During the holiday season, we would stop for a treat or two. The older woman who owned the store always let my sister and me watch them mix huge batches of whatever confectionary they were making (with a sample here and there!).

Besides an enormous display case of every kind of chocolate you could think of, they also had the most amazing roasted nuts that glistened attractively under the heat lamps. When you walked into Mary's all you could smell was salt and chocolate. I remember specifically that the cashews were expensive, but we always bought a little bag for our Christmas Eve meal. They were creamy and oily, and no other cashew to date has rivaled their perfection.

So on National Cashew Day, I pay homage to Mary's Candies (and all the mom-and-pop stores that are most certainly missed every day).

DID YOU KNOW?

Cashews are in the same family as pistachios, mangoes, and poison ivy.

Today is also National Cranberry Relish Day.

NATIONAL EAT A CRANBERRY DAY

"It has been an unchallengeable American doctrine that cranberry sauce, a pink goo with overtones of sugared tomatoes, is a delectable necessity of the Thanksgiving board and that turkey is uneatable without it." —Alistair Cooke

Admit it: As a kid you were completely enamored with canned cranberry sauce—both the deep, crimson hue and the perfectly circular, ridged slabs were absolutely mesmerizing, especially against the earthen tones and misshapen spoonfuls of other Thanksgiving dishes. And if you're like me, you're probably still besotted!

What a more perfect food to celebrate this time of year than the humble cranberry, which is one of three fruits native to North America. (The blueberry and the Concord grape are the other two.) Native Americans—the first to harvest cranberries—used them for food, medicine (cranberries are awesome for bladder infections, heart health, and ulcers, for example), dyes, and as a symbol of peace.

Cranberry sauce/relish is very easy to make (and the leftovers are awesome in grilled peanut butter sandwiches, too). If you're heading off to your first Thanksgiving as a contributing adult, or were just lucky enough to have not drawn the short straw for turkey prep this year at your family's mega feast, making a cranberry relish from scratch is definitely one way to impress.

Today is also National Espresso Day.

GRANDMA KUTER'S CRANBERRY RELISH

Makes 6 to 8 side servings

Note: This dish needs to be made the day before serving. Any leftover portions may be frozen the next day.

- 1 pound fresh cranberries
- 3 stalks celery, cut into chunks
- 1 medium seedless orange, peeled and sectioned
- 1 large apple, any kind, peeled, cored, and cut into chunks
- 1 (20-ounce) can crushed pineapple, drained (juice reserved)
- 1½ cups granulated sugar
- 1 (3-ounce) box lemon gelatin
- 1 (3-ounce) box orange gelatin
- 2 cups boiling hot water

Put the cranberries, celery, orange, and apple into a food processor and pulse until finely chopped (visually it will look shredded). Empty the pulsed ingredients into a large bowl. Mix in 1 cup of the crushed pineapple and sugar. Be sure to mix the sugar in well. Cover the bowl and let set for 2 hours.

After the cranberry mixture is set, dissolve the lemon and orange gelatins into the hot water and 1 cup of the reserved pineapple juice. Mix this into the cranberry mixture until everything is well combined, and then divide the mixture equally into six to eight small bowls or containers. Refrigerate overnight.

NOVEMBER 24

NATIONAL SARDINES DAY

"Remember that a very good sardine is always preferable to a not that good lobster." —Ferran Adrià

I never had a problem eating fish when I was younger. It helped that my grandfather used to take me fishing, so I'd be a part of the entire process; it started with catching worms after it rained, segued to sitting in the boat for hours waiting patiently for a bite on said worms, and finished with my grandmother who'd stuff the caught salmon with lemons, onions, and pads of butter before grilling it. The cycle made sense to me.

But I never understood sardines. It didn't help that my dad would take me to the wildlife park—specifically to the hatchery—to teach me about how they would raise trout to put back into, and support, our water ecosystems. A couple weeks later when he'd roll back the top of a sardine tin and slip the strong, oily, intense-tasting fish into his mouth, I'd be confused. Fish wasn't meant to come out of a can—wasn't that the opposite of what he had just taught me?

If you're as confused as I was, or if sardines are off-putting to you, keep in mind that they don't *have* to come out of a can. They're full of omega-3 fatty acids, which is *really* good for your heart! Toss some sardines with pasta, on a Caesar salad, or use them to make fritters for a different take today.

DID YOU KNOW?

Sardines are also called "pilchards."

NOVEMBER 25 · NATIONAL PARFAIT DAY

"One of the delights of life is eating with friends, second to that is talking about eating. And, for an unsurpassed double whammy, there is talking about eating while you are eating with friends." —Laurie Colwin, Home Cooking

Today is the perfect day.

No, literally! *Parfait* means "perfect" in French. The word originally described a frozen dessert made from layers of sugar syrups, eggs, and creams back in the late nineteenth century. Here in the States we've certainly morphed the idea of parfaits into just about whatever we want it to mean. Some places use the terms *parfait* and *sundae* interchangeably.

But since we already celebrated National Chocolate Parfait on May 1st, maybe you should stick to a healthier alternative, like a parfait made from layers of yogurt, fresh fruit, and granola. During this time of year, your body is probably aching for something so nutritious!

Or if you've still got a bunch of leftovers from Thanksgiving (assuming it's happened early this year), you could always celebrate today by making a savory parfait made with layers of mashed potatoes, shredded turkey, peas (for color), and gravy.

Don't pretend you haven't seen pictures of similar dishes before and secretly wished you could dive into one!

NOVEMBER 26 — NATIONAL CAKE DAY

"Your good friend has just taken a piece of cake out of the garbage and eaten it. You will probably need this information when you check me into the Betty Crocker Clinic." —Cynthia Nixon, Sex and the City

Cake has been around forever. Okay, not forever—Velociraptors were definitely not daintily snacking on a slice of Bundt cake and a cuppa with their pinky extended. But almost forever! As long as there's been bread, there's basically been cake, too—and it was sweetened with things like honey and fruit. Obviously, if you've turned on any food-based TV channel in recent years, you'll see that cakes have changed quite a bit over time.

It seems that there are a lot of cake-related holidays on the food calendar. And well there should

be, considering every region in the world has contributed their own version of the sweet treat. Today, instead of repeating any of the ones we've already celebrated this year, why not think outside the box (the Atlantic ocean, Canadian border, Pacific ocean, Mexican border box, that is) and try something like *pavlova* (similar to meringue and topped with fresh fruits) from Australia and New Zealand or red bean cake (made with red bean paste using azuki beans) from parts of Asia?

UPSIDE DOWN SALAMI CAKE

Makes one 4- to 5-inch "cake"

Note: This dish needs to chill for 1 hour before serving and is best if made in a medium-size plastic container with a lid.

8 slices salami (packaged or deli)
1 (8-ounce) package cream cheese, at room temperature
1 (3- to 4-ounce) jar green olives with pimientos, drained (juice reserved)
1 box of durable crackers

Place the salami on paper towels to soak up any moisture.

In a small bowl, combine the cream cheese and enough olive juice to make the combination a spreadable consistency. Set the bowl aside.

Take the lid from a medium-size container (about the size of 1 quart or larger) and turn it upside down to use it as a plate. Put 1 to 3 teaspoons of the cream cheese mixture onto the center of the "plate" and spread it out thinly. Lay one slice of the salami onto the cream cheese to "stick" it onto the "plate."

Spread the cream cheese mix thinly across the entire slice of salami, add another slice of salami, spread the cream cheese mix across that slice of salami, add another slice of salami, and repeat until all eight slices of salami have been used. Spread the rest of the cream cheese mix across the top and sides of the "cake" as if you were "frosting" it, until no salami is showing.

Slice the green olives and press them gently into the top of the "cake." Flip the bowl part of the container upside down and put it over the "plate" lid. Place the salami cake in the refrigerator to set for 1 hour.

Remove the "cake" from the refrigerator, remembering that the container is upside down and that the "cake" is being served on the lid! Gently remove the bowl part of the container, cut it in wedges like a cake, and serve it on the crackers.

Tip! Wanna make this veg-friendly? Use Yves Meatless Deli Salami or something comparable.

NATIONAL BAVARIAN CREAM PIE DAY

"The homemade pie has been under siege for a century, and surely its survival is endangered." —Janet Clarkson, Pie: A Global History

This is a week that's heavy in sweet foods, and today is no different: Traditional Bavarian cream (*bavarois*, or Crème Bavaroise,) is a very rich, creamy custard made with gelatin and whipped cream. Spread it into a pie shell and top it with additional whipped cream and fruit, and you've got the start of a really good night in. (Unless you're sharing . . . which you probably should!) While it may have originally started off as something on the fancier end of the dessert spectrum in the nineteenth century, it's become a pretty commonplace treat in modern days—most people have had it in the ever-classy Bavarian cream doughnut.

I thought I would try and be clever today by adding some liquor to my Bavarian cream pie. Adding it to the cold pudding mixture I used, though, meant that the booze didn't burn off. So it was basically like eating bourbon-flavored pie with a hint of vanilla.

I suppose there are worse ways to celebrate a food holiday!

NATIONAL FRENCH TOAST DAY

"I went to a restaurant that serves 'breakfast at any time.' So I ordered French Toast during the Renaissance." —Steven Wright

Bread. Eggs. Milk.

If you're a New Englander, then you know that these three staples are what you buy in preparation for a blizzard. Why these three things instead of beer, chips, and salsa? I don't know. But if the power goes out and I'm stuck inside freezing my bum off, I'm definitely going to want a beer (probably many of them) over a glass of moo juice.

For most everyone else, a shopping basket filled with bread, eggs, and milk screams only one thing: "I'm making French toast! Would you like to come over?" Okay, maybe not that latter part, but I'm definitely *that* creeper in the grocery store who makes remarks like, "Wish I was going to your house tonight!" when I see what the person in front of me is purchasing.

French toast, like French fries and French kissing, didn't originate in France. Most likely it originated during ancient Roman times. (Those soldiers just couldn't resist a bit of eggy bread, could they?) Today you can find French toast in frozen food sections and fast-food joints, as well as in fancy-shmancy restaurants as a gourmet breakfast item.

NOVEMBER 29 — NATIONAL LEMON CREAM PIE DAY

"When life gives you lemons, squirt someone in the eye." —Cathy Guisewite

One of the best parts about this time of year is that calories don't count. (Actually, haven't I been saying this all year?) Your metabolism goes into this cryogenic state or something where whatever your weight and body shape was the day before Thanksgiving is how it will remain until the day after New Year's. How awesome would that be? No, you're definitely getting a holiday bulge. And if you're attempting to eat the year on top of celebrating the season like I did, then most likely Santa will be getting you a muffin top for Christmas and he probably will deliver early (not that I'm speaking from experiences or anything)!

Lemon has been used to flavor desserts since the Middle Ages. Probably a smart move as citrus prevents scurvy, and lemon in particular is great for bolstering your immune system, helping with digestion, and offering serious antibacterial properties.

So don't be a lemon today—eat a lemon! And what a better way than in a pie shell with some whipped cream?

DID YOU KNOW?

India is the world's largest producer of lemons.

Today is also National Chocolate Day and National Rice Cake Day.

NATIONAL MOUSSE DAY

"The stubby French painter Toulouse-Lautrec supposedly invented chocolate mousse—I find that rather hard to believe, but there you have it." —Alton Brown

If someone invites you over to celebrate National Mousse Day—be careful! You may not be sitting down to a dish filled with something chocolaty or fruity. Instead, you may find your bowl filled with a fleshy-colored seafood-based mousse!

Mousse—which is French for "foam" or "froth"—has been around since at least the eighteenth century in France. And while many of us consider it a lighter, airier version of pudding, it most likely originated as a savory dish, similar to a pâté. Pâté is a dense mixture of ground-up or puréed seasoned meat, seafood, or vegetables that's formed into a thick, spreadable pastelike substance, while mousse—which is similar—also introduces beaten egg whites, or whipped cream, into the mixture to give it that foamy or frothy texture. It also sometimes has gelatin in it to keep the whole thing stabilized.

Since today is just National Mousse Day without any specific kind mentioned, you've got plenty of options for how you might celebrate. Sure, you could play it safe and stick to something like raspberry white chocolate mousse, or you could really spice things up and try smoked salmon mousse, shrimp mousse, asparagus mousse, avocado mousse, or even blue cheese mousse!

DECEMBER IS...

DECEMBER IS ALSO...

National Fruitcake Month
National Eggnog Month
National Pear Month

NATIONAL PIE DAY

"Almost everything that I behold in this wonderful country bears traces of improvement and reform—everything except Pie." —George Augustus Sala, America Revisited

During the year, we celebrate almost two dozen pie-related food holidays. Based on that, I think it's safe to assume we're a country that doesn't just kinda like pie . . . we're completely enamored with it! Any flavor or texture you're craving can be tossed into a pie, and has over the course of our history.

I don't know about you, but I'm a little tired of sweet pies. The savory pie deserves some love, too! One of my family's beloved holiday traditions includes eating *tourtière*, which is a meat pie made with pork and potato. It's one of the foods that brings us together and allows us to carry on our cultural traditions despite whatever changes are happening in the rest of the world. And, in a way,

doing so allows us to (whether we realize it or not) continue to honor those loved ones who fought so hard to give us a better life than they had.

That being said, it was important for me to celebrate National Pie Day without compromising my personal gastronomical beliefs. The result? A delicious (but far healthier and more compassionate) trip down memory lane (*v'ourtièr* equals vegetarian *tourtière*).

Which is exactly how food should make you feel this time of year!

Today is also National Eat a Red Apple Day.

V'OURTIÈRE

Makes one 9-inch pie

2 premade 9-inch piecrusts, at room temperature

4 medium potatoes, peeled and quartered

2 tablespoons olive oil, divided

1½ pounds soy sausage (like Lightlife Gimme Lean)

¼ cup milk

2 tablespoons unsalted butter

¼ teaspoon salt

¼ teaspoon black pepper

2 teaspoons ground cinnamon

½ teaspoon ground clove

1 teaspoon ground nutmeg

Ketchup (optional but highly recommended)

Preheat the oven to 375°F.

Press one piecrust into the bottom of a pie plate.

In a large pot of water, boil the potatoes until a fork inserts easily into them.

While the potatoes are boiling, place 1 tablespoon of the olive oil in a skillet. Brown the soy sausage until cooked through and set it aside.

Drain the water from the potatoes, add the milk, butter, and other tablespoon of olive oil. Mash the potatoes until creamy. Mix the "meat" into the potatoes. Stir in the salt, pepper, cinnamon, clove, and nutmeg. Spread the mixture into the piecrust.

Place the second piecrust onto the pie and crimp it to the bottom crust along the edges. Pierce the top crust with a fork several times for venting steam. Bake the pie for 60 to 70 minutes, or until the crust is brown. Serve hot with a drizzle of ketchup if desired.

Tip! Wanna make this omnivore-friendly? Use ground pork; just make sure to drain off any fat before adding the meat to the mashed potatoes.

NATIONAL FRITTERS DAY

"There are men that will make you books, and turn them loose into the world, with as much dispatch as they would do a dish of fritters." —Miguel de Cervantes Saavedra, Don Quixote

Fritters are one of those universal foods where anything goes. Basically you just need to make patties out of some crab, ground lamb, potatoes, cauliflower, apple, pineapple rings—seriously, whatever you want!—and dredge it through flour or a batter (similar to that of a pancake), pan or deep-fry it, and you're good to go.

It seems corn and apple fritters are two of the more popular options in the United States, but I really wanted to do something special for National Fritters day. And different. Twelve months into eating the year, I knew I had to do *something* to keep each day unique and interesting. So when I celebrated today, I just tossed all my remaining Thanksgiving leftovers into one big bowl, used my hands to mash it all together (playing with your food never gets old), and made fritters from sweet potatoes, mashed potatoes, stuffing, peas, and cranberry sauce.

It made a dozen fritters.

I ate a dozen fritters.

Best decision I made all year!

NATIONAL PEPPERMINT LATTE DAY

"It is the destiny of mint to be crushed." —Waverley Lewis Root

Ever walk into some quaint art house-meets-coffee shop, where indie music you've probably never heard of is playing overhead while everyone around you is wearing impossibly skinny jeans? Already feeling uncomfortable, you take a glance at the menu to find that the only word you really understand is "coffee."

Well, today is your day to try something new. (Or maybe not; I understand—coffee, just coffee, is serious nectar from the gods most of the time!) But if you'd like to try something else or are a little intimidated by all those foreign-sounding coffee drinks and hipsters staring at you, here's a quick breakdown of just the basics:

- Espresso: It's basically a stronger, thicker coffee. The beans are ground into a consistency similar to powdered sugar and tightly packed into a very small basket in an espresso machine that generates up to fifteen atmospheres of pressure forcing water through the grounds.
- Caffè Misto: Hot coffee and frothy, steamed milk. Also goes by *café con leche* in Spain or *café au lait* in France.
- Cappuccino: Espresso with steamed milk and lots of foam.
- Latte: Espresso with a lot of steamed milk and only a little foam.
- Caffè Mocha: Coffee or espresso mixed with chocolate.
- Caffè Americano: Espresso and hot water. This is the one you're getting the most ripped off from, since you're paying for water to be added to your drink. Save yourself some change, order a triple espresso or whatever, and just add the water yourself.

Now go forth and order yourself a coffee drink in confidence!

DID YOU KNOW?

What do you get when you cross spearmint and water mint? Peppermint!

Today is also National Apple Pie Day and National Ice Cream Box Day.

NATIONAL COOKIE DAY

"When I buy cookies, I eat just four and throw the rest away. But first I spray them with Raid so I won't dig them out of the garbage later. Be careful, though, because that Raid really doesn't taste that bad." —Janette Barber

My mom used to host an annual cookie swap during the holiday season when she'd invite some of her closest friends over for coffee, chitchat, laughter, and to trade treats with one another. It was a lot of work to host, but it was a great way to be introduced to new desserts (and a taste of someone else's traditions) that weren't necessarily something you celebrated the season with.

Want to host your own? Invite six or seven friends over for a few hours—like nine a.m. to twelve p.m. on a Saturday morning. Have each person package and bring equal amounts of cookies for everyone. Everybody leaves with one of everything (except what they made), and as a result, you won't have to do any baking for the holidays. What a fun way to celebrate National Cookie Day, right?

You don't have to limit it to just cookies, either; white chocolate gorp, biscotti, rum balls, dipped pretzels, or even mini pies all work, too!

CORY'S CROWNIE BROOKIES

Makes about 2 dozen

1 ounce unsweetened baker's chocolate, chopped

½ cup (1 stick) unsalted butter, at room temperature

8 ounces chocolate chips (about 2 cups), divided

2 cups all-purpose flour, sifted

¾ teaspoon baking powder

¼ teaspoon salt

4 large eggs

1½ cups granulated sugar

1 tablespoon vanilla extract

Preheat the oven to 350°F.

Grease the baking sheets and set them aside.

In a saucepan, melt the chocolate, butter, and 1 cup of the chocolate chips. Set the pan aside to cool.

In a bowl, combine the flour, baking powder, and salt. Set it aside. In a separate bowl, beat together the eggs, sugar, and vanilla. Add the flour mixture slowly to the wet ingredients until well mixed, and then stir in the melted chocolate. Stir in the other cup of chocolate chips. Drop the dough by spoonfuls onto the baking sheets and bake for about 10 minutes, or until the cookies have set. These cookies are best eaten while still warm!

DECEMBER 05 NATIONAL COMFORT FOOD DAY

"Food, like a loving touch or a glimpse of divine power, has that ability to comfort."
—Norman Kolpas

What smells or flavors are conjured when I say "comfort foods"? To everyone it's something different, but the meaning behind the phrase is the same: foods that physically put us at ease and have either sentimental value or distinct (and fond) memories attached to them. For many people, an automatic response to stress is to emotionally eat—and the foods they turn to tend to be those that have been consistent throughout their lives (both in presence and flavor) and may even remind them of a more stable time, thus making them happy.

Popular comfort foods in the U.S. are all things you would probably expect, like macaroni and cheese, mashed potatoes, pizza, grilled cheese and tomato soup, ice cream, hot chocolate, and cookies.

So whether you're missing someone or somewhere (geographically or in time), today is the perfect day to indulge with some simpler fare that—while it may not be good for your hips—will be good for your heart!

Today is also National Sacher Torte Day.

DEBRA'S BUBBE'S LATKES

Makes 2 to 4 servings

3 medium potatoes, peeled and cut into small chunks (about 3½ cups)

½ large yellow onion, peeled and cut into small chunks (about 1¼ cups)

1½ cups matzo meal

1 large egg

1 teaspoon kosher salt

Pinch of garlic powder, if you want to enhance the flavor (optional)

¼ vegetable oil, divided

Line a baking sheet with paper towels and set it aside.

Blend the potatoes, onion, matzo meal, egg, salt, and garlic powder (if desired) in a blender until everything has broken down and has the consistency of oatmeal (be patient, this is going to take some time).

Pour 2 tablespoons of the vegetable oil into a skillet and bring it to medium heat. Pour the latke batter into the skillet ¼ cup at a time, leaving space around the latkes in the skillet. Fry on one side for 4 minutes, flip them, and fry the other side for an additional 4 minutes, until golden-brown on both sides and cooked through. If the latkes brown too fast, turn the heat down. Transfer the cooked latkes to the baking sheet to absorb any excess oil. Make a second batch of latkes and transfer them to the baking sheet, too. Before frying the next batch, place the rest of the oil into the pan, and then continue frying batches of latkes until the batter is gone. Eat and enjoy!

Tip! Eat these latkes warm with a sprinkle of salt and pepper, or topped with sour cream, apple sauce, ketchup, or salsa!

NATIONAL GAZPACHO DAY

"Worries go down better with soup than without." —Jewish proverb

You know why gazpacho rocks?

Because it's fun to say. Personally, I like to drag out the first syllable and then say the rest of the word really fast. Gaaaaaaaazzzzzz . . . pacho! Try it. It's linguistically loveable.

It's also culinarily appealing. A traditional gazpacho is a classic Spanish soup that's served cold. Original versions of the dish were made from water, olive oil, garlic, and bread; crushed tomatoes and spices were eventually added. Sounds absolutely delicious to me, though perhaps seasonally out of place. I'm not sure I need something so summery and refreshing during the first week of December, but we know that these food holidays are often arbitrarily assigned!

Don't be tempted by gazpacho's sister, warm and creamy tomato soup, or influenced by the weather outside. If you've never had a chilled soup before, today is as good a day as any to try it! If you're not feeling tomatoes, try a white gazpacho, which is similar to the original version mentioned above but with the addition of nuts and fruit. A green gazpacho can be made with avocados, cukes, jalapeños, spinach, etc.

Cold soup during cold weather? How rebellious!

Today is also National Microwave Day.

DECEMBER 07

NATIONAL COTTON CANDY DAY

"I am a cynical optimist. Big opening weekends are like cotton candy. The films you will remember over time are the films that stick in the consciousness of the audience in a good way." —Robert Redford

Cotton candy is so beloved by everyone in the United States that it's celebrated twice throughout the year—July 31st *and* December 7th—giving those afflicted with a sweet tooth multiple reasons to indulge for a reason.

But where does this gloriously colored sugar-on-a-stick come from?

Food lore says that it gained its popularity from a dentist named William Morrison in 1897. (Clever money-making scheme for him, or genuine goodwill act toward the children of the world?) He and a friend, John Wharton, introduced their "fairy floss"—as it was then called—at the World's Fair in St. Louis in 1904. It was a hit, although expensive; and it was reintroduced to the world a couple decades later as "cotton candy."

Don't limit yourself to just celebrating with the wispy, sugary confection. In this day and age, the flavor of cotton candy can be found in unexpected places like vodka and frosting, too!

DID YOU KNOW?

Cotton candy really only contains one ingredient—sugar!

NATIONAL BROWNIE DAY

"I hear Angela's party will have double fudge brownies. It will also have Angela."
—Kevin Malone, The Office

When I found out a wine tasting was happening at a chocolate confections and gourmet brownie store, my mind was nearly blown at the amount of epicness that was going to be happening under one roof. I needed to be a part of it, but I couldn't round up any friends at the last minute so I ended up taking myself on a date. That afternoon, I ate my weight in different flavors of malted milk balls (which included peanut butter, blueberry, and pumpkin), discovered that I was in love with port, and was asked to stop eating the brownies (which is less embarrassing when you have a cohort helping you polish off the free samples and aren't just doing it yourself).

But I couldn't resist—it was the first time I had ever been introduced to brownies that weren't just plain ol' chocolate. I got to try bourbon brownies with caramel and sea salt, brownies made with orange marmalade, and even sweet potato cheesecake brownies. They were moist, dense, and intensely flavorful.

It may have been the best one-person date I have ever been on!

JINGLE BELL BROWNIES

Makes an 8 x 8-inch pan

Brownies:

⅓ cup cocoa powder

½ cup all-purpose flour

¼ teaspoon salt

¼ teaspoon baking powder

½ cup (1 stick) unsalted butter, melted

1 cup granulated sugar

2 large eggs

1 tablespoon vanilla extract

Frosting:

3 tablespoons salted butter, at room temperature

3½ tablespoons cocoa powder

1 tablespoon honey

1 teaspoon vanilla extract

1 cup confectioners' sugar

1 cup circular peppermint candies

Preheat the oven to 350°F.

In a large bowl, mix together the cocoa powder, flour, salt, and baking powder.

In a medium bowl, mix the butter with the sugar, eggs, vanilla, and 1 tablespoon hot water until well blended. Beat the wet ingredients into the dry ingredients until well combined. Pour the batter into an 8 x 8-inch greased pan and bake for 30 minutes, or until a toothpick inserted in the center comes out dry.

While the brownies are baking, mix together the butter, cocoa powder, honey, vanilla, and confectioners' sugar until everything blends together and forms a smooth frosting. Set it aside.

Unwrap the peppermint candies and place them in a plastic baggie. Use a hammer or rolling pin to crush the mints until they are in tiny pieces, crumbs, and dust. Set them aside.

Frost the brownies when they have finished baking but while they're still warm. Sprinkle the crushed peppermints on the frosting. Let the brownies cool before cutting. Enjoy!

DECEMBER 09 — NATIONAL PASTRY DAY

"Desserts are like mistresses. They are bad for you. So if you are having one, you might as well have two." —Chef Alain Ducasse

When I was in college for culinary arts, our class was split into two groups each week: half worked on baking, the other half worked on cooking. At the time, I was completely disinterested in cooking. (It probably didn't help that I had failed the tests on how to make a proper roux and how to make the perfect omelet.) On more than one occasion, I was reprimanded for sneaking over to the baking side when it wasn't my day. But I was just fascinated by the entire process, which seemed so much more methodical. Do it right and you could masterfully create elegant desserts that had centuries of history attached to them. And when it went wrong—you knew it, because there was no hiding any mistakes under garnishes, pretty presentations, or extra seasoning.

In all honesty, I think my obituary might sound something like: "She lived a life full of good romances and better pastries." And I have! I don't know what it is about the treat, but it seems each chapter of my life has been marked by a different pastry. My youth was filled with éclairs from the local bakery; during my teen years and into college I discovered lemon Danish (*swoon*); and when I lived in Europe, I was besotted with *pain au chocolat*. Lately, it seems that I haven't met a pastry I don't like (well, except maybe for cream puffs)!

DID YOU KNOW?

King Louis XVI loved pastries so much that he'd eat them until he got sick.

DECEMBER
10

NATIONAL LAGER DAY

"Alcohol is like Photoshop for real life." —Will Ferrell

Lager and ale are two of the most popular styles of beer globally. But what's the difference? Ales are brewed with top-fermenting yeast. They ferment quickly in warm temperatures. Lagers (which come from the German word *Lagerbier*, which roughly translates to "storehouse" or "cellar") are lightly hopped and brewed with bottom-fermenting yeast. They ferment slower and require cooler temperatures. For those of you non-beer-inclined-folks, it may seem trivial, but those differences are where all the flavor and aroma are created.

Now... what do Budweiser, Miller, and Coors all have in common?

They're all lagers.

Unfortunately, as a result, there are many folks in the U.S. who associate tasteless, cheap, sex-in-a-canoe beer with the lager style. (Not my words—just repeating what I've heard while working as a beer spokesmodel! And for the record, one of the best promos I ever did was an '80s weekend at a ski resort where I worked as a Bud Light Girl with a Guns N' Roses cover band). Don't let these adjunct macro lagers negatively influence the entire style of beer for you. Lots of smaller breweries are producing some pretty exceptional lagers, so support your local economy and maybe go for a brewery tour today. Or there are *plenty* of other options available to celebrate today: Try pilsners, bocks, or dunkels (darks) for example!

DID YOU KNOW?

Zythology is the study of beer.

| DECEMBER 11 | # NATIONAL NOODLE RING DAY |

"Oh, look, it's Mr. Noodle's brother, Mr. Noodle." —Elmo, Sesame Street

I don't know about you, but "noodle ring" sounds suspiciously to me like someone wanted to celebrate *SpaghettiOs* without naming a brand. I mean, let's call a spade a spade! What other pasta do you consider *noodle rings*?

Wouldn't you know that today *wasn't* meant to be a trip down memory lane. (Unless you want it to be of course. Remember: No one should tell you how to celebrate *your* holiday!) There's actually a noodle ring dish! It's a casserole of sorts made with noodles, egg, breadcrumbs, and cheese that's shaped in a circular, ring-shaped mold and baked. If the hole in the center is big enough, you can fill it with vegetables or meat, too.

Actually, that sounds pretty delicious, doesn't it?

DID YOU KNOW?

The Pope set quality standards for pasta in the thirteenth century.

NATIONAL AMBROSIA DAY

"In the wintertime, in the snow country, citrus fruit was so rare, and if you got one, it was better than ambrosia." —James Earl Jones

A fan of fruit salad, but looking to change things up? Just want a break from the heavy foods of the holiday season? You should try "the food of the Gods." (Supposedly if you eat it, you'll become immortal according to Greek mythology.)

Ambrosia is made with whipped cream, sour cream, yogurt (or a combination of the three if you want), marshmallows, shredded coconut, and fruits like—but not limited to—pineapple, oranges, maraschino cherries, and/or grapes. It may sound like a really bizarre combination of textures, but it's actually a beloved dessert here in the States (and apparently one of my ancestors' favorite eats at get-togethers). While you can buy ambrosia premade at most grocery stores, I highly encourage you to make your own. It's not that difficult to assemble—just be sure to refrigerate before serving.

After a bite or two, you'll be feeling divine in no time!

Today is also National Cocoa Day.

NATIONAL ICE CREAM AND VIOLINS DAY

"If you like ice cream, why stop at one scoop? Have two, have three. Too much is never enough." —Morris Lapidus

National Ice Cream and Violins Day may have been the first food holiday I ever heard of. I was working as the marketing director for a local gelato company and was looking for unique ways to promote our brand. (I've always thought that the Internet is similar to the white rabbit's hole in *Alice in Wonderland*; you start looking up one thing, but it leads to something else, then something else, and you just tumble further and further in before you wonder, "What was I looking up in the first place?")

I came upon a list of ice cream–related holidays. It was late October and the next one in the calendar was today, National Ice Cream and Violins Day. I pitched to the owners that we use it as a marketing tool to get more customers in during the cold months—I suggested that we have some local musicians in to play the violin while we offered a special batch of gelato for the event. The owners said *no*—I guess they didn't think food holidays were going to catch on.

Oh, how wrong they were.

DID YOU KNOW?

Mashed potatoes were (and sometimes still are) used as ice cream in commercials because set lights would melt real ice cream.

NATIONAL BISCUITS AND GRAVY DAY

"To fulfill a dream to be allowed to sweat over lonely labor, to be given a chance to create, is the meat and potatoes of life. The money is the gravy." —Bette Davis

When my mom was in her early twenties, she had the opportunity to travel the continental U.S. She spent some serious time living in the South before eventually relocating back to New England. Having never had biscuits and gravy before today's food holiday, I asked her to describe them to me, knowing she had eaten authentic ones before. She said: "When I was down South, biscuits and gravy—like grits and sweet tea—were a part of every meal. Sometimes it was meat gravy, sometimes not. Usually it was white and served on fresh homemade biscuits. It was warm, comforting,

roll-your-eyes-back-and-swoon good. Made with such love and such tenderness, too. Biscuits and gravy are heaven."

Well then . . . I'm sold.

I can count the number of times I've eaten breakfast in the past few years on one hand. It's just not a meal that thrills me—it never really has. But I know that breakfast really is the most important meal if you're someone who's constantly on-the-go. And, after trying biscuits and gravy, I can honestly say that if every day started this delicious, I might become a breakfast convert!

Today is also National Bouillabaisse Day.

DECEMBER 15 · NATIONAL LEMON CUPCAKE DAY

"The spirit cannot endure the body when overfed, but, if underfed, the body cannot endure the spirit." —St. Frances de Sales

Do you know why I like today's food holiday? (FYI: Some people just call it "Cupcake Day," while others call it "Lemon Cupcake Day.") If you're celebrating the latter version, then it's a step outside the norm. Chocolate and vanilla cupcakes are so mainstream that anything just a little different is really exciting—and why shouldn't we celebrate that? Especially during this time of year when our taste buds are oversaturated by traditional sweets. Lemon cupcakes sound like a refreshing, tangy break from all of that!

Personally, I'm a sucker for anything citrus, specifically limes and lemons. To me, the perfect lemon cupcake can be summed up in one word:

lush. The lemon flavor needs to be the perfect balance of tang and sweet; the cupcake itself needs to be light and soft; and the frosting must be creamy enough to tempt anyone into indulging (and not just on National Lemon Cupcake Day!).

Cupcakes are essentially small cakes created for one person, making them the perfect take-a-break-for-yourself-from-holiday-madness treat. Plus, they are very, *very* trendy. Whether it's super-hip food trucks selling apple cider cupcakes with salted caramel frosting on the corner of your street, reality TV shows about cupcake competitions, or cookbooks entirely dedicated to the single-serve desserts . . . cupcakes are "in"!

DECEMBER 16

NATIONAL CHOCOLATE COVERED ANYTHING DAY

"Las cosas claras y el chocolate espeso." *(Ideas should be clear and chocolate thick.)* —Spanish proverb

Wait . . . wait . . . chocolate-covered *anything* day? Like . . . *anything*? I could celebrate today with chocolate-covered pretzels if I wanted? Or chocolate-covered bacon, rippled potato chips, Cheddar cheese cubes, blueberries, or espresso beans? 'Cause that's *exactly* how I want to celebrate December 16th every year for the rest of my life, please and thank you!

The word "covered" might trap you into thinking you should be encasing something in a coating of chocolate. Let the word, instead or also, mean "topped" or "enveloped," because today could easily and simply be celebrated with Belgian waffles drenched in chocolate sauce. You could also make or go out for a mole (a Mexican sauce made with chilies, spices, and bittersweet chocolate). A stuffed bean and cheese chile relleno smothered in the sauce? It's sweet, spicy, creamy—what's not to love?!

And hey, if you're a hardcore chocoholic, don't be afraid to celebrate with chocolate covered chocolate, either! While you might get strange looks any other time of the year, today anything goes!

CH'CHEESE, CH'CHIPS, CH'BACON

Makes one large tray of goodies!

Note: This dish needs to chill for at least 2 hours before serving.

1 (10-ounce) block New York extra sharp cheese, cut into 24 cubes

8 ounces chocolate chips (about 2 cups)

2 tablespoons unsalted butter

2 teaspoons vanilla extract

4 tablespoons milk

6 slices bacon, or ½ package tempeh bacon slices, cooked crisp, drained, cooled, and halved

1 (8-ounce) bag rippled potato chips (about 2 cups)

Line a baking sheet with waxed paper and set it aside.

Skewer the cubes of cheese with toothpicks and set them aside.

In a saucepan, mix the chocolate chips, butter, vanilla, and milk on medium-high heat. When the mixture is melted and creamy, lower the heat to a simmer. Hold the cheese cubes by the toothpicks and dip each of them into the chocolate until they are covered. Place them on the waxed paper. Gently dip each piece of bacon into the chocolate, coating them as much as possible, and transfer them to the waxed paper. Lastly, dip the potato chips in the chocolate, coating them as much as possible, and transfer them to the waxed paper.

Transfer the baking sheet to the refrigerator and chill for 2 hours before serving. Store any leftovers in an airtight container to eat later.

Tip! The cheese cubes (which are best served cold) will get the most quizzical look from people, but once they try them, they'll be believers, too!

DECEMBER 17 — NATIONAL MAPLE SYRUP DAY

"I happen to know everything there is to know about maple syrup! I love maple syrup. I love maple syrup on pancakes. I love it on pizza. And I take maple syrup and put a little bit in my hair when I've had a rough week. What do you think holds it up, slick?" —Jeremy Grey, Wedding Crashers

I'm from a region of the world that makes a lot of maple syrup. When the sap is running the heaviest, we have a statewide festival called Maine Maple Sunday. It's usually held on the last Sunday of March, and it's an opportunity for folks to explore the local sugarhouses to learn how maple syrup is made. Usually there are live demonstrations, free tastings, wagon rides, live music, pancake breakfasts, etc. Many states actually celebrate their own maple-based festivals around the same time, too.

So why is National Maple Syrup Day in the middle of December?

Who knows, right? More importantly: Who cares? Maple syrup is awesome any time of the year! Back in the seventeenth century, the colonists adopted the process of tapping, harvesting, and boiling the sap of a maple tree into a thick syrup from the Native Americans. Some maple trees have been tapped for over 150 years!

When I first celebrated today, we got our first major snowstorm of the season, so I thought the perfect way to eat today would be by making maple taffy, aka sugar on snow, where boiling maple syrup is drizzled directly onto fresh snow and eaten. It feels like clouds in your mouth; weird description, but it's true!

---

18 NATIONAL ROAST SUCKLING PIG DAY

"To eat is a necessity, but to eat intelligently is an art." —La Rochefouchauld

Every family has its own holiday traditions that are cultural, were inherited from older generations, or were simply incorporated because they were liked. For example, my loved ones and I have cinnamon rolls and coffee early on Thanksgiving morning before any cooking marathons begin. And on our table later that day is *always* a bowl of sweet potatoes and broccoli casserole. Our Christmas meal, on the other hand, is a lot more relaxed and changes from year to year depending on what we feel like eating.

Many cultures, though—including parts of Latin America, Northern Europe, and even Greece—celebrate Christmas dinner with a slow-roasted pig. A suckling (or "sucking") pig, more specifically, was basically a piglet that was still drinking its mother's milk or was only very recently weaned before slaughter. Properly cooked, the meat is incredibly tender and the skin is crispy, making it a culinary delight for some people.

Could be quite the interesting way to celebrate—and probably surprise your guests!—during the holidays this year.

Today is also National Bake Cookies Day.

NATIONAL HARD CANDY DAY

"Knowledge was like candy: You never turned it down, especially if you didn't have to work too hard to get it." —Robert Liparulo, House of Dark Shadows

I've always been a bit competitive. I was an athlete most of my life, and I would thrive off the adrenaline rush that I would get during the last few minutes of a game. (Especially during penalty corners, as I think many other former field hockey goalies will tell you!) But my favorite competitions have always been against myself. And when I was younger, never was that more prevalent than at the arcade. How many tickets could I collect playing Skee-Ball in an hour's time?

And how many pink lemonade–flavored Jolly Ranchers would I be able to get with said tickets?

Hard candy may not seem like a big deal to you, but it wasn't something I ate a lot of growing up. I had a retainer as a kid, and the list of what I *was* allowed to eat was a mere fraction of the list of things I *wasn't* allowed to eat. (I couldn't even bite into a sandwich—they had to be cut into small pieces I could just pop into my mouth.) When I was finally retainer-free, I gorged myself on hard-earned pink lemonade Jolly Ranchers. So when I think about hard candy, it takes me back to that moment in time!

Jawbreakers, mints, rock candy, butterscotch discs, or root beer barrels—how will you eat today?

Today is also National Oatmeal Muffin Day.

NATIONAL SANGRIA DAY

"The problem with the world is that everyone is a few drinks behind." —Humphrey Bogart

Let's take a break from all the holiday craziness and celebrate that it's not quite winter yet (because technically it's not—most years it starts either December 21 or 22) with some refreshing, fruity sangria. You in?

Sangria, a punch that comes to us from the Iberian peninsula of Spain, is a mix of wine (usually red—white makes it "sangria blanca"), sliced fruit (like lemons, limes, oranges, apples, peaches, mangoes—whatever you want!), a sweetener of some kind (think honey, agave, or simple syrup), brandy, and seltzer water. As you can imagine, with so many variables, sangria really can taste different depending on who makes it or the mood they're in.

When I lived in Spain, I drank *a lot* of sangria. I wasn't in the Canary Islands to celebrate today's food holiday, but drinking is drinking no matter where in the world you are. So I cobbled together my own version of the drink and raised a glass to the places I've been and will visit again someday.

Salud!

Today is also National Fried Shrimp Day.

C'ANGRIA

Makes 4 to 6 servings

1 (750 ml) bottle Syrah or Cabernet Sauvignon
1 large orange, sliced
1 lemon, sliced
2 limes, sliced
½ grapefruit, sliced
¼ cup brandy
1 teaspoon granulated sugar
Ice, to fill
Club soda, to taste

In a very large bowl or pitcher, mix together the bottle of wine with the orange, lemon, lime, and grapefruit slices, along with the brandy and sugar. Stir everything together until the sugar dissolves completely. It's okay if your fruit takes a little bit of a beating in the process—it'll enrich the fruit infusion.

Pour the liquid into an airtight container and refrigerate for 12 to 24 hours to let the flavors combine.

To serve, pour in tall glasses over ice and add club soda to taste.

NATIONAL KIWIFRUIT DAY

"A table, a chair, a bowl of fruit and a violin; what else does a man need to be happy?" —Albert Einstein

What's small, brown, and hairy?

If you guessed the kiwi bird—you're right! And if you guessed kiwifruit—you're also right! And while one inspired the other, the other inspired today's food holiday.

Kiwifruit originated in China. When they were introduced to New Zealand in the early twentieth century, the country really embraced the fruit (which, by the way, is part of the berry family). So much so, they named it after their beloved flightless bird because of their semi-similar appearance.

As off-putting as it might seem, the furry skin of the kiwifruit is actually edible. So go ahead and bite right into one, especially since the brilliantly green fruit are filled with fiber, antioxidants, and more Vitamin C than an orange!

DID YOU KNOW?

The national fruit of China is the kiwi.

Today is also National Hamburger Day.

NATIONAL DATE NUT BREAD DAY

"That is an artist as I would have an artist be, modest in his needs: He really wants only two things, his bread and his art—panem et Circen." —Friedrich Nietzsche

One of my goals when eating the year was to celebrate as many different food holidays as I could. And I think I did a pretty excellent job, especially since it was no easy task because many foods (or variations on themes) are celebrated more than once. Date nut bread, for example, has two days to honor it: September 8th (page 287) and today, December 22nd. And as far as I know, there are no other foods celebrated on either of these days. But perhaps they're totally different days, and I'm missing something. After all, if you Google *When is Date Nut Bread Day?*, it will tell you today. If you Google *When is Date-Nut Bread Day?* (notice the hyphen), it will tell you September 8th. Interesting, yeah?

All I know is this: It's National Date Nut Bread Day Redux! And it's time to get my boxed quick bread mix out once again!

Many folks agree that date nut bread is a perfect treat during the holiday season; it's naturally sweet and makes for an amazing breakfast before shopping or impending family craziness!

NATIONAL PFEFFERNÜSSE DAY

"A plate of cookies is a great way to end dinner and really nice to share at the holidays." —Bobby Flay

Despite my (very, *very* small) German heritage, until today I had never heard of Pfeffernüsse. If you had asked me to guess what I might think it was, I'd probably have said some kind of pretzel product or even a spiced, whipped mousse—neither of which are as far off the mark as guessing "potato salad" or "pork shoulder" would have been.

Pfeffernüsse, which is German for "pepper nuts," are traditionally small, round, hard cookies. They're usually spice-filled (think cinnamon, allspice, etc.) and sometimes also made with ground nuts. Did I mention they were hard? So hard that some people dunk them into a hot beverage before eating, while others just wait—the cookies usually soften within a week of aging.

I tried to cobble together a recipe for Pfeffernüsse to celebrate today and, well, mine didn't come out hard. Mine came out like chewy lemon-pepper cookies. I found redemption a few days later, though, when my stepdad bought me cherry-flavored, chocolate chip-filled Pfeffernüsse-like cookies covered in powdered sugar.

Und sie waren lecker! (And they were tasty!)

NATIONAL EGGNOG DAY

"Eat well, drink in moderation, and sleep sound, in these three good health abound." —Latin proverb

I don't think I've ever actually had *real* eggnog; y'know, the kind with milk, sugar, raw eggs, and nutmeg. That just sounds like a bad stomachache to me. But I used to love the pasteurized stuff my local dairy farm made every year. And now? I look forward to a glass or four of soy-based nog (with a little splash of rum) during the holiday season. Especially since toasting my loved ones on Christmas Eve with a glass of nog is the equivalent to toasting with Champagne on New Year's Eve in my book!

So as far as I'm concerned, the universe couldn't have more appropriately placed a food holiday than today!

Tonight, don't forget to leave Santa a glass of eggnog sans the liquor. *Eat the Year* doesn't endorse drinking and flying. (Side note: My parents always had my sister and me leave Santa some milk or water instead; they told us that Santa liked the break from the heavy stuff!) And remember some carrot sticks and celery for the reindeer, too—they're really the ones doing all the work to get Santa around the world in a timely fashion!

DID YOU KNOW?

The name "eggnog" may have come from the Old English word "nog," which referred to "noggin"—a small, wooden mug that was used to serve alcohol (specifically an egg inside a small cup of booze in this instance).

NATIONAL PUMPKIN PIE DAY

"One cannot think well, love well, sleep well, if one has not dined well."
—*Virgina Woolf*, A Room of One's Own

For centuries, people have loved pumpkin pie. The fruit-as-dessert is sweet, creamy, features spices appropriate to the season, and it's a gentle reminder of the end of another harvest. During the Thanksgiving-to-Christmas stretch, I've always felt very strongly about the idea of taking a break from our daily grind to recognize everything we're blessed with and to break bread with loved ones. To me, pumpkin pies are symbolic of that time.

My family usually celebrates the holidays with a homemade chocolate cream pie *and* a pumpkin pie made from a local bakery. It isn't uncommon for each of us to have a sliver of both with a dollop of whipped cream plopped right on top uniting the two as if they were one piece. It's a happy, happy marriage—after all, pumpkin and chocolate are flavors that go beautifully together.

I hope your day is filled with love, laughter, and a decadent piece of pie or two!

DID YOU KNOW?

Geumophobia is the fear of taste.

Today is also National Kiss the Cook Day.

NATIONAL CANDY CANE DAY

"We elves try to stick to the four main food groups: candy, candy canes, candy corns, and syrup." —Buddy the Elf, Elf

I'm a big fan of candy canes. They're one of the only decorations allowed on my Christmas tree (green tree, white lights, red glittering balls, a red bow on top, a single red stuffed lobster, and candy canes here and there). What makes me angry are the candy-flavored versions like blue raspberry. That is *not* a candy cane. It's a cane-shaped candy that doesn't taste like *any* flavors associated with Christmas. Blue raz, go back to summer, y'hear me?! Shame on you, friends, if you like these. I cannot support this terrible culinary decision.

Original candy canes were just long, hard, white sticks that tasted of mint. It's believed that a choir director at the Cologne Cathedral in Germany during Christmas Eve around 1670 got a local candy maker to shape them into what looked like a shepherd's staff (a more appropriate shape, given the season). He then handed out the candy to children during the very long church worship service, which no doubt helped keep them quiet.

Brilliant mind, if you ask me.

How will you celebrate today? I think I'm going to snatch one of the candy canes off my Christmas tree and use it to stir my hot chocolate.

'Tis the season (for a few more days), right?

Today is also National Coffee Percolator Day.

NATIONAL FRUITCAKE DAY

"The worst gift is fruitcake. There is only one fruitcake in the entire world, and people keep sending it to each other." —Johnny Carson

Poor fruitcake. It's been the unfortunate butt of Christmas jokes for generations. It was in our family. In 1990 or 1991, one of my uncles bought a fruitcake as a gift for our annual post-holiday meal Yankee Swap. The rules were that whoever received it had to come up with a creative way to regift it at the following year's Yankee Swap. (One year, someone created a T-shirt with an image of a fruitcake, and that's how it was passed off that year—to me, by the way, because I thought the shirt was really cool.) As far as I know it's still in rotation. The box is nearly ruined, but the fruitcake itself? Still in perfect, glistening condition.

I'm not sure why the fruitcake has gotten the reputation it has; after all, the modern fruitcake has been around for *centuries* (though primitive versions were found in tombs of ancient Egyptians).

The cakes themselves vary from region to region, depending on what ingredients were local and seasonably available.

So today, instead of mocking this generations-old traditional holiday food, try a bite. If it's great, then save it for your grandchildren to try in a few decades. And if it's awful (and mine was—then again, anything with dye Blue No. 1 is usually questionable), wrap it up and save it for your grandchildren anyway!

DID YOU KNOW?

Some superstitions state that if you're unmarried, putting a slice of fruitcake under your pillow will help you dream about who you're supposed to marry!

NATIONAL CHOCOLATE DAY

"The greatest tragedies were written by the Greeks and Shakespeare . . . neither knew chocolate." —Sandra Boynton

Today's food holiday shouldn't be too difficult to celebrate, considering we're just coming off a slew of holidays; it's National Chocolate Day, so bust out that leftover pie or the truffles you found in your stocking and eat up!

If you're eating the year through, today might seem overwhelming. At this point in time we've had roughly *fifty* chocolate-themed food days. With only a few days left in the year, don't give up now. What's one more piece of chocolate after all we've gone through together this year, right? Besides, for those of you with large families or busy schedules, you may just be getting to your holiday celebrations today—if that's the case, you have no excuse not to take your auntie up on the sweets she's offering you!

I know you want to, but you can't start your post-holiday diet quite yet. Catapulting yourself into some crazy diet and exercise routine immediately after the holidays is bad; going cold turkey from a high-calorie diet to a restricted one just sets us up for failure. (Sound familiar? I believe I told you the same thing back in early January about dieting and New Year's resolutions!) I think gradually weaning ourselves off holiday foods back into normal diets makes much more sense.

So one . . . or two . . . pieces of candy won't hurt you today.

HOMEMADE IRISH CREAM LIQUEUR

Makes two 750 ml bottles worth

Note: This recipe must be made the day before serving.

- 2 large eggs
- 1 (14-ounce) can sweetened condensed milk
- 1 pint light cream
- ¼ cup chocolate syrup
- 4 cups inexpensive whiskey

In a blender, blend the eggs, milk, cream, and syrup together on low until well blended. Add the whiskey one cup at a time until completely blended. Pour immediately into bottles, or an airtight pitcher with a lid, and refrigerate for 24 hours. Enjoy over ice or in coffee.

Tip! For an excellent drink, pour some of this Irish cream over the orange juice ice cubes from the Citrus Champagne Punch (page 421).

DECEMBER
29

NATIONAL PEPPER POT DAY

"Americans can eat garbage, provided you sprinkle it liberally with ketchup, mustard, chili sauce, Tabasco sauce, cayenne pepper, or any other condiment which destroys the original flavor of the dish." —Henry Miller

Sprinkle some black pepper onto some soil in a flowerpot today, and within moments a magical little plant will spring to life to grant you three wishes!

Today's actually all about a pretty delicious food that can be interpreted in one of two ways.

Option #1: Philadelphia Pepper Pot was first created during the Revolutionary War (and food lore states it was even created on December 29th). The Continental Army was low on supplies and suffering through a pretty brutal winter when the baker general threw together a thick, spicy soup made from what was on hand: tripe, meat scraps, and peppercorns. It invigorated the men and was considered "the soup that won the war."

Option #2: Pepper Pot is a West Indian seasoned stew; very popular in the Caribbean now. It's made with—just to name a few ingredients—coconut milk, collard greens/kale/callaloo, sweet potato or yam, and a Scotch bonnet pepper (or any other pepper you can find that's gonna add some heat). And it's how I chose to celebrate today. After all, nothing's better than a hot (temp) and hot (spice) dish in a blizzard!

Today is also National Get on the Scales Day and National Chocolates Day.

NATIONAL BICARBONATE OF SODA DAY

Rachel: "Okay, that would be two cups of tarragon, one pound of baking soda, and one red onion?" Monica: "What the hell are you cooking?" —Friends

Bicarbonate of Soda Day? What's this science stuff doing in my foodstuff? Let's go with the name most people know it as—it's National Baking Soda Day!

It may seem bizarre that baking soda gets its own food holiday, but just think of how often you've used it throughout the food calendar. Sodium bicarbonate is a white, odorless, fine-powdered, water-soluble chemical compound ($NaHCO_3$). And it's used in many different avenues of life, including baking as a leavening agent (meaning your cupcakes, or whatever rises), to deodorize (if your fridge ever smells, stick an open box of baking soda in it), to clean (not just your counter—try sprinkling some on your toothbrush and give them old chompers a scrub), to extinguish grease and oil fires, to have fun (baking soda + vinegar = instant volcano), and—my personal favorite—as an antacid—which was exactly how I celebrated with it today.

Listen, even foodies who attempt to eat the year and irrationally think they have iron stomachs get indigestion and heartburn from time to time. It's okay if you do, too!

NATIONAL CHAMPAGNE DAY

"Champagne, if you are seeking the truth, is better than a lie detector. It encourages a man to be expansive, even reckless, while lie detectors are only a challenge to tell lies successfully." —*Graham Greene*, Travels with My Aunt

When I think about New Year's Eve, I *definitely* think about toasting to the health and happiness of my loved ones with Champagne at midnight. The sound of the cork popping, the tickling of the bubbles, the reflection of another year gone and the hope for new beginnings—never was there a more appropriate food holiday!

Real Champagne is a sparkling wine made from (primarily) a blend of Pinot Noir, Pinot Meunier, and Chardonnay grapes in the Champagne region of France. The Comité Interprofessionnel du Vin de Champagne (CIVC)—a trade association that represents grape growers in Champagne—developed specific rules to protect its economic interests regarding the production of the drink. As a result, despite the popular nomenclature, not all sparkling wines are actually Champagnes. Only when the drink has met the requirements by the CIVC (which includes, but isn't limited to, grape varieties and several viticulture aspects) is it labeled as such.

Recent research has also shown that drinking Champagne in moderation is actually good for your health. Yes, please: I definitely want to live in a world where scientists have discovered that dark chocolate, red wine, and Champagne are all good for me!

And now you're all the wiser, foodies.

Tonight, crack open a bottle of bubbly and celebrate to your heart's content. After all, tomorrow is another day, and I hear Bloody Marys are an awesome hangover cure.

CITRUS CHAMPAGNE PUNCH

Makes 6 to 8 drinks

Note: The juice cubes will need to be made the night before serving.

- 1 quart orange juice
- 1 lemon, peeled and cut into small chunks
- 1 cup pineapple juice
- 4 cups cranberry ginger ale
- 1 bottle Champagne
- 1 large orange, peeled and sliced

The night before:

Make two trays of ice cubes with some of the orange juice and a small chunk of lemon in each. It's okay if the lemon pieces stick out of the cubes. Reserve the leftover orange juice until the day the punch is made.

The day you serve:

In a punch bowl or pitcher, pour in the remaining orange juice, pineapple juice, cranberry ginger ale, Champagne, and add the orange slices. Add the premade citrus ice cubes to the punch. Stir and serve. It's New Year's Eve—try not to drink it right outta the punch bowl!

Tip! The little pieces of lemon will get so soft (and lose their bitterness) that they'll become edible!

FORMULAS FOR METRIC CONVERSION

Ounces to grams .... multiply ounces by 28.35
Pounds to grams .... multiply pounds by 453.5
Cups to liters .... multiply cups by .24
Fahrenheit to Centigrade .... subtract 32 from Fahrenheit, multiply by 5 and divide by 9

METRIC EQUIVALENTS FOR VOLUME

U.S.	Metric
⅛ tsp.	0.6 ml
¼ tsp.	1.2 ml
½ tsp.	2.5 ml
¾ tsp.	3.7 ml
1 tsp.	5 ml
1½ tsp.	7.4 ml
2 tsp.	10 ml
1 Tbsp.	15 ml
1½ Tbsp.	22 ml
2 Tbsp. (⅛ cup/1 fl. oz)	30 ml
3 Tbsp. (1½ fl. oz)	45 ml
¼ cup (2 fl. oz)	59 ml
⅓ cup (3 fl. oz)	79 ml
½ cup (4 fl. oz)	118 ml
⅔ cup (5 fl. oz)	158 ml
¾ cup (6 fl. oz)	178 ml
1 cup (8 fl. oz)	237 ml
1¼ cups (10 fl. oz)	300 ml
1½ cups (12 fl. oz)	355 ml
1¾ cups (14 fl. oz)	425 ml
2 cups (1 pint/16 fl. oz)	500 ml
3 cups (24 fl. oz)	725 ml
4 cups (1 quart/32 fl. oz)	.95 liters
16 cups (1 gallon/128 fl. oz)	3.8 liters

OVEN TEMPERATURES

Degrees Fahrenheit	Degrees Centigrade	British Gas Marks
200°	93°	–
250°	120°	½
275°	140°	1
300°	150°	2
325°	165°	3
350°	175°	4
375°	190°	5
400°	200°	6
425°	220°	7
450°	230°	8

METRIC EQUIVALENTS FOR WEIGHT

U.S.	Metric
1 oz	28 g
2 oz	57 g
3 oz	85 g
4 oz	113 g
5 oz	142 g
6 oz	170 g
7 oz	198 g
8 oz	227 g
16 oz (1 lb.)	454 g
2.2 lbs.	1 kilogram

METRIC EQUIVALENTS FOR BUTTER

U.S.	Metric
2 tsp.	10 g
1 Tbsp.	15 g
1½ Tbsp.	22.5 g
2 Tbsp. (1 oz)	27 g
3 Tbsp.	42 g
4 Tbsp.	56 g
4 oz. (1 stick)	110 g
8 oz. (2 sticks)	220 g

METRIC EQUIVALENTS FOR LENGTH

U.S.	Metric
¼ inch	.65 cm
½ inch	1.25 cm
1 inch	2.50 cm
2 inches	5.00 cm
3 inches	6.00 cm
4 inches	8.00 cm
5 inches	11.00 cm
6 inches	15.00 cm
7 inches	18.00 cm
8 inches	20.00 cm
9 inches	23.00 cm
12 inches	30.50 cm
15 inches	38.00 cm

ACKNOWLEDGMENTS

Thank you, God, for your faithfulness, grace, and sense of humor!

To Elisa Stanford of Edit Resource for making my proposal (and me!) sparkle; Kim Perel (fellow dino lover and rock star agent extraordinaire) and Wendy Sherman for believing in and fighting for my concept and me; and Jordana Tusman for your invaluable input and patience. (Did I mention the patience thing?) Also, Ashley Haag for bringing my book to life and Mike Lowery for your whimsical illustrations. (Who knew catfish could be so sassy-looking?)

A heartfelt thanks to my friends and family who helped me every step of the way, and to all the wonderful companies who assisted me in my adventure to eat the national food holidays as compassionately and animal-free as possible.

Thank you Joshua Bankhead, Amy Bilodeau, Lisa Fields, Erika Martinez, Norma Potenzo, Debra Ross, Cory and Tammy Stoker, Sol Fresneda, Sylvane Treible, and Tara Vetrone for sharing a part of yourselves with me via your recipes. You've all played an incredibly influential role in my own style of cooking, and I am happy to know each and every one of you!

Finally, this journey would have *never* been possible without three very important people: Jeffrey Remick, Dell Gray, and Cari Deschenes. In your own ways, you each ate the year along with me, and I think you all know how indebted I am to you for the individual help you gave me along the way. Thank you for loving me and supporting me every time I come up with some crazy new project. Ready for the next?

INDEX